Alan Howard, Daniel Nussbaum, Brenda Shaffer
Operational Energy

Alan Howard, Daniel Nussbaum,
Brenda Shaffer

Operational Energy

—

DE GRUYTER

ISBN (Paperback) 978-3-11-079650-6
ISBN (Hardcover) 978-3-11-079647-6
e-ISBN (PDF) 978-3-11-079810-4
e-ISBN (EPUB) 978-3-11-079833-3

Library of Congress Control Number: 2024935793

Bibliographic information published by the Deutsche Nationalbibliothek
The Deutsche Nationalbibliothek lists this publication in the Deutsche Nationalbibliografie; detailed bibliographic data are available on the Internet at http://dnb.dnb.de.

© 2024 Walter de Gruyter GmbH, Berlin/Boston
Cover image: Photo courtesy of the U.S. Army

www.degruyter.com

Acknowledgements

Operational Energy is the first textbook on the planning for energy needs in modern warfare. We thank RuthAnne Darling, Director, Operational Energy – Innovation, US Department of Defense and Jim Caley, Director for Operational Energy, US Navy, for the vision and support for this research project and book. Ms. Darling, along with Dr. Clint Novotny developed the OE Innovation ontology framework. Colonel (retired) Mace Carpenter further developed the framework and authored the description of the framework elements.

Colonel (retired) Mace Carpenter and Lt. Col. (retired) Eric Turner provided extensive insightful commentary and feedback on our research and manuscript and we are grateful and acknowledge their extensive expertise.

It was great to work with De Gruyter Press, which early on in the development of this book recognized the importance of publication of this first textbook on operational energy. We especially thank at De Gruyter Press Michaela Göbels, Gerhard Boomgaarden, Faye Leerink and Antonia Mittelbach.

Miles Pomper and Jonathan Hoare each provided very useful comments on the book manuscript and we appreciate this input. Miles also conducted research for the project. Rabia Haider Khan also provided useful edits. Thank you to John Fleming, Frank Chezem, and Brandon Wall for their work on the graphics.

We also are grateful to students at the US Naval Postgraduate School that provided us with insights from their operational experiences that enhanced our knowledge on OE.

We would also like to thank our team at the Energy Academic Group for supporting this work. Several colleagues at the Energy Academic Group at the US Naval Postgraduate School contributed extensive research and writing to this book. Lawrence Walzer authored Chapter 4, "Military Threats to Operational Energy" and the case study on the attack on the Metcalf electricity substation. Dr. David Alderson and Dr. Daniel Eisenberg authored Chapter 6, "Operational Energy Vulnerability and Resilience." Dr. Arnold Dupuy led the research of Chapter 7 "Education and Training and his research contributed greatly to the case study on the cyberattack on the Colonial Pipeline. Charles "Jay" Lynn contributed significantly to Chapter 8 "Operational Energy Challenges to the Armed Services Branches." The case study in chapter 3 on nuclear power plants in war drew upon the research of Prof. Theresa Sabonis-Helf from Georgetown University.

Alan Howard, Dan Nussbaum and Brenda Shaffer

Preface

It is a commonplace to say that "energy is the lifeblood of civilization." Energy fundamentally orders the global landscape, including geopolitics, economics, and the conduct of military operations.

Despite the critical role of energy in the outcome of battles and wars, this is the first textbook on operational energy (OE). Operational energy is "the energy required for training, moving, and sustaining military forces and weapons platforms for military operations." Until recently, most militaries treated OE needs as a subset of logistics. Today, the US military views operational energy not only as ensuring supplies to enable the military's operations, but as a component of war strategy that increases the power and lethality of American troops, while denying energy supplies to US adversaries.

Energy is an enabler of – and a constraint on – military power. Operational Energy superiority requires the ability to fully exploit one's own energy capabilities while preventing the adversary from doing the same.

As stated in this book, "Throughout history, militaries have sought to gain energy supplies and deny them to their adversaries" and that energy "has played a role in military conflicts and the determination of their outcomes. Energy supply options have shaped decisions in battles; and commanders have leveraged and sought out energy advantages to gain an edge on opponents. Enemy energy supply lines are regularly targeted as part of battle and war. In many instances, access to energy also played a role in the initiation of conflict."

Operational Energy provides military officers with knowledge and skills to plan effectively for the OE needs of their forces. The authors of this textbook have begun to repair the gap in the energy and logistics literature. *Operational Energy also* examines multiple cases and lessons learned on the role of OE in the battlespace.

Military historians recount that 150 years ago, OE took the form of food stocks to feed horses. Today OE takes the form of the enabling power for just about everything – military aircraft, ships, land vehicles, space platforms, electrical grids for automation and communications, forward bases, and directed energy has even become a new weapon.

Operational Energy needs have grown rapidly over the twentieth century. We require ever-larger overall levels of energy: The operational energy needs of the US military has increased with the introduction of each new weapon system and platform. This growth is not only in volumes but in the need for specific types of fuels. The US military is also facing growing operational energy challenges due to the increased geographic spread of its missions around the globe.

Throughout most of its history, the United States has enjoyed access to almost undisrupted energy supplies and operational energy superiority. However, this has changed. As pointed out in this book, US adversaries—China, Iran and Russia—all intend in conflict to target US energy supplies, both at home and abroad. The United States is especially vulnerable to threats to its energy supplies in conducting operations in Asia, in contrast to the European theater.

Today, energy is a critical pillar of national defense and a major factor in military power. In modern warfare, attaining energy superiority over one's adversaries is a critical condition for success on the battlefield. Operational energy planning is an integral part of all combat and regular operations. The centrality and vulnerability of OE is a major reason that we must educate service members and military civilians on OE throughout their careers and at all levels of conflict—tactical, operational, and strategic. US Department of Defense personnel must be experts in OE, in any given battlespace. Since operational energy will undoubtedly remain essential for almost all forms of combat and at all levels of combat, the need to educate, at all ranks, is urgent and persistent.

While no text can profess to be a complete compendium on OE, this text makes the requisite start. Comments from the future readership will undoubtedly shape future editions. For now, this text is the correct beginning.

Dr. Dan Nussbaum
Chair, Energy Academic Group, US Naval Postgraduate School

Contents

1 Introduction — 1
1.1 Definition of Operational Energy — 3
1.1.1 OE Superiority — 4
1.2 OE Needs Are Increasing and Will Increase Further — 4
1.3 Establishment of OE Planning in the US Military — 7
1.4 OE versus Civilian Energy Security — 7
1.5 Energy as a Weapon in the Emerging Battlefield — 8
1.6 OE: Long-Term and Short-Term — 8
1.7 OE as a Vulnerability — 8
1.8 Critical Infrastructure and Critical Energy Infrastructure — 9
1.9 DOD OE Guidance and Tools — 10
1.10 Textbook Structure — 10
1.11 For Study — 10
1.12 Topics for Discussion and Research — 10

2 Operational Energy throughout History — 12
2.1 Energy Transitions and Militaries — 12
2.2 Energy Transitions and War — 13
2.3 Energy Affects Military Decisions and Outcomes — 16
2.3.1 Energy as a Constraint — 18
2.3.2 Energy as an Advantage — 18
2.4 Anticipating and Developing the Next Energy Transition as Part of Military Power — 20
2.5 For Study — 21
2.6 Topics for Discussion and Research — 21
2.7 Case Study: Operation Edelweiss 1942 — 21
2.7.1 Questions for Discussion — 26

3 Geopolitics of Operational Energy — 27
3.1 Energy Basics — 27
3.1.1 Global Fuel Mix — 27
3.1.2 Global Energy Total Consumption Trends — 28
3.1.3 Energy Density — 29
3.1.4 Energy Transportation and Markets — 29
3.1.4.1 Oil — 29
3.1.4.2 Coal — 30
3.1.4.3 Natural Gas — 31
3.1.4.4 Renewable Energy — 31
3.1.4.5 Nuclear Energy — 32
3.1.4.6 Electricity — 33

3.2	Global Geopolitics of Energy —— 34	
3.2.1	Geopolitics of Different Fuel Sources —— 35	
3.2.1.1	Geopolitics of Oil —— 36	
3.2.1.2	Changing Geopolitics of Oil —— 36	
3.2.2	Geopolitics of Natural Gas —— 37	
3.2.3	Geopolitics of Minerals and Metals for Renewable Energy —— 38	
3.2.4	Energy and Maritime Delimitation Conflicts —— 38	
3.2.5	Maritime Energy Transportation: International Waterways and Chokepoints —— 39	
3.2.6	US Adversaries Seek to Influence US's and Allies' Energy Policies —— 39	
3.2.7	Economic Tools of Geopolitics of Energy —— 40	
3.2.8	Energy Security Policies —— 40	
3.3	Geopolitics of OE —— 41	
3.3.1	US Government and Public Limitations on OE —— 43	
3.3.2	Hybrid Warfare: OE Threats —— 45	
3.3.3	Reliance on Civilian Energy Supply Lines —— 46	
3.3.4	International Legal Conventions Affecting OE —— 47	
3.3.5	OE and Sea Chokepoints —— 47	
3.3.6	OE Implications of the "Pivot to Asia" —— 47	
3.4	Protection of Energy Infrastructure of US Allies and Partners —— 48	
3.4.1	Identification and Planning to Exploit OE Vulnerabilities of American Adversaries —— 50	
3.5	OE Planning: Geopolitical Factors —— 50	
3.6	Necessary Intelligence on Geopolitics of Energy for OE —— 51	
3.6.1	Cross-Agency Cooperation: OE Supplies and Infrastructure —— 51	
3.7	International and Regional Institutions —— 52	
3.8	For Study —— 52	
3.9	Topics for Discussion and Research —— 53	
3.10	Case Study: Energy in Conflict – the 2020 Armenia-Azerbaijan War —— 53	
3.10.1	Background: The Armenia-Azerbaijan Conflict —— 54	
3.10.2	Energy Export —— 55	
3.10.3	Energy – the Catalyst for Reignition of War —— 56	
3.10.4	Attacks on International Pipelines during the War —— 59	
3.10.5	Weaponization of Energy Infrastructure —— 60	
3.10.5.1	Armenia's Threats to the Mingachevir Hydropower Station —— 60	
3.10.5.2	Azerbaijan's Threat to the Metsamor Nuclear Power Plant —— 61	
3.10.6	Energy Post-war —— 62	
3.10.7	Conclusions —— 62	
3.10.8	Questions for Discussion —— 63	
3.11	Case Study: Nuclear Power Plants in War – The Case of Ukraine —— 64	
3.11.1	The Russia-Ukraine War and the Zaporizhzhya Nuclear Power Plant —— 65	
3.11.2	IAEA Plays a Role —— 67	
3.11.3	Russian and Ukrainian Aims —— 70	

3.11.4 Case Conclusions —— 70
3.11.5 Topics for Discussion and Research —— 71

4 Military Threats to Operational Energy —— 72
Lawrence M. Waltzer
4.1 What Is a Threat? —— 72
4.2 Thinking About Threats —— 73
4.3 Center of Gravity Analysis —— 74
4.4 Connecting the JIPOE with Planning and Targeting —— 76
4.5 Control and Weaponization of Energy —— 77
4.6 Deliberate versus Non-deliberate Threats to OE —— 78
4.7 Non-deliberate Threats to OE —— 78
4.7.1 Geography —— 78
4.7.2 Accidents/Safety —— 80
4.7.3 Aging or Poorly Constructed, Maintained, and/or Operated Infrastructure —— 81
4.7.4 Poor Decision-Making and Policies —— 81
4.7.5 Theft —— 81
4.8 Deliberate Threats to OE —— 82
4.8.1 Terrorism —— 82
4.8.2 Looting —— 87
4.8.3 Sabotage —— 87
4.8.4 Cyberattack —— 88
4.8.5 Blockade —— 92
4.8.6 Aerial Bombings / Indirect Military Fires —— 93
4.9 US Adversaries' Views on Disruption of Opponents' OE Supplies —— 94
4.9.1 China —— 94
4.9.2 Russia —— 97
4.9.3 Iran —— 97
4.9.4 Conclusions on US Adversaries' Views of American Operational Energy Vulnerabilities —— 99
4.10 For Study —— 100
4.11 Questions for Discussion —— 100
4.12 Case study: Destroying the Enemy's Energy Supplies in the Twenty-First Century —— 100
4.12.1 Details of Cases —— 101
4.12.1.1 Russia – Ukraine (from February 2022) —— 101
4.12.1.2 Israel-Hamas (from October 7, 2023) —— 103
4.12.2 Case Conclusions —— 104
4.12.3 Questions for Discussion and Research —— 105
4.13 Case Study: The Attack on the Metcalf Electricity Substation —— 105
4.13.1 Background: Metcalf and the Role of Transformers in the Energy Grid —— 106
4.13.2 Attack on Metcalf —— 107

4.13.3 Assessment of the Attack —— 108
4.13.4 Discussion —— 110

5 Operational Energy Policy, Strategy, and Institutions —— 111
5.1 Congressional Interest —— 111
5.2 DOD Interest —— 111
5.3 National Defense Authorization Legislation —— 113
5.4 National Security, Defense, and OE Strategies —— 113
5.5 OE Institutions —— 115
5.6 Requirements of the Different Services —— 116
5.7 US DOD Institutions —— 117
5.7.1 US Transportation Command and the Defense Logistics Agency —— 117
5.8 For Study —— 118
5.9 Topics for Discussion and Research —— 118
5.10 Case Study: The Colonial Pipeline Cyberattack —— 118
5.10.1 Background —— 118
5.10.2 The Colonial Pipeline —— 119
5.10.3 Importance to US National Security —— 119
5.10.4 Pipeline Performance —— 120
5.10.5 IT Performance —— 121
5.10.6 Anatomy of the Attack: Events of May 7, 2021, and After —— 122
5.10.6.1 Pipeline Recovery Actions —— 123
5.10.6.2 What Was Targeted and How? —— 124
5.10.6.3 The Perpetrators —— 124
5.10.7 Impact and Recovery —— 125
5.10.7.1 Fuel Hoarding —— 125
5.10.8 US Federal and State Government Response —— 126
5.10.8.1 Balance between Commercial and Government Oversight —— 127
5.10.9 Topics for Discussion and Research —— 128

6 Operational Energy Vulnerability and Resilience —— 129
Daniel A. Eisenberg and David L. Alderson
6.1 Background on Vulnerability and Resilience in OE Systems —— 129
6.2 Vulnerability Analysis for OE Systems —— 131
6.3 Reliability, Risk, and Adversarial Analysis —— 134
6.3.1 The Basics —— 134
6.3.2 The Details —— 136
6.3.2.1 Reliability Analysis —— 136
6.3.2.2 Risk Analysis —— 137
6.3.2.3 Adversarial Analysis —— 138
6.3.3 Example for How Reliability, Risk, and Adversarial Analyses Produce Different Results —— 140
6.4 Resilience Strategies for OE Systems —— 141

6.5	Resilience Outcomes: What Should Systems Do (Rather than Fail) —— 143	
6.6	A Final Thought: Efficiency vs Resilience —— 145	
6.7	Topics for Discussion and Research —— 146	
6.8	Case Study: The US Virgin Islands – the Hurricanes of 2017 —— 146	
6.8.1	Vulnerability Analysis of the USVI Energy System —— 148	
6.8.2	Case Conclusions —— 150	
6.8.3	Topics for Discussion and Research —— 151	

7 Education and Training —— 152

7.1	The Importance of OE Education to the Military Mission —— 152
7.2	Current Gap in OE Education —— 153
7.3	Training Requirements and Structure —— 154
7.3.1	A Multi-Tiered Solution —— 154
7.3.1.1	Tier 1: Foundational Instruction —— 155
	OE Introduction, Level I —— 155
7.3.1.2	Tier 2: Advanced OE Instruction —— 155
	OE Introduction, Level II —— 155
7.3.1.3	Tier 3: Future or Specialized Instruction —— 156
7.3.2	Potential Additional Curriculum Topics —— 156
7.3.2.1	Decision Support Tools —— 156
7.3.2.2	Enhanced or Future OE Instruction —— 156
7.3.3	Critical Infrastructure Operators and Resilience Specialist Training —— 157
7.3.4	Climate and Weather Impact on OE —— 157
7.4	An OE Education and Training Implementation Plan —— 157
7.5	Education Tools: Wargames, Tabletop Exercises, Case Studies, Best Practices and Enhancing Cooperation with Allies and Partners —— 158
7.5.1	Wargames —— 158
7.5.2	Exercises —— 158
7.5.3	Case Studies —— 159
7.5.4	Best Practices Analysis —— 159
7.6	OE Education Cooperation with Allies and Partners —— 159
7.7	Conclusions —— 160
7.8	For Discussion in the Classroom and Study —— 160

8 Operational Energy Challenges of the Armed Service Branches —— 161

8.1	OE Challenges for Today's Military —— 161
8.1.1	The Costs of Energy —— 162
8.2	What Changed? —— 164
8.2.1	Appearance of Digital Devices on the Battlefield —— 165
8.3	Military Approach to Energy Use —— 170
8.4	Service-Specific OE Challenges —— 171
8.4.1	The US Air Force —— 171
	The Air Force's Approach to Reducing Energy Consumption —— 172

8.4.2   The US Naval Services —— **175**
8.4.3   The US Army —— **179**
8.5   Conclusion —— **181**
8.6   Case Study: Closure of the Red Hill Fuel Storage Facility at Pearl Harbor —— **182**
8.6.1   Questions for Discussion —— **187**

9   Looking Ahead: Operational Energy Adoption of Technology —— 188

Appendix —— 191
A.1   OE Ontologies —— **191**
A.2   Operational Energy Ontology —— **191**
A.2.1   Energy Sub-Systems —— **192**
        Sources —— **192**
        Controls and Power Management —— **193**
        Power Generation / Conversion —— **193**
        Distribution —— **194**
        Storage —— **195**
A.2.2   Enablers —— **195**
        Tools and Analytics —— **195**
        Training and Education —— **195**
A.2.3   Systems —— **196**
        Weapons Systems —— **196**
        Platforms and Propulsion —— **196**
        Auxiliary Systems —— **196**
A.2.4   Operations —— **196**
        Weapon Capability —— **196**
        Platform Capability —— **197**
        Mission —— **197**
        Operational Effect —— **197**

Index —— 199

1 Introduction

Energy is an enabler of – and a constraint on – military power. *Operational Energy* provides military officers with knowledge and skills to plan effectively for the operational energy needs of their forces. The US Department of Defense (DOD) defines operational energy (OE) as the "energy required for training, moving, and sustaining military forces and weapons platforms for military operations."[1] It includes energy used by ships, aircraft, combat vehicles, and power generators that serve military operations.

Operational Energy is a textbook for use primarily in DOD courses in US military universities, colleges, and training programs; US service academies; and US senior service academies. *Operational Energy* also provides researchers on US and global energy security a resource to understand military energy needs. Scholars of geopolitics can learn from the book about a critical source of military power, as well as a potential national security vulnerability and source of strength of states.

Energy has always played a role in battlefield outcomes. Over the twentieth and early twenty-first centuries the importance of energy in warfighting has grown. Today, energy is a critical pillar of national defense and a major factor in military power. In modern warfare, attaining energy superiority over one's adversaries is a critical condition for success on the battlefield. Correct OE policies optimize missions and affect the strategic outcome of conflicts.

OE planning goes far beyond logistics. OE is emerging as an element of US military strategy. OE strategy affects US military effectiveness and lethality and that of opponents. OE planning is an integral part of all combat and regular operations. OE strategy requires identifying and planning for the challenges of US military global power projection and the risks posed to the energy supply chain in support of America's global missions.[2] OE strategy requires identifying and planning ways to foil opponents' access to energy supplies.

Energy is both a major constraint and at the same time one of the most important enablers of military missions. As stated in the 2016 *Department of Defense Operational Energy Strategy:* "Energy is a fundamental enabler of military capability, and the ability of the United States to project and sustain the power necessary for defense depends on the assured delivery of this energy. It must be available at home and abroad, over

---

[1] Office of the Law Revision Counsel, "United States Code: 10 US Code § 2924 (4): Operational Energy" (https://uscode.house.gov/view.xhtml?req=granuleid:USC-prelim-title10-section2924&num=0&edition=prelim).
[2] Department of Defense, *2016 Operational Energy Strategy*, December 3, 2015, page 7 (https://www.acq.osd.mil/eie/Downloads/OE/2016%20OE%20Strategy_WEBd.pdf).

great distances, through adverse weather, and across air, land, and sea, often against determined adversaries."[3]

> "Operational energy in the battlespace is about improving combat effectiveness. It's about increasing our forces' endurance, being more lethal, and reducing the number of men and women risking their lives moving fuel."
>
> – Gen. John Allen, USMC, Commander, US Forces in Afghanistan, in a December 2011 policy memorandum

Energy supply capacities determine the time, length, and physical distance of military operations. Energy is the main limit on military operational reach. More efficient use of energy means the capacity for longer military operations and at farther distances. Lower fuel needs mean less risk from operations to supply the fuel and decrease the ability of US adversaries to disrupt supplies and thus operations.

OE can also be a vulnerability, intentionally disrupted by adversaries, and a source of causalities. OE needs are an integral input into both tactical and strategic planning processes and the overall risk identification process. In parallel, America's adversaries also have OE vulnerabilities that the US military can exploit.

With the increase in hybrid warfare, the threat of potential disruption of US domestic energy supplies and targeting of domestic US energy infrastructure has emerged. The 2023 *US Department of Defense Operational Energy Strategy* recognizes this threat and states: "The dual realities of a homeland that is no longer a sanctuary and increasingly contested logistics ensure that access to energy will only grow more challenging over time."[4]

OE consumes approximately 85 percent of the US military's overall energy consumption, with the remainder spent on supporting and running fixed installations. Under the DOD, the Air Force is the largest consumer of OE. The Air Force consumes close to half the fuel used by DOD, while the US Navy consumes approximately a third of the fuel.

General advances in how energy is produced and consumed translate into changes in warfighting. Each historical energy transition profoundly changed the battlefield. And vice versa, developments in the battlefield have triggered energy transitions or significant changes in how the civilian sector produces and consumes energy.

---

[3] Department of Defense, *2016 Operational Energy Strategy*, December 3, 2015, page 3 (https://www.acq.osd.mil/eie/Downloads/OE/2016%20OE%20Strategy_WEBd.pdf).

[4] Department of Defense, *2023 Operational Energy Strategy*, May 2023, page 1 (https://www.acq.osd.mil/eie/Downloads/OE/2023%20Operational%20Energy%20Strategy.pdf).

Decisions on weapons and platform design lock the military into needs for certain types of fuel and quantities for several decades. For instance, a fighter plane design based on access to energy-dense petroleum derived liquid fuels cannot likely be adapted to electricity as a fuel source. Thus, the design decisions should take into consideration the desired future fuel needs of the US military and vice-versa. In addition, the military's decisions on main fuel sources impact weapon and platform design options, and thus need to take into consideration this impact.

> "Coalition forces possess the ability to project power around the globe for extended periods, often times in the harshest environments. Inherent to this capability is our need for fuel, which is greater than at any time in history. This 'operational energy' is the lifeblood of our warfighting capabilities."
>
> – Gen. David Petraeus, in a 2011 Memorandum to the Force

1.1 Definition of Operational Energy

Operational energy (OE) is:

> The energy required for training, moving, and sustaining military forces and weapons platforms for military operations. The term includes energy used by forward bases, mobile forces, tactical power systems, communications, cyber systems, and energy weapons platforms.[5]

OE includes all the energy used in military operations, in direct support of military operations, and in training that supports unit readiness for military operations, and includes the energy used at non-enduring locations (contingency bases).

OE differs from *installation energy*, which is "the energy used to power installations and enduring locations, as well as the non-tactical fleet vehicles used at those locations."[6] Installation energy is referred to at times as facility energy. However, there is some overlap as energy consumed at installations that directly support military operations falls under the definition of OE.

As operational missions are increasingly performed from US bases and installations, the distinction between operational and installation energy is becoming less clear. This distinction is further eroded as warfare becomes more digital.

---

5 Office of the Law Revision Counsel, "United States Code: 10 US Code § 2924 (4): Operational Energy" (https://uscode.house.gov/view.xhtml?req=granuleid:USC-prelim-title10-section2924&num=0&edition=prelim).
6 Department of Defense, *2016 Operational Energy Strategy*, December 3, 2015, page 4 (https://www.acq.osd.mil/eie/Downloads/OE/2016%20OE%20Strategy_WEBd.pdf).

US Congressional legislation requires that "the Secretary of Defense shall ensure the types, availability, and use of operational energy promote the readiness of the armed forces for their military missions in contested logistics environments." The legislation states that "The Secretary of Defense shall

(1) require the Secretaries concerned and the commanders of the combatant commands to assess the energy supportability in contested logistics environments of systems, capabilities, and plans;
(2) authorize the use of energy security, cost of backup power, supportability in contested logistics environments, and energy resilience as factors in the cost-benefit analysis for procurement of operational equipment; and
(3) in selecting equipment that will use operational energy, give favorable consideration to the acquisition of equipment that enhances energy security, energy resilience, energy conservation, and reduces logistical vulnerabilities in contested logistics environments."[7]

1.1.1 OE Superiority

Success in the OE domain occurs when (1) there is efficient, effective, and sustained production of combat power when and where it is required by friendly forces, while (2) the enemy combat power production is disrupted, degraded, or destroyed. OE superiority is the ability to fully exploit one's own energy capabilities while preventing the adversary from doing the same.[8]

> OE superiority is the ability to fully exploit one's own energy capabilities while preventing the adversary from doing the same.

1.2 OE Needs Are Increasing and Will Increase Further

War and conflict have become more energy intensive over the years. OE needs are increasing in both quantity and the need to provide more specific fuels and energy sources, due to the increased sophistication and range of diversity of weapons systems. Greater use of electronics in the battlefield also entails increased energy demand for cooling and heating equipment. All digital functions and modern communications

---

7 Office of the Law Revision Counsel, "United States Code: 10 US Code § 2926 section 2911(a) Operational Energy" (https://uscode.house.gov/view.xhtml?req=granuleid:USC-prelim-title10-section2926&num=0&edition=prelim).
8 RuthAnne Darling and Paul Mason Carpenter, "Energy: An Essential Element for Winning Future Wars – Operational Energy Part 1," *Surge*, Summer 2020, Naval Postgraduate School (https://nps.edu/web/eag/future-wars).

are dependent on energy supplies. Energy is now used directly as a weapon as well on the modern battlefield.

> "Every major system that the U.S. is developing, requires higher fuel demands. Not only more fuel, but different types of fuel."
>
> – Eric Turner, Lt. Col USAF retired

The nature of the modern battlefield increases OE needs and vulnerabilities. For instance, the twenty-first-century battlespace requires that the US and allied forces place a larger number of forward-deployed assets. Energy needs have grown over time: during World War II, the average fuel demand per soldier was a gallon a day. In contrast, Operations Iraqi Freedom and Enduring Freedom required 15–20 gallons a day per soldier. In addition, in recent decades, new weapons systems are generally more energy intensive than the systems which they replace. For instance, the F-35, which replaces the F/A-18s, and the Littoral Combat Ship (LCS), which replaces legacy frigates in the US Navy, both use substantially more energy than their predecessors.

OE needs are increasing: the newer generation of weapons demands higher volumes of energy; the US military is operating over larger operating areas; with flat or declining fuel logistics capacity[9] and amidst increasing threats to infrastructure. Due to the ever-increasing geographic spread of US military missions, and the likelihood of multiple conflicts taking place in different geographies, OE needs are anticipated to increase. American adversaries target and will continue to target these longer-stretched energy supply lines.

OE needs themselves also create increased demands for new military ships and other vehicles. Ships and other vehicles must not only power themselves, but serve as a power station for the weapons systems they carry and potentially for troops and other vehicles in their vicinity. Engineers now design this power provision function into ships and other vehicles, creating new design demands.

The US military continually strives to increase energy efficiency. However, when the military becomes more energy efficient, it rarely reduces the volumes of energy it consumes, but rather translates the efficiency gained into longer and more distant missions and increased energy use in weapons systems.

Since the conclusion of World War II, the US has not fought in a conflict where strategic logistical supply lines were seriously threatened or disrupted by an adversary.

---

9 Department of Defense, *2016 Operational Energy Strategy*, December 3, 2015, page 9 (https://www.acq.osd.mil/eie/Downloads/OE/2016%20OE%20Strategy_WEBd.pdf).

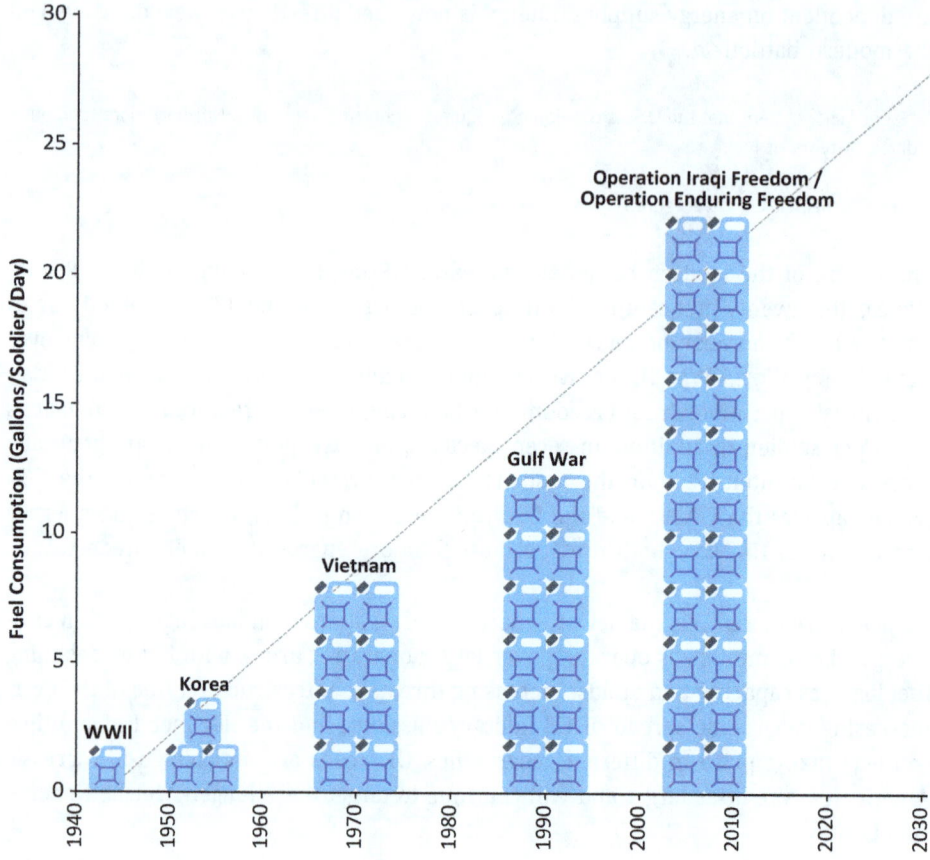

Figure 1.1: Historic Fuel Consumption. Source: DESC Rand Corporation, AMSAA, Deloitte Analysis.

This may have resulted in creating several generations of military leaders and troops who have become complacent in their views and practices regarding access to OE.

> "Operational energy requires not only meeting the energy needs of our forces, but complicating the enemy's access to energy, and creating problems for the enemy.
>
> For example, destroying the power grid at your enemy's base is the best way to keep aircraft from lifting off the ground from that base. Least risky and usually most cost efficient.
>
> Every conflict from World War Two until now demonstrates that we're going to a posture of more distributed forces. This allows carrying out missions at higher speeds and at greater ranges. However, this creates new challenges to fuel the distributed forces. This also means the US military needs to access energy from commercial networks.
>
> We need to increase the monitoring and measurement of energy use in the military in order to reduce consumption and raise efficiency.

> In order to reduce our energy consumption, we need to measure the energy needs of a weapon system or platform across its lifecycle, not just during military operations.
>
> Weapon system designers need to also account the energy requirements of their designs.
>
> Hybrid systems and vehicles that incorporate electricity and fuels can enhance the operational energy performance."
>
> - Interview with James C. Caley, Director of Operational Energy, Department of the Navy.

1.3 Establishment of OE Planning in the US Military

While militaries throughout history have planned to ensure supplies of their energy needs (see Chapter 2), up until 2010 the DOD treated OE as a subset of logistics planning. That year, the DOD established OE strategy and planning as a separate discipline from logistics planning, with the establishment of the Operational Energy Plans and Programs directorate within the Office of the Under Secretary of Defense of Acquisition, Technology & Logistics (see Chapter 5). Congress requires each service to have a similar office.

The OE strategy of the DOD is codified in the DOD *Operational Energy Strategy*. The first *Operational Energy Strategy* was issued in 2011 and new strategies are required by law to be issued every five years (see Chapter 5).[10] Despite the importance of OE to warfighting, at the time of publication the DOD had not developed an OE doctrine.

1.4 OE versus Civilian Energy Security

OE planning is very different from energy security planning in the civilian sector. The civilian sector can endure "blackouts" and other energy supply disruptions. Civilian energy supply disruptions generally result in economic damage. In contrast, the costs for supply disruptions to the military often result in significant loss of life, failure of military operations, the loss of battles, and failure in war. In addition, in contrast to the civilian sector, OE needs to provide for the peak power needs of the military. While the civilian sector can tolerate some disruptions during peak power needs, disruptions to the military are not tolerable since those peak needs are usually critical to the fulfillment of military missions.

> OE must provide for the peak power needs of the military. While the civilian sector can tolerate some disruptions during peak power needs, disruptions to the military are not tolerable since those peak needs are usually critical to the fulfillment of military missions. Since energy disruption carries such

---

10 Department of Defense, *2016 Operational Energy Strategy*, December 3, 2015 (https://www.acq.osd.mil/eie/Downloads/OE/2016%20OE%20Strategy_WEBd.pdf).

> high costs to militaries, optimal OE planning requires a much larger margin of backup, diversification, and system redundancy than the civilian sector.

Since energy disruption carries such high costs to militaries, optimal OE planning requires a much larger margin of backup, diversification, and system redundancy than the civilian sector. The US military also needs highly specialized fuels, and often at short notice and thus can't rely on commercial markets alone to supply them. Moreover, unlike the civilian sector, the military also is required to supply energy over long distances – essentially anywhere on the globe, at short notice, all the time.

1.5 Energy as a Weapon in the Emerging Battlefield

Another reason OE needs are increasing is that the emerging battlefield involves greater use of directed energy weapons, such as lasers, particle beam weapons, microwave arms, and railguns and electronic warfare capabilities. In the coming years, it is likely that directed energy weapons will play a major role in the battlespace.[11]

With directed energy, electronic warfare, and the future use of new tools like power beaming, forces will need to adapt their approach to energy planning. The energy used for powering energy weapons is becoming the "bullets." When you get low on energy, you run out of bullets. Optimizing energy use will become analogous to the conservation of ammunition for the future warfighter.

1.6 OE: Long-Term and Short-Term

OE planning involves long-term and short-term components, which generally occur at different command levels. Senior commanders need to plan for the acquisition and development of fuel sources that increase US military power and to foil enemy access to energy. At the same time, operational commanders need to plan for short-term OE needs that maximize performance in a specific operation and/or theater, while denying fuel supplies to enemy forces.

1.7 OE as a Vulnerability

In post-World War II warfighting, the United States military rarely encountered serious challenges to its energy supply lines. However, this likely has changed. The large geo-

---

[11] Mason Carpenter, Paul Sullivan, and Dan Nussbaum, "Operational Energy: Essential Knowledge for Military Officers" (https://nps.edu/web/eag/operational-energy-essential-knowledge-for-military-officers).

graphic spread of US military missions, many in regions where the US cannot count on access to energy supplies such as Asia, has created new vulnerabilities. In addition, US rivals – China, Russia, Iran – have growing technological abilities that can challenge American energy supplies, especially those close to their territory in Asia and the Middle East.

Moreover, US adversaries plan to target American military energy supply lines to disrupt and deny energy supplies. They will use a variety of tools, including physical disruption, cyberattacks, and coopting of civilian suppliers of energy, especially outside the United States.

Furthermore, the US military uses civilian supply lines and energy systems and sources energy from civilian entities at home and abroad. These civilian lines are more vulnerable to threats from adversaries, especially cyber attacks, due to a lower level of protection in force than that in military units and military supply lines. Accordingly, adversaries are likely to target these civilian energy supply sources, in order to undermine US military energy supplies.

In addition, in the battlespace military units delivering fuel are often vulnerable targets, as they are usually large, slow-moving vehicles, laden with explosive and flammable materials.

1.8 Critical Infrastructure and Critical Energy Infrastructure

OE planning requires identifying the critical infrastructure and critical energy infrastructure in a theater of operations.

American critical infrastructure is defined as "systems and assets, whether physical or virtual, so vital to the United States that the incapacity or destruction of such systems and assets would have a debilitating impact on security, the national economy, national public health or safety, or any combination of those matters."[12]

OE infrastructure often is dependent on general infrastructure, such as civilian supply chains, creating a challenge to protect and maintain the infrastructure and obligating cooperation with commercial and civilian government authorities (see Case Study Colonial Pipeline Attack, Chapter 5).

---

12 US Government Publishing Office, "42 USC. 5195c(e), Critical Infrastructures Protection," 2010 (https://www.govinfo.gov/app/details/USCODE-2021-title42/USCODE-2021-title42-chap68-subchapIV-B-sec5195c/summary).

> Critical Energy Infrastructure: Systems and assets so vital to the functioning of an energy system that the incapacity or destruction of such systems and assets would have a debilitating impact on security, national economic security, national public health or safety, or any combination of those.

1.9 DOD OE Guidance and Tools

The US DOD has developed guidance and tools to plan the OE of missions. The Office of the Secretary of Defense Operational Energy-Innovation Directorate has developed an *energy ontology model* for analysis of OE tasks. The full OE ontology appears in the appendix of this textbook.

1.10 Textbook Structure

The textbook comprises of chapters focusing on different aspects of OE. At the end of each chapter, there is a summary of major topics for study and for discussion in the classroom. Most chapters have case studies, which are useful for deepening understanding of OE challenges and generating new thinking on OE. Instructors can assign many of the questions and topics for discussions in the chapters and case studies as papers and other research project topics for course work.

1.11 For Study

- Memorize the definition of OE.
- Understand the difference between OE and installation energy.
- Memorize the definitions of critical infrastructure and critical energy infrastructure.

1.12 Topics for Discussion and Research

- Explain why energy is both an enabler and constraint on military operations.
- Discuss how energy is a vulnerability of the US military.
- Why are energy supplies a target in military operations?
- How does OE strategy differ from logistics strategy?
- Explain why lower fuel consumption allows the US military to conduct longer and more distant missions.
- Why is OE fundamentally different from the security of supply of civilian energy systems?

- Why will US adversaries likely target civilian energy supply systems in the US and abroad in order to disrupt American OE supplies?
- Why are OE needs growing over time? What can be done to change this?
- What are some examples you are aware of that illustrate the role of OE in conflict?
- Examine and share examples of the role of OE from your military experience.

2 Operational Energy throughout History

Throughout history, OE has played a role in military conflicts and the determination of their outcomes. Energy supply options have shaped decisions in battles; and commanders have leveraged and sought out energy advantages to gain an edge on opponents. Enemy energy supply lines are regularly targeted as part of battle and war. In many instances, access to energy also played a role in the initiation of conflict.

In recent decades, OE needs have changed fundamentally and are increasing in importance. Energy needs are growing and the need for specific fuel types is expanding. Energy not only serves as a means of moving and powering combatants and their equipment but is also a weapon itself.

Energy transitions have sparked military transitions. Militaries' strategies, tactics, and reach have changed as energy technology has advanced. At the same time, war has played a role in catalyzing energy transitions in the civilian sphere and technological advances in energy. The arrow points in both directions: energy transitions create new battlespace conditions, while at other times, battlespace developments generate new energy transitions.

> The arrow points in both directions: energy transitions create new battlespace conditions, while at other times, developments in the battlespace generate new energy transitions.

This chapter examines the impact of OE on military developments throughout history. The chapter also discusses how energy transitions generate developments in the battlefield and technological developments in the military trigger energy transitions.

2.1 Energy Transitions and Militaries

Throughout history, energy transitions have occurred that fundamentally changed how humans produce and consume energy. An energy transition is a change in the primary energy source or group of sources to a different primary energy source or fuel mix and the resulting economic, industrial, geopolitical, societal, technological, and environmental changes.[13] Significant technological and/or commercial developments that create widespread and affordable access to an energy source are the catalysts for energy transitions.

Energy transitions have had direct effect on the predominant fuels in use in warfare, OE needs, and warfighting itself. These changes in OE uses and requirements have also

---

[13] Definition of *energy transition* in Brenda Shaffer, *Energy Crisis* (forthcoming, 2025).

had significant geopolitical impact, determining the physical range of conflicts and distances of overseas wars and conquests. The nineteenth-century energy transition from wood and animal products to coal, and the early twentieth-century transition from coal and animals to oil, fundamentally changed the international political system, as states that were separated over long distances now interacted.

> An energy transition is a change in the primary energy source or group of sources to a different primary energy source or fuel mix and the resulting economic, industrial, geopolitical, societal, technological, and environmental changes.

Energy transitions create a variety of changes, including supply chain routes and scope, needs for materials, commercial trends, workforce composition, regulatory and legal frameworks, environmental impact, and foreign relations.

Energy transitions create new opportunities, but also new challenges for militaries. Militaries need not only to be resilient to the changes brought on by energy transitions, but to position themselves to increase their power in a new energy era.

Energy transitions are not always easy to identify when they are taking place. Over the twentieth century and early twenty-first century, many myths have been propagated about how the globe's population uses energy and future trends indicating imminent transitions that did not emerge. There was "peak oil," which purported in the 1980s and 1990s that the globe would soon run out of oil, leading to oil scarcity. Instead, the shale revolution emerged, leading to rapid and significant growth in global oil and natural gas volumes and to the emergence of the United States as the global energy superpower. Then in the 2010s, came "peak demand" concept proponents who claimed that global demand for fossil fuels had peaked and was soon to be replaced by renewable energy, in the early twenty-first century. However, despite spending trillions of dollars on subsidies on renewable energy generation and infrastructure in the early twenty-first century, at the time of publication, renewable energy provided less than 10 percent of the globe's energy needs.

Accordingly, military planners need to correctly identify the emerging energy transitions in order to build forces that best adapt and harness the new dominant energy form. At the same time, they must exert caution and correctly assess which ideas, that policymakers and the media promote, will actually materialize.

2.2 Energy Transitions and War

Until the late nineteenth century, humans and animals were the core source of OE. Commanders calculated food and water needs not only for the soldiers, but for the energy needs of warfighting. Commanders also harnessed wind and water to move troops and goods.

Two major energy transitions took place in the late nineteenth century and early twentieth century, and they had a significant impact on warfare. These two energy transitions were based on the use of hydrocarbons – coal and oil. These two energy transitions had significant impact on the OE needs and capabilities of armed forces.

Up until the eve of the twentieth century, the predominant energy sources were wood and animal products, including dung and whale blubber. This changed over the course of the 1800s, with the widening use of coal. The widespread use of coal to produce steam in the second half of the nineteenth century ushered in the Industrial Revolution. As a result, militaries could power and move larger and heavier weapons and propel them for greater distance and with increased firepower. In addition, the Industrial Revolution enabled the mass production of weapons. Moreover, steam power emerged to propel rail and sea vessels, lengthening the distances that forces could be deployed and reducing the time to reach locations.

This energy transition enabled power projection across vast distances and thus changed the nature of international engagements and the international security system. The increased range of sea vessels led to increased volumes of international trade and new exchanges of goods. This increased range also enabled the establishment of vast empires overseas, generating new military engagements and security needs.

The use of railroads, enabled by the use of coal to produce steam power, to transport soldiers and equipment had a major impact on the American Civil War and the Austro-Prussian War of 1866, in which Prussia used the rail system to great advantage, moving men and material.

The next energy transition, which began early in the twentieth century, was to the widespread use of crude oil and refined products. One of the most monumental shifts in warfighting enabled by this energy transition came when Winston Churchill, then First Lord of the Admiralty, decided to transition the British Royal Navy from coal-fired propulsion to oil. While this provided the British Navy greater range and speed, it meant that the UK needed to acquire oil abroad to meet its OE needs, rather than rely on domestically produced coal. This change was initially resisted by the Navy because of the dependence on oil imports. Eventually, over time the British Navy recognized the advantages of faster cruising speeds and longer duration patrols enabled by the switch to petroleum. Many other countries switched to petroleum following the British, making access to oil a necessary component of an effective modern naval force. This fundamentally changed OE needs and global geopolitics.

The transition to refined crude oil for transportation led to widespread use of cars and trucks in the battlespace. Trucks were also easier to maintain than large numbers of horses, which required extensive support, medical treatment, and shelter. The entrance of vehicles powered by gasoline changed the nature of the battlefield during World War I. On the ground, armored cars, trucks, self-propelled artillery, and tanks contributed to the evolution of the battlespace away from trench warfare to more dynamic warfighting. By the second full year of the war in 1916, petroleum-consuming cars and trucks became commonplace on the battlefield. By 1917, commanders used trucks to move soldiers to rapidly exploit breakthroughs in the static lines of defense.

At the end of World War I, the British Minister of Foreign Affairs Lord George Curzon declared that "The Allies were carried to victory on a flood of oil." A French senator similarly stated that, "Oil – the blood of the earth was the blood of victory." The Allies, who had access to oil especially from the United States, acquired large numbers of motorized vehicles which consumed petroleum. In contrast, the Germans only had a few trucks, planes, and tanks and did not have access to the required petroleum to power more.[14] Reliant on a modest amount of southeast European oil, German General Erich Ludendorff admitted that Germany "should not have been able to exist, much less to carry on the war, without Romania's corn and oil."[15]

In addition to the widespread use of cars and trucks in the battlefield, access to petroleum added the air dimension to the battlefield. Use of dense liquid fuels produced from petroleum enabled air travel in the early twentieth century. This development dramatically changed the battlefield, lifting combat and intelligence forces into the skies during World War I. Airplanes were initially used in much the same manner as the observation balloons which they replaced. As the war progressed, pilots added aerial combat and bombing runs to their observation missions.

World War II catalyzed the development of nuclear technologies. In this case, the development of nuclear weapons contributed to an energy transition with the advent of nuclear energy. The US Navy began examining the use of nuclear power for naval vessels only a year after the war ended. Soon thereafter, Admiral Hyman Rickover, the so-called "father of the nuclear Navy" advocated for the use of nuclear power in naval submarines and aircraft carriers to allow them to deploy for much longer periods of time and with less detectable "noise." The first naval submarine, the *USS Nautilus* was launched and commissioned in 1954, three years before the first US commercial

---

14 RuthAnne Darling and Paul Mason Carpenter, "Energy: An Essential Element for Winning Future Wars – Operational Energy Part 1," *Surge*, Summer 2020, Naval Postgraduate School (https://nps.edu/web/eag/future-wars).
15 RuthAnne Darling and Paul Mason Carpenter, "Energy: An Essential Element for Winning Future Wars – Operational Energy Part 1," *Surge*, Summer 2020, Naval Postgraduate School (https://nps.edu/web/eag/future-wars).

reactor (the Shipping Port Atomic Power Station) began operation in Pennsylvania. That reactor used a core from a canceled nuclear-powered aircraft carrier for its first fuel load. More generally, the predominant US commercial nuclear power design – the light water reactor – stemmed from a naval design and the nuclear Navy has been and remains a major training ground for the personnel operating the civilian nuclear power industry.

2.3 Energy Affects Military Decisions and Outcomes

Throughout history, access to energy has affected military outcomes as both a constraint and force enabler.

During World War I, regular access to oil gave the Allies a significant advantage over the German forces. The alliance with the United States enabled the Allies access to oil. During World War I, the United States was the top producer of crude in the world. The US also possessed an extensive tanker fleet, which facilitated the delivery of the American-produced oil to the Allies in Europe.

Recognizing the Allied advantages in the battlefield from their access to oil supplies and in attempt to break the supply blockade on Germany during World War I, Berlin dispatched submarine "U-boats" (*unterseeboots*) that prowled the Atlantic armed with torpedoes, targeting boats that were supplying the Allies with oil and other supplies. Only after defeating the U-boat threat did the Allies in Europe have uninterrupted oil supplies.

France, a country whose prewar economy had been powered by coal, provides the starkest example of the increased demand for oil that occurred during World War I. As the war progressed, and fuel consumption increased exponentially, so too did the amount of oil that France imported to meet this growth in demand.[16] Clearly in this situation of import dependency, ties with the United States, the top producer of crude at the time of the war, were crucial.

During World War I, artillery emerged as an important element in the battlefield, and this created further demand for oil. In addition, this and other battlefield innovations using oil and oil products, such as lubricants, required the need for units of logicians to regularly supply oil and these products to the front.

---

16 W.G. Jensen, "The Importance of Energy in the First and Second World Wars," *The Historical Journal*, vol. 11, no. 3, 1968, page 543.

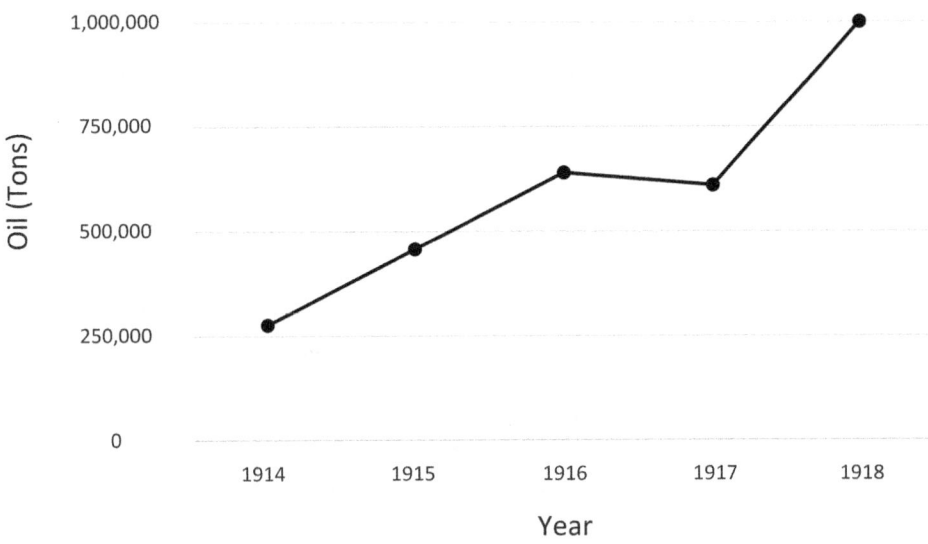

Figure 2.1: French Oil Imports during WWI. Source: W.G. Jensen, "The Importance of Energy in the First and Second World Wars," *The Historical Journal*, vol. 11, no. 3, 1968, page 543.

During World War II, the quest to attain oil supplies was a major factor determining battle plans to gain control of oil producing regions (see case study Operation Edelweiss, this chapter). In addition, lack of access to energy was a major factor in the outcome of troop advances and battles. During World War II, both the Allies and Axis powers at times suffered from lack of access to energy. German Field Marshal Erwin Rommel, who moved his Afrika Corps through North Africa, ran out of fuel near El Alamein, Egypt. His failure signaled the beginning of the end for Rommel's forces and the fall of North Africa to the Allies.

Access to energy has at times served as a catalyst for war. One of the primary goals of the Japan in attacking the United States at Pearl Harbor and other Pacific posts in 1941 was to remove US forces from the Philippines so that much needed petroleum (a need exacerbated by the US embargo) could be supplied unfettered through the South China Sea from oil fields in Malaysia and other locations in Southeast Asia to Japan to fuel expansion ambitions.[17] In addition, denial of energy supplies to an adversary is also a military goal: as described in the case study in Chapter 3, in 2020 Russia sought via its ally Armenia to prevent Azerbaijan from exporting significant new quantities of natural gas to Europe, by attempting to occupy the hills above the Southern Gas Corridor natural gas pipeline to Europe, on the eve of its initiation of operations.

---

[17] Daniel Yergin, "Blood and Oil: Why Japan Attacked Pearl," *Washington Post*, December 1, 1991.

2.3.1 Energy as a Constraint

Energy needs have served as a constant constraint on the reach and ability to sustain engagement of militaries. During the US Civil War, a conflict that bridged pre-industrial and industrial warfare, horse-drawn supply wagons were the primary means of moving material for operations. Large, centralized supply depots provided convenient stockpiles of materials, but wagon trains were still the principle means of getting materials from those depots to the fighting arena. A team of four to six mules or horses typically pulled the wagons. Food was the "fuel" and determined how much weight a wagon could transport. Part of that cargo also had to include forage for the draft animals if the distance to be traveled was more than half a day from the supply depot. On average a six-mule or six-horse team could only pull between 1000 to 2500 pounds of supplies. This number was dependent on the health of the animals and the road conditions, which were often both poor: "To move one ton twenty miles on a level road at 2.9 miles per hour in one day required 3,421 calories for an 1,100-pound horse."[18]

To achieve that caloric intake, by Army regulation, each horse or mule required fourteen pounds of hay and somewhere between twelve and nine pounds of grain per day.[19] A single day's movement for one wagon team required that 138 pounds of that wagon's 1000-pound load capacity, or just over 13 percent, be forage for the animals. Using the information above, the amount of forage that a corps would have had to carry to move twenty miles in one day would have been an astounding 28.75 tons.

2.3.2 Energy as an Advantage

Throughout history, access to OE supplies has served as an important determinant of battle and war outcomes. This was evident in the US Civil War and World War I. During the US Civil War, the Union's possession of mobile electric power to power telegraph systems gave the Union an advantage over the Confederacy. One of the earliest requirements for a military force to have a sustainable source of OE on the battlefield, other than the food and water needed to sustain caloric energy, was the need of US Civil War combatants to maintain a source of electrical power to operate their telegraph systems. Resource and manufacturing shortfalls prevented the Confederacy from fully integrating the telegraph system into operations. In contrast, the Union Army was able to significantly enhance command and control of Union forces using the telegraph as a principle means of rapidly communicating between the Army and civilian leaders. To do

---

18 Clay McShane and Joel A. Tarr, *The Horse in the City: Living Machines in the Nineteenth Century* (Baltimore: Johns Hopkins University Press, 2007), page 127.
19 Colonel Theo S. Case, *The Quartermaster's Guide: The Army Regulations of 1863 and the General Orders of the War Department from May 1, 1861 to April 10, 1865* (Saint Louis, MO: P.M. Pinckard, 1865), chapter IX.

Figure 2.2: Union Wagon Trains Entering Petersburg, Virginia in 1864. Source: Library of Congress.

this successfully, the Union developed techniques for rapidly constructing telegraph networks in the field, often laying miles of telegraph wire immediately behind an advancing Army vanguard. Telegraph battery wagons supplied the electrical power for this field telegraph system. The wagons were horse-drawn and outfitted with banks of lead acid batteries and the necessary equipment to send and receive telegraphic signals.

Illustrating recognition of the importance of telegraph communications to the battlefield outcomes during the US Civil War, the Confederate forces frequently cut the telegraph wires behind the lines and then lay in ambush awaiting parties of linemen who would be sent out to locate and repair the cut. During the war, one in ten linemen were killed while either laying or repairing telegraph wire, a casualty rate on par with infantry casualties on the front lines.[20]

Through history, combatants have frequently targeted fuel convoys. In Iraq and Afghanistan, over 3000 American military members or contractors died within fuel convoys between 2003 and 2007. "Our ability to sustain military operations is increasingly threatened," Deputy Secretary of Defense William Lynn said at a Pentagon briefing unveiling a new strategy. "Our adversaries are increasingly employing asymmetric tactics, and energy can be a soft target."[21]

---

20 Eric Ethier, "The Operators," *Civil War Times*, vol. 45, no. 10, January 2007, pages 17–18.
21 Steve Hargraves, "Ambushes Prompt Military to Cut Energy Use," CNN Money, August 16, 2011 (https://money.cnn.com/2011/06/14/news/economy/military_energy_strategy/index.htm).

Figure 2.3: Union Telegraph Battery Wagon near Petersburg, Virginia in 1864. Source: Library of Congress.

2.4 Anticipating and Developing the Next Energy Transition as Part of Military Power

As illustrated in this chapter, military innovations have played an important role in catalyzing general energy transitions. And, energy transitions have dramatically changed the battlespace and determined battle and war outcomes. Accordingly, military strategists and planners need to study, identify, and correctly assess the impact of emerging energy transitions. Future energy transitions will determine OE needs and supply opportunities. The military needs to build its forces to best harness the advances in the next energy transition and to deal with the challenges they create. This will require constant study of the technological developments in the sphere of energy.

In the twenty-first century, military planners design weapons and platforms for use over several decades. These designs lock the military into needs for certain fuels and can prevent adoption of new forms of energy enabled by energy transitions. However, relying on technologies that have not been developed or are not commercial or producible on a military scale is also hazardous. As energy continues to grow in importance as a component of military power, planners need to identify ways to incorporate energy advances into their existing weapons and platforms and the wider battlespace, while at the same time providing for energy needs based on current technologies.

2.5 For Study

– Definition of an energy transition.

2.6 Topics for Discussion and Research

– How do energy transitions affect the battlespace? And, how do technological developments in the battlespace generate energy transitions? Give examples of both.
– Discuss how the energy transition to oil affected developments in the battlespace during World War I.
– How did the energy transition to coal and oil affect the international security system?
– What factors should planners take into consideration in their planning for future energy transitions?
– What are the indicators of an emerging energy transition? Set a methodology for identifying an emerging energy transition.
– What will be the next energy transition? When will it take place?
– What are the constraints and opportunities generated by the next anticipated energy transition?
– How do OE needs affect geopolitics?
– Analyze historical cases that illustrate the role of OE in conflict. Consider examples such as the Battle of the Bulge, Patton's attack across Europe, the Allied strategic air campaign against Germany, and the "highway of death" in Operation Desert Storm.

2.7 Case Study: Operation Edelweiss 1942

During World War II, the importance of access to energy in battlefield outcomes was evident in dozens of cases. Accordingly, in the European theater, the Allies frequently bombed oil production sites, including the Romanian oil fields, and oil and coal depots that were in reach of German forces during the war. The US targeted German controlled railroad marshaling yards in order to disrupt German coal supplies and thus their electricity used for both war production and OE. During the Battle of the Bulge, German forces were ground to a halt, largely due to the lack of fuel. Starting in the spring of 1944, the Allies carried out "The Oil Plan," which targeted German fuel sources and refineries.[22] During the war, the Axis and Allies engaged in efforts to develop new energy supplies and sources, including replacements for oil.

The Allies and Axis also determined their conquest plans based on the need to access oil supplies. One of the clearest cases during World War II of a battleplan based on the desire to access energy supplies was Hitler's Operation Edelweiss. This operation aimed to capture the oil fields in Russia's North Caucasus and Baku, the capital of Soviet Azerbaijan, in 1942. This case illustrates that gaining access to energy plays a major role in battle goals. Combatants seek energy supplies and also seek to deny supplies to their adversaries. The case illustrates that gaining control of the territory where energy is produced or stored is not sufficient to harness these supplies, but rather plans need to be in place and executed to transport the newly controlled energy supplies to the troops.

Azerbaijan is the cradle of the modern global oil industry. At the beginning of the twentieth century, wells in and around Baku were producing half of the global oil production. During World War II, Soviet Azerbaijan was the main source of oil and refined products in the USSR. In 1940, Soviet Azerbaijan was the source of 72 percent of the USSR's oil supplies.[23] These supplies were essential to the Soviet war effort. In addition to the quantities of oil produced in Soviet Azerbaijan, Azerbaijan's unique light oil grade was especially useful for military purposes, especially for the production of jet fuel.

Aware of the need to deprive the USSR of its main supplies, and the desire to access new supplies for Germany's army, Hitler decided to capture Russia's North Caucasus (also a source of Soviet oil production and refineries) and Baku. Control of Ukraine and Azerbaijan played a major role in Hitler's vision for a new German empire. Hitler viewed capturing Baku's oil and Ukraine's rich farmlands as essential for the new German empire to be self-sufficient.[24]

Hitler was quite fixated on the importance of oil as an element of economic and military power. While the German generals reportedly advised him to aim to capture Moscow following the opening of the front with the USSR, Hitler preferred to focus on cap-

---

[22] RuthAnne Darling and Paul Mason Carpenter, "Energy: An Essential Element for Winning Future Wars – Operational Energy Part 1," *Surge*, Summer 2020, Naval Postgraduate School (https://nps.edu/web/eag/future-wars).
[23] Vagif Agayev, Fuad Akhundov, Fikrat T. Aliyev, and Mikhail Agarunov, "World War II and Azerbaijan," *Azerbaijan International*, vol. 3, no. 2, Summer 1995, pages 50–55, 78 (https://www.azer.com/aiweb/categories/magazine/32_folder/32_articles/32_ww22.html).
[24] Daniel Yergin, *The Prize: The Epic Quest for Oil, Money, & Power* (New York: Free Press, 2008), page 334.

turing the Soviet oil fields in the Caucasus, stating "My generals know nothing about the economic aspects of war."[25]

Thus, in 1942 Germany's war efforts focused on reaching the Soviet oil supplies in the Caucasus. Hitler believed it would accomplish the two goals of OE: gaining access to supplies while denying them to one's enemy. Capturing Soviet oil production in the Caucasus would inflict a mortal blow to Soviet war production,[26] as well as provide the German army with much needed oil.

The German war planners named the mission to capture the Caucasus from the Soviet Union Edelweiss (a flower that grows on the alpine slopes of Germany and Austria), since the German army would have to cross the Great Caucasus Mountain range to reach the Baku oil fields. During 1942, Germany's triumphs in capturing wide swaths of Soviet territory put the Caucasus in reach of the Nazi forces. In July 1942, Germany captured Rostov – a major city in the Russian Caucasus – and in August 1942, German forces captured the oil production at Maikop. In mid-August, German mountain troops planted the swastika at the summit of Mount Elbrus, the highest point in the Caucasus and in Europe.[27]

In 1942, Hitler's army executed two-front battle plans to capture in parallel Stalingrad and the Caucasus. The Nazis set the date of September 25, 1942 for the attack and capture of Baku. A few days prior to the planned attack, Hitler's generals presented him with a cake, decorated with a map of the Caspian Sea and Baku. Hitler picked for himself the piece of cake where the word Baku was written.[28]

German's two-front war against the USSR was very risky. Field Marshal Erick von Manstein implored Hitler to transfer German forces from the Caucasus to the front at Stalingrad.[29] However, Hitler's quest for oil, superseded the battlefront threats: "Unless we get Baku's oil, the war is lost."[30] He then proceeded to discuss the central importance of

---

25 Daniel Yergin, *The Prize: The Epic Quest for Oil, Money, & Power* (New York: Free Press, 2008), page 334.
26 Joel Hayward, "Too Little, Too Late: An Analysis of Hitler's Failure in August 1942 to Damage Soviet Oil Production," *The Journal of Military History*, vol. 64, no. 3, 2000, page 770.
27 Daniel Yergin, *The Prize: The Epic Quest for Oil, Money, & Power* (New York: Free Press, 2008), page 337.
28 Documentary, "Objective Baku: Hitler's War on Oil," DTX (State Security Service of the Republic of Azerbaijan) YouTube Channel (https://www.youtube.com/watch?v=CWc6dgVvbAA).
29 Vagif Agayev, Fuad Akhundov, Fikrat T. Aliyev, and Mikhail Agarunov, "World War II and Azerbaijan," *Azerbaijan International*, vol. 3, no. 2, Summer 1995, pages 50–55 (https://www.azer.com/aiweb/categories/magazine/32_folder/32_articles/32_ww22.html).
30 Daniel Yergin, *The Prize: The Epic Quest for Oil, Money, & Power* (New York: Free Press, 2008).

oil in warfare.[31] "'If I can no longer get you the oil for your operation,' he purportedly told the Field Marshal, 'you will be unable to do anything.'"[32]

Paradoxically, Hitler's drive to conquer the oil fields of the Caucasus was largely impeded by the German armies' stretched supply lines, including a shortage of oil. In the end, Hitler's fixation on reaching Baku, contributed to major battlefield reversals for the Nazi forces. Hitler's two-front strategy of conquering in tandem Stalingrad and the Caucasus led his forces to be spread too thin and to fail in both missions. Stalingrad became Germany's first major defeat in World War II and Berlin failed to capture Baku.

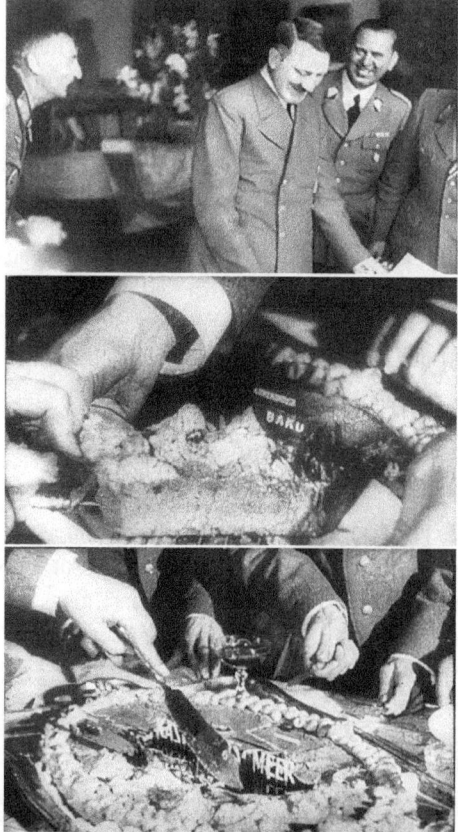

Figure 2.4: Hitler Pictured with Cake of Baku. Source: Documentary, "Objective Baku: Hitler's War on Oil," DTX (State Security Service of the Republic of Azerbaijan) YouTube Channel.

---

31 Vagif Agayev, Fuad Akhundov, Fikrat T. Aliyev, and Mikhail Agarunov, "World War II and Azerbaijan," *Azerbaijan International*, vol. 3, no. 2, Summer 1995, pages 50–55 (https://www.azer.com/aiweb/categories/magazine/32_folder/32_articles/32_ww22.html).
32 Vagif Agayev, Fuad Akhundov, Fikrat T. Aliyev, and Mikhail Agarunov. "World War II and Azerbaijan," *Azerbaijan International*, vol. 3, no. 2, Summer 1995, pages 50–55 (https://www.azer.com/aiweb/categories/magazine/32_folder/32_articles/32_ww22.html).

Hitler's quest to access Baku's oil was likely doomed from the beginning. Prior to their retreat from other oil production sites, such as Maikop, the Soviets burned and destroyed the oil wells. Accordingly, it is likely that even if Hitler succeeded in reaching close striking distance of Baku, the Soviets would have destroyed Baku's oil wells as well before retreating. In fact, the Soviets undertook preparations to destroy the wells in Baku and much of the stored oil there was dumped into the Caspian Sea, to deny the enemy access.

Moreover, military historian Joel Hayward claims that Hitler and his advisers never discussed in detail and did not have a plan for how to transport the Caucasus oil to Germany or to the German forces once captured.[33] During World War I, General Erich Ludendorff and the German High Command also assessed the problem of the transport of oil to Germany and did not identify a solution.[34] Thus, even if Hitler had succeeded in capturing Baku, his army most likely would not have been able to transport the oil to the German forces. Though he could have denied the USSR access to this important source of oil. During the war, Moscow prepared for the possibility that Hitler would capture Baku, and moved much of the oil production equipment to other parts of the USSR, where there were oil fields.

An interesting page in the history of the drive to control the oil fields in the Soviet Caucasus during World War II is that the Allies contemplated bombing Azerbaijan's oil fields. The Allies wanted to deny Germany access to the Soviet oil fields. The Allied discussions on bombing Baku were especially active while the USSR was still a formal ally of Nazi Germany following the Molotov-Ribbentrop Pact (August 1939) and prior to Hitler's attack on the Soviet Union in Operation Barbarossa (June 1941). The Allies eventually dismissed this idea and assessed that even if Hitler captured the Baku oil fields, the Allies could disrupt transit of the oil in the Black Sea and prevent it from reaching Germany's forces. This illustrates that even if a combatant possesses access to energy, its successful transport to its troops is not ensured, and the transport is also an essential part of OE planning.

World War II also catalyzed Soviet technological developments in the sphere of oil production and transport. For instance, during the war, there was an insufficient number of oil tankers to transit the oil from the site of production in and around Baku across the Caspian Sea to the battlefront in Russia. To overcome this obstacle, Soviet Azerbaijani engineers developed special canisters for oil transport that were tugged by regular boats across the Caspian Sea. This is an example of how military needs generate new technologies for energy use by the civilian sector.

---

33 Joel Hayward, "Too Little, Too Late: An Analysis of Hitler's Failure in August 1942 to Damage Soviet Oil Production," *The Journal of Military History*, vol. 64, no. 3, 2000, page 773.

34 E. Ludendorff, *My War Memoirs, 1914–1918* (London: Hutchinson), pages 658–660, quoted in Hayward "Too Little, Too Late," page 773.

Figure 2.5: Oil Cannisters Being Tugged. Source: DTX (State Security Service of the Republic of Azerbaijan).

2.7.1 Questions for Discussion

- What were Hitler's main goals in his quest to control the oil fields of Baku?
- How did the quest to gain control of Baku's oil fields contribute to the German defeat in World War II?
- Discuss the fact that OE was a high priority for Hitler, yet he was unable to achieve adequate supplies to his forces.
- Hitler and his military advisers evidently did not have a plan for the transport of Baku's oil to the German forces after conquering Baku. Look at a map of the Caucasus and greater Europe. What were the potential routes for transporting oil from Baku to the German forces? What types of modes of transportation were able to transport significant quantities of oil from the Caspian to Germany's troops? Was it likely the oil could have been successfully transported on a large scale from Baku to the German forces?
- The case points out that the Soviets destroyed oil production in areas they retreated from. Does contemporary military planning involve plans to deny adversaries access to energy?

3 Geopolitics of Operational Energy

This chapter examines the global dynamics of the geopolitics of energy and the geopolitical factors that specifically affect US OE in the first half of the twenty-first century. The chapter opens with a discussion of energy basics.

3.1 Energy Basics

This section presents the major global trends in energy consumption, production, markets, and transportation. The use of different sources of energy create different geopolitical challenges.

3.1.1 Global Fuel Mix

The major global sources of energy have changed over time. Through the first half of the nineteenth century, wood and various animal products were the primary fuel sources. In the last half of the nineteenth century, coal emerged as the major energy source in industrialized countries. In the twentieth century, oil became the major fuel source. In the first half of the twenty-first century, natural gas is emerging as a leading fuel source. The prevailing major fuel source shapes lifestyles, economies, and trade; the relative power of various states; and the battlefield and other military operations.

Trends in fuel mix consumption change based on economics, technology developments, domestic and international politics, environmental and health concerns, and more. In addition, different countries and regions utilize very different fuel mixes, based on both demand needs and supply opportunities, geography and climate of the location, as well as political and economic preferences. Fuel mix composition is far from universal: while the industrial centers in the world rely primarily on fossil fuels, over two billion people use primarily animal products, wood and other biomass as their main sources of energy.

In studying data on the energy fuel mix, it is important to differentiate between actual volumes and the relative proportion of an energy source that is produced or consumed. For instance, from the 1970s until 2000, the volumes of oil consumed in the world increased significantly. However, oil's share of the global fuel mix declined from half of the world's total energy consumption to a third.

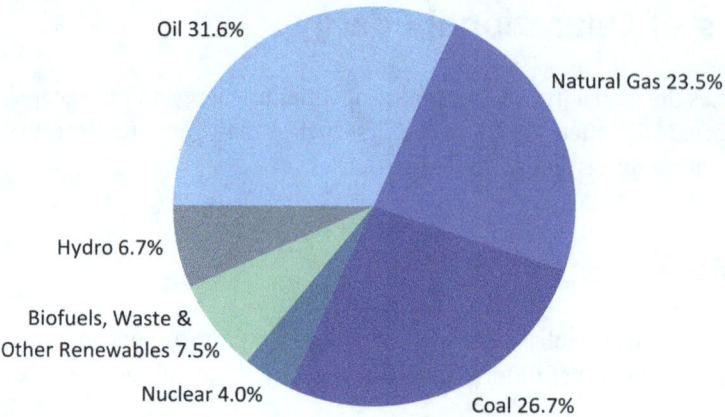

Figure 3.1: Global Share of Total Energy Supply by Source, 2022. Source: Energy Institute, *2023 Statistical Review of World Energy* (https://www.energyinst.org/statistical-review).

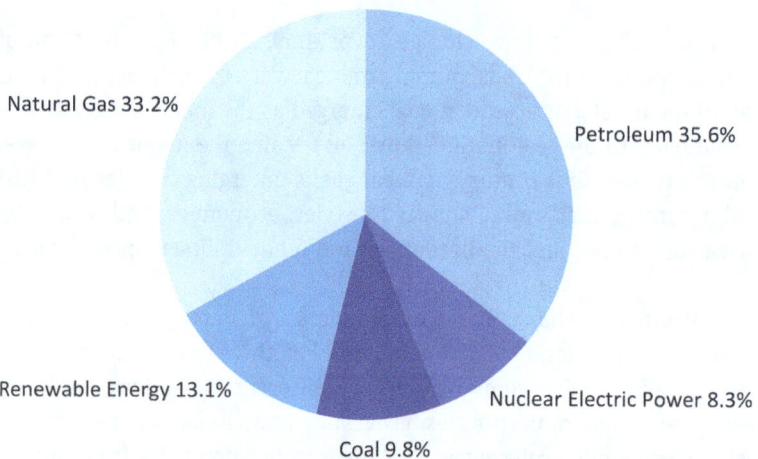

Figure 3.2: US Primary Energy Consumption by Source, 2022. Source: US Energy Information Administration, US Department of Energy (https://www.eia.gov).

3.1.2 Global Energy Total Consumption Trends

The major source of energy consumed globally and by the United States and its allies is fossil fuels (oil, natural gas,[35] and coal, also referred to as hydrocarbons). Fossil fuels are anticipated to remain the major source of energy for the first half of the twenty-

---

[35] Americans commonly refer to gasoline as "gas." However, gasoline is a refined petroleum product. In contrast, natural gas is composed of gases (mostly methane). Cooking and heating gas used in most American homes is primarily propane, a gas product of petroleum.

first century and likely beyond. In 2030, fossil fuels are expected to comprise approximately 70 percent of global energy consumption, with renewable energy, waste,[36] and nuclear energy comprising the remaining 30 percent. The three fossil fuels – oil, natural gas, and coal – are anticipated to each provide a third of the fossil fuel supply in 2030. Electricity production represents the fastest growing energy demand sector. Electricity is a product of energy, not an energy source.

Fossil fuels have continued to dominate energy use for over a century for several reasons. One, fossil fuels possess high energy density (see below), especially liquid fuels. Next, these fuels have built-in storage, which does not require the expense or technology of storing them in a separate form. In contrast, existing renewable energy requires separate storage and backup mechanisms. In addition, fossil fuels are found in abundance in many geographic locations. Moreover, fossil fuels are relatively easy to transport from the places they are produced to the consumption centers (in contrast to renewable energy).

3.1.3 Energy Density

Energy density is the relative volume per unit of energy. Energy density highly affects fuel choices and the mass and weight needed to produce, transport, and store fuels. Fossil fuels and uranium have high energy density. Today's renewable energy sources have very low energy density. Energy density is an especially important factor in OE, as it determines the size of vessels, planes and vehicles needed for energy transport and the size of storage facilities. Energy density considerations are especially important for military forces, which are required to supply energy over long distances, at quick pace, to multiple locations around the globe. Volume of energy supplies is highly limited by the military's energy transport vessels and vehicles, as each inch and pound on a ship or plane.

> Energy density considerations are especially important for military forces, which are required to supply energy over long distances, at quick pace, to multiple locations around the globe. Volume and weight of energy supplies is highly limited by the military's energy transport vessels and vehicles.

3.1.4 Energy Transportation and Markets

3.1.4.1 Oil
As a liquid, oil can be shipped easily, and thus is a fungible commodity traded on a global market. Oil is traded primarily between commercial entities, in most cases with-

---

36 Waste refers primarily to animal dung and other biomass.

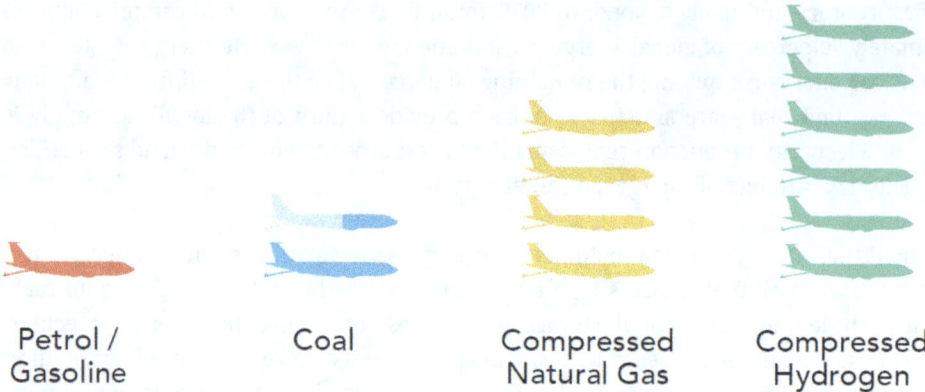

Figure 3.3: Tank Size Matters – Fuel Sources Have Different Volumetric Energy Density. Data source: Advanced Biofuels USA.

out government involvement. Oil is a global commodity. Most oil is traded based on spot market prices, without long-term contracts. There are differences in the price of different grades of oil, based on their density and percentage of sulfur content. There are two major benchmarks for oil prices: Brent (which reflects global trends) and West Texas Intermediate (which represents the price of the main oil sales in the United States). In the twenty-first century, the transportation sector is the primary consumer of oil.

Tankers at sea transport most oil traded internationally. Major waterways for oil (and LNG) transport are critical geopolitical arteries.

Oil is consumed primarily through refined petroleum products. Refineries differ in their capacity to process different grades of oil and produce different types of products. Thus, not all types of oil are compatible for refining in all refineries. Accordingly, the existence of a refinery in a location does not mean it can process any source of petroleum or produce a desired product. The different processing capacities of refineries have geopolitical impact, since they limit the kinds of oil that can be processed and likely traded.

> Refineries are tooled to process specific types of crude and produce different products. Refineries are not easily retooled to refine different types of crude or produce different products. Thus, availabiliy of crude and access to refineries in a location does not necessarily provide access to the operational enery supplies necessary in a certain geographic location.

3.1.4.2 Coal

Coal is a fungible commodity like oil, with similar global market dynamics. Like oil, coal trade is conducted primarily by commercial entities, based on spot markets, with few long-term contracts or governments involved in the trade. Power plants are tooled to process certain types of coal, thus different grades are consumed in specific markets. Coal is transported primarily by ship, but also by rail, truck, and barge. Coal consumption declined in most Western countries in the early part of the twenty-first century. By contrast, in China and India and many developing regions, coal consumption continued to rise in the early twenty-first century.

Coal is easy and inexpensive to store. Thus, like in the case of oil, it is easy to back up coal supplies. Coal can be used to produce liquid fuels, such as synthetic oil.

3.1.4.3 Natural Gas

In the first half of the twenty-first century, natural gas stood out as the fastest growing fuel, with demand growing in most markets. Natural gas has become especially commercially attractive due to its low air pollution and relatively low climate impact. Moreover, multiple additional locations and volumes of gas have been found in recent decades, facilitating access for more consumers.

Due to the high costs and complications of its transport, there is not a global market for natural gas, and each market is priced separately, though trends in different gas markets affect each other.

Natural gas is supplied by two main methods: in gas form by pipeline or in a liquid form as liquefied natural gas (LNG). Approximately two-thirds of the internationally traded national gas is supplied by pipeline, with the remainder transported as LNG by sea vessels. LNG requires two types of coastal facilities: liquefaction plants where the LNG is produced through cooling, and regasification plants that convert the LNG back into gas for use by the consumer. LNG is produced through cooling natural gas to -260 degrees Fahrenheit to liquefy it.

LNG vessels transit global waterways and many of these main routes have geopolitical significance, like the main sea transit routes of oil. Adversaries may target LNG liquefaction and regasification plants, and disrupt LNG sea transit routes, especially during active conflict.

Most natural gas used for electricity production is composed primarily of methane. Natural gas generally is treated to remove impurities such as water, carbon dioxide, and helium, before use in power or heat production.

3.1.4.4 Renewable Energy

Renewable energy comprises less than 10 percent of the global consumption of energy. The main source of renewable energy is hydropower. Other sources of renewable energy include geothermal power, solar power, wind power, and energy from waste and biomass, including animal dung and wood. Most renewable energy is used to produce electricity.

While the percentage of electricity production from renewable energy is growing, it is anticipated that in 2030, renewable energy will still supply less than 30 percent of global electricity production.

It is important to distinguish between the percentage of renewable energy in electricity consumption and in total energy consumption. Many sources, especially in the media, regularly mix up electricity and total energy consumption data.

Delivering stable electricity supplies requires a constant baseload and backup capacity. Accordingly, electricity produced by intermittent and non-storable renewable energy is paired with electricity produced by more reliable natural gas, coal, or nuclear. Therefore, the current generation of renewable energy technologies cannot replace fossil fuels but are used in tandem with fossil fuels or nuclear energy to deliver electricity.

The baseload can also be produced by oil, but only a small number of locations use oil in electricity production, due to its high costs and generation of air pollution.

In contrast to fossil fuels, renewable energy cannot be stored on an industrial scale. A large portion of R&D efforts in both the private and public sectors focus on identifying ways to store energy on a large scale that is commercially viable. Breakthroughs may take place in the future. But, the current technologies of renewable energy still require a corresponding baseload fuel to deliver stable electricity.

Like fossil fuels, the price of renewable energy is volatile, especially due to the changing prices of the minerals and metals that are necessary to produce renewable energy and electrical grids.

3.1.4.5 Nuclear Energy

Nuclear power plants produce energy through nuclear fission. Nuclear energy comprises less than 10 percent of the global consumption of energy. Nuclear energy is used to produce electricity and, in some places, heat.

Global nuclear power capacity is declining, mainly due to cost. This decline is especially steep in the United States and Europe. Nuclear energy is attractive as it does not emit carbon emissions and air pollution. However, the high price of generating nuclear energy relative to alternatives, the challenges in most Western countries of attaining permits to establish nuclear power plants (and legal challenges to these permits), and the safety concerns regarding nuclear waste have all led to a lack of investments in new plants in the United States and strengthened support for policies against continued operations of nuclear power plants in Europe. As part of the Biden administration's quest to lower US carbon emissions, the administration provided government incentives for increased nuclear power generation. However, those incentives will not likely reverse the decline in nuclear capacity in the United States.

Proponents of nuclear energy contend that Small Modular Nuclear Reactors (SMRs) will give a boost to the nuclear energy industry. However, by early 2024, no SMR projects have been established in the United States or Europe.

> **Renewable, clean, green energy: what's the difference?**
>
> Renewable energy: energy that is produced from sources that are not depleted through usage and are naturally replenishing, such as solar and wind energy.
>
> Clean energy: energy whose production and usage generate low levels of carbon emissions and other greenhouse gases.
>
> Green energy: energy whose production and usage have low environmental impact.
>
> **The terms are not interchangeable.** For instance, *renewable energy is not necessarily green energy or clean energy.*
>
> Policymakers, journalists, and activists often use the terms renewable energy, clean energy, and green energy interchangeably, and in debates on US energy policy, the three terms are often meshed. However, renewable energy, clean energy, and green energy are three distinct categories. Renewable energy, for instance, can have high negative environmental impact, and thus is not necessarily green energy. Hydropower, the leading source of renewable energy in the United States and globally, is an important example of a renewable source that causes significant environmental damage. Wind and solar power often have high environmental impact, especially due to their extensive land use. In addition, many sources of renewable energy release significant amounts of carbon emissions, such as burning wood or waste. Accordingly, in energy policy analysis, it is important to distinguish between renewable energy, green energy, and clean energy.

3.1.4.6 Electricity

Electricity is a product produced by an energy source, and is not itself an energy source. However, electricity can be used to displace direct fuel in many uses, such as gasoline and diesel in transportation or natural gas and fuel oil in heating. Thus, in some policy calculations and energy use assessments electricity is evaluated in comparison to primary energy sources.

Electricity is produced in power plants (coal, natural gas, nuclear, hydropower, geothermal, biomass) or generated at solar energy and wind energy plants. Electricity is supplied from power plants via electrical grids.

Like natural gas, electricity supply has limited flexibility. Electricity is supplied via dedicated infrastructure and cannot be diverted to different locations if there is no grid connection, or the grid does not have sufficient capacity or appropriate technical capacity or relevant commercial arrangements. In addition, electricity supplies are limited by distance: electricity loss in transmission is significant and thus costs increase significantly when electricity is transmitted over long distances, rendering many proposed electricity transmission projects technically feasible but not commercially.

The lack of storage is a major factor affecting the security of supply of electricity. Based on current technology, electricity cannot be stored in sufficient volumes to serve as a backup for major electricity supplies. However, small-scale electronics and some microgrids can be backed up with batteries.

As noted in the section on renewable energy, delivering stable electricity supplies requires a constant baseload fuel. An electricity supply system requires that a certain percentage of production (often at least 50 percent) is non-variable/dependable, such as from natural gas, coal, or nuclear energy. The current generation of renewable energy cannot provide the baseload function. In addition, due to lack of storage ability, the volatile supplies produced by renewable energy need backup capacity, generally supplied by fossil fuels or nuclear energy. Today, renewable energy does not remove the need for fossil fuels or nuclear energy in electricity production. In addition, the addition of renewable energy adds costs to grid operations, due to the need to keep baseload and backup capacity operating.

In electricity production data, it is important to differentiate between production capacity and actual consumption. Many US states and foreign countries require mandatory percentages of electricity production capacity from renewable energy. Often the required capacity is established, yet electricity systems often do not fully utilize this capacity. Accordingly, some states and countries maintain renewable capacity that they do not use, in order to fulfill these commitments to renewable energy policies.

> **Baseload**
>
> Delivering stable electricity supplies requires a constant baseload and back-up capacity. Accordingly, electricity produced by intermittent and non-storable renewable energy is paired with electricity produced by natural gas, coal, or nuclear. Accordingly, the current generation of renewable energy technologies cannot replace fossil fuels but are used in tandem with fossil fuels or nuclear energy to deliver electricity. Many governments and private industry are investing efforts in developing electricity storage capacity, and a breakthrough may take place in the future. But, with current technologies, renewable energy still requires a corresponding baseload fuel.

3.2 Global Geopolitics of Energy

Adequate energy supply is essential to maintaining national security, functioning economies, and modern lifestyle and mobility. As stated above, energy is an enabler of – and a constraint on – military power. Energy use is also a major factor impacting the state of the environment, global economy, geopolitics, and public health. The state of the security of supply and price level directly affects economic growth trends. Energy is the most traded good in the global economy; thus, energy prices are a significant determinant of global economic trends. Energy prices reverberate onto the costs of all goods: agriculture, manufacturing, transportation, electricity and more. Accordingly, energy prices are one of the most, if not the most, important inputs in economic growth and inflation trends. Energy is also the most important input in manufacturing costs; thus, the cost of energy supplies directly determines a state or company's relative position in manufacturing. In addition, changes in global economic trends directly affect energy demand trends.

Stable access to energy is a vital national interest in all countries. Insufficient or expensive energy supplies often lead to economic and political breakdown, as well as making countries vulnerable to external intervention. According to international law, restricting energy supplies is a *casus belli*. However, due to the changes over time in how energy is traded, from the 1970s countries can generally access energy supplies supplied by commercial entities, and governments don't need to produce them or control production locations, as in the past. However, safe passage in global trade routes is vital to energy trade. The US military ensures global freedom of the seas.

> Safe passage in global trade routes is vital to energy trade. The US military ensures global freedom of the seas.

3.2.1 Geopolitics of Different Fuel Sources

The most significant determinant of the state of energy geopolitics today is the physical state of an energy source and consequently how it is transported and stored. Oil as a liquid and coal as a solid enable flexible transportation and easy storage. In contrast, natural gas requires dedicated and largely fixed transportation and complicated and expensive gas storage. Consequently, achieving security of supply of natural gas requires significant policy effort and government involvement, in contrast to security of supply of oil and coal. Electricity, a product of energy sources, shares with natural gas transportation and thus increased geopolitical challenges. Large-scale storage of electricity is not commercially viable at the time of publication, adding to the geopolitical challenges of security of supply of electricity.

Different energy sources create fundamentally different geopolitical and energy security challenges. A major trend in the first half of the twenty-first century is that the relative portion of natural gas and use of electricity is growing in global total energy consumption, while the relative portion of oil and coal is declining. Accordingly, energy security challenges are growing, and the geopolitics of energy is becoming ever more important to national security and economic prosperity.

> **Terms**
>
> Energy security: the level of (1) reliability, (2) affordability, and (3) environmental sustainability of energy supply systems
>
> Geopolitics: the impact of geographic factors (including commodities like energy) on foreign policy and national security.

3.2.1.1 Geopolitics of Oil

For most of the twentieth century, the United States and other countries focused energy security policies on oil. However, the nature of international oil trade has changed dramatically since the mid-twentieth century, and thus the geopolitical concerns. Today, governments are not involved in most oil trade, removing most foreign policy considerations from oil trade. Liberalization of oil trade, beginning in the late 1960s, has contributed to the increase in proved global oil volumes and improved security of supply of oil. In addition, as a liquid, oil is easily stored, and maintaining oil storage greatly reduces the prospects of supply disruptions.

However, the price of oil is the most volatile of any traded commodity, and thus while oil supply challenges have decreased tremendously in the first decades of the twenty-first century, the oil price is still a major geopolitical and policy challenge.

3.2.1.2 Changing Geopolitics of Oil

The geopolitics of oil has changed considerably over the past century. While all over the globe, humans have consumed oil throughout the twentieth century, proved oil reserves have grown in parallel. The global oil market has changed dramatically since the 1970s, when OPEC members produced close to 70 percent of the world's oil. In the early twenty-first century, the oil producers are much more diversified, and non-OPEC producers account for about 65 percent of global oil production. The United States became the world's top oil producer in 2018, significantly changing the global oil market and geopolitics.

From the 1970s to the 1990s, OPEC, which was established in 1960, was the major actor shaping oil supply. In 1973–1974, the Arab members of OPEC conducted a boycott of oil supplies to the USA, Israel, and the Netherlands following the 1973 Yom Kippur Middle East War. The 1973–1974 boycott raised global concerns about the potential security of oil supply. Indeed, while the OPEC boycott contributed to an extreme oil price increase in the 1970s, it did not deny oil to any consumers. Rather, the one-time use of oil as a weapon resulted in long-term negative ramifications for the oil producers themselves. Consumers took steps to lower demand for oil with some sectors, such as power generation, almost eliminating permanently demand for oil in that sector.

Another important development in the geopolitics of oil was the forging of strategic cooperation between OPEC and Russia in 2016. OPEC and Russia, and several other states, established the OPEC-Plus format. Since the establishment of this cooperation, Russia and Saudi Arabia have coordinated oil production policies. The Russia-OPEC coordination effort has increased the power of Russia and OPEC in the global oil market.

The US, NATO members, China, and many other states store volumes of oil for use in the event of supply disruptions. The United States, as mandated by law, stores oil in the Strategic Petroleum Reserve (SPR). The American legislation which established the SPR envisioned the use of the supplies only to prevent supply disruptions. However, some US administrations have released supplies in order to affect the global oil price.

The United States coordinates stored supplies of oil with allies and partners within the framework of the International Energy Agency (IEA), which is based in Paris. The US and allies from NATO established the IEA following the 1973 oil crisis, to ensure security of oil supply. Since its establishment, several non-NATO members that are American security partners, including Japan and South Korea, have joined the IEA.

The use of the "oil weapon" has shifted from a tool of the producers in the 1970s to mostly a tool of the consumers. Since the 1990s, consumers have wielded the "oil weapon" through sanctions to deny market access to oil producing states, or technology for the oil and natural gas sector, in order to coerce a change in their foreign policy and national security behavior. The United States (often in tandem with Europe and the United Nations) has applied sanctions targeting oil production from and/or exports to: Russia, Iran, Iraq, Sudan, and more.

3.2.2 Geopolitics of Natural Gas

Natural gas trade is far more affected by geopolitical factors and impacts geopolitical developments far more than oil and coal trade. This is mostly due to the complexities and costs of transporting natural gas. Natural gas trade is not flexible like that of oil and coal, since most natural gas is supplied via permanent pipelines. Even LNG trade is not entirely flexible because of the use of dedicated LNG vessels and long-term supply relationships. In addition, most LNG trade takes place within the framework of long-term contracts.

In addition, natural gas storage is complicated and expensive to establish; thus there is insufficient gas storage in use to offset potential disruptions, including from geopolitics.

Governments are necessarily involved in international gas trade, in contrast to oil and coal trade. Due to the need to establish infrastructure and acquire associated permits, governments are involved in natural gas trade agreements that establish infrastructure in their countries and link to foreign countries. Natural gas production requires much more time to recoup investment than oil or coal production; thus, investing companies assess the host government policies and longevity as part of their political risk calculations and investment decisions. Secure supplies of natural gas require extensive infrastructure, such as storage, and backup systems, that are often not provided by the private sector. Thus, government needs to be involved in either mandating or establishing the infrastructure to ensure security of supply of natural gas.

Due to the relative inflexibility of natural gas trade, supplies or markets can be denied as a means of political coercion. Russia has used the "natural gas weapon" several times with markets in Europe and in neighboring post-Soviet countries.[37]

3.2.3 Geopolitics of Minerals and Metals for Renewable Energy

Countries no longer wage wars to gain access to energy supplies. There is enough oil available through commercial entities that countries no longer need to "put a flag" on an oil field, to ensure access to oil. The same is true for natural gas and coal. However, in the case of the rare earth and other minerals that are necessary to produce batteries, grids, and other components of electricity systems, countries have acted to ensure dedicated access to these materials, as was common with oil and coal in the first half of the twentieth century.

China got in early in this "great game" and controls and produces the lion's share of these strategic minerals, metals, and processing capacity. Accordingly, access to rare earths and other strategic metals is an energy security concern. The US and its allies established policies aimed to reduce vulnerability from potential lack of access to strategic minerals and metals. However, it is not clear if these policies will overcome the American disadvantage.

3.2.4 Energy and Maritime Delimitation Conflicts

Offshore exploration and production of oil and natural gas has led to a significant increase in the number of maritime delimitation conflicts. Prior to the advent of offshore drilling, maritime conflicts focused on fishing rights and freedom of navigation, especially for military vessels. The ability to reach valuable hydrocarbons below the ocean, however, has created many new maritime disputes.

---

[37] For more on natural gas trade and foreign policy, see Brenda Shaffer, "Natural Gas Supply Stability and Foreign Policy," *Energy Policy*, vol. 56, May 2013, pages 114–125.

3.2.5 Maritime Energy Transportation: International Waterways and Chokepoints

Most of the international trade in energy – oil, coal, and LNG – transits the world's waterways, adding to the importance of keeping these waterways open and secure. Moreover, the ability to disrupt energy supplies through control of the world's major chokepoints – such as the Straits of Hormuz, the Red Sea, and the Malacca Straits – increases the geopolitical significance of these waterways.

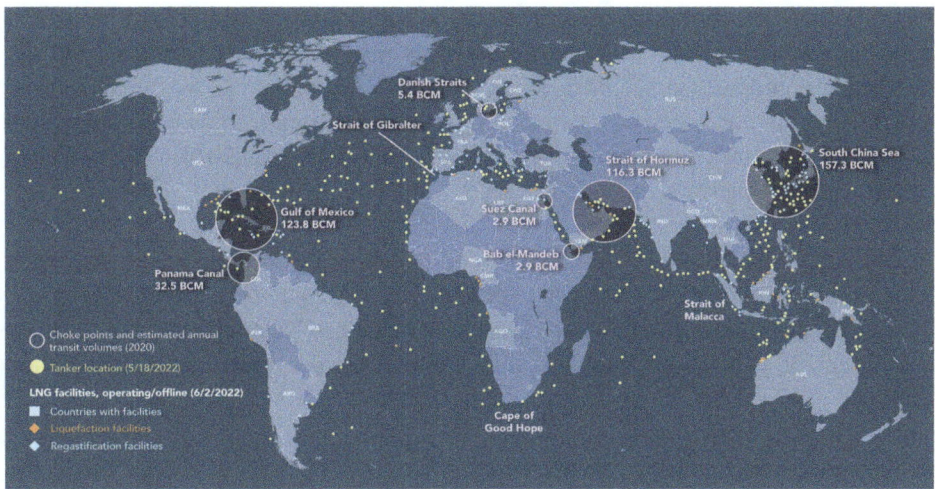

Figure 3.4: Global LNG Tanker Trade Chokepoints. Source: Presentation of Michael Ratner, GEST seminar, Doha, Qatar, May, 2023.

3.2.6 US Adversaries Seek to Influence US's and Allies' Energy Policies

As part of hybrid warfare, US adversaries, especially Russia and China, sponsor clandestine influence campaigns in the US and American allied countries, aimed to turn public opinion against fossil fuel production and other policies that enhance energy security. Some US adversaries have sponsored bogus environmental movements and campaigns in attempts to limit energy production in the US and allied and partner nations. For instance, Russia sponsored covert campaigns aimed at influencing countries in Europe, such as Bulgaria, to adopt legislation to ban hydraulic fracking as increased production of natural gas in European countries would reduce dependence on gas imports from Russia.[38] Through campaigns in the Western media and financial support

---

[38] Keith Johnson, "Russia's Quiet War against European Fracking," *Foreign Policy*, June 20, 2014.

for campaigns of American non-governmental organizations,[39] China has encouraged Western countries to lower their carbon emissions at great economic cost, while China continues to use coal and other fossil fuels with no inhibitions, increasing its carbon emissions.

3.2.7 Economic Tools of Geopolitics of Energy

Disruption or threat of disruption of energy supplies often is conducted through the use of economic instruments. Not only energy producers use energy as a geopolitical tool, but energy consumers and transit states. The United States has repeatedly applied sanctions on oil and other energy exports, from adversaries such as Iran. The US, together with partners, has also applied sanctions to technologies for use in the energy sector of producing states, such as Russia.

Some energy exporting states use a variety of economic tools to promote their geopolitical interests. Russia has often released and denied supplies to hub gas markets in Europe, to affect the price and availability of natural gas. Russia has also used direct suspension of natural gas supplies as a geopolitical tool, such as to Georgia and Ukraine.

Market structure and energy trade policies affect the geopolitics of energy. For example, in the 1990s and 2000s, the EU took policy steps to transfer natural gas trade from within the framework of long-term contracts to spot trade at gas hubs. In contrast to Brussel's expectations, hub trade endowed Russia with increased influence over price and supply trends in Europe: as the largest supplier and the only one with spare capacity, Gazprom was the swing producer in Europe's gas market. Moreover, elimination of long-term contracts meant that less dedicated gas supplies would be available to Europe, creating larger dependency on Russian supplies and Europe's exposure to the price volatility of LNG trade.

3.2.8 Energy Security Policies

Traditionally, energy security was achieved or at least improved through following several state-led policies. These included diversifying fuel mixes (both diversified fuel type and geographic origin of energy supplies), establishing redundancies in critical infrastructure, and maintaining ample energy storage. Dual-fuel power and heat plants are also energy security tools. In recent years, however, many Western countries, in-

---

[39] Colling Anderson and Joseph Simonson, "Meet the Green Energy Group behind the Study That's Driving Calls to Ban Gas Stoves," *The Washington Free Beacon*, January 16, 2023.

cluding the United States and Europe, have instead opted to rely on market forces to deliver energy when needed and ended government-led energy security policies. These policies have had a significant negative impact on their energy security. For instance, it ended mandates requiring natural gas storage in Europe (only to be re-instated after the 2022 energy crisis). Relying on market forces alone to deliver energy supplies contributed to the extended Texas power outage in February 2021.[40]

In the 2020s, Washington and Brussels promoted rapid expansion of electrification of transportation, heating, and other sectors. This policy aimed to increase use of renewable energy, which produces electricity. There are energy security implications, as US and European policies promoting concentration of most energy use in electricity rather than relying on diverse energy sources contradicts the principle of diversification.

3.3 Geopolitics of OE

This section discusses the energy geopolitical factors that constrain and provide opportunities for US military OE.

The United States has had a significant edge over adversaries for the last century because of its ample domestically produced energy supplies. Under the current global energy system, where fossil fuels are dominant, the US enjoys tremendous economic and military advantages over adversaries, especially China. China imports most of its oil and natural gas.

However, in the early 2020s, the United States decided to promote a change in the prevailing energy system from one based on fossil fuels to one based on solar, wind, hydropower, and nuclear energy in order to lower its greenhouse gases. In an energy system based on the current generation of renewables and nuclear energy, China dominates. If this transition is made, the US likely will lose its energy advantage, which will impact its economic and military power. This change can also affect American OE capacity.

> In the early 2020s, the United States decided to promote a change in the prevailing energy system from one based on fossil fuels to one based on solar, wind, hydropower, and nuclear energy to lower its carbon emissions. In an energy system based on the current generation of renewables and nuclear energy, China dominates. If this transition is made, the US likely will lose its energy advantage, which will impact its economic and military power. This change can also affect American OE capacity.

Even under a fossil fuel-based system, where the US has global dominance, the US will be challenged to access OE supplies, in certain theaters, especially Asia, where China is able to pose a threat to US energy supply chains.

---

[40] Brenda Shaffer, "Lessons for the States on Energy Security," *Real Clear Energy*, February 23, 2021.

Threats to civilian energy supplies impact OE during missions abroad since the US military relies primarily on civilian supply lines for its energy supplies. Close to half of those supplies are procured outside the United States, including in the Middle East and Asia. The US Department of Defense generally purchases refined energy products as close to the point of consumption as possible. While this reduces opportunities for disruption of the supply lines by enemies, it makes the US dependent on the reliability of local, foreign suppliers. In wartime, adversaries will likely attempt to disrupt these supplies, including through non-military means, including bribery and co-option. Thus, as part of OE, planners should assess the state of US relations with local suppliers. In addition, policy makers on many levels of the US DOD and US military need to plan for the ability during wartime to procure energy from locations that are not vulnerable to disruption by adversaries.

The geographic location of a mission creates different OE constraints and opportunities. Geographic locations have different climates, which affect and constrain energy use. For instance, cooling and heating needs of forces and equipment differ widely based on the climates of different locations. Batteries, for instance, are highly affected by weather conditions. Moreover, significant heating and cooling needs require greater amounts of energy.

The military applies different OE doctrines to different battle geographic locations. For instance, in recent years US ongoing operations have taken place in landlocked countries (Afghanistan) or semi-landlocked states which have limited coastal access (Iraq). This limits the logistic options, including for energy supplies.[41] The number of landlocked states grew significantly over the twentieth century and states of this type have a higher propensity for conflict, and thus are more likely to be sites of US military operations.

> Ashton Carter, when he headed Pentagon acquisition, technology, and logistics, said that the success of the war in Afghanistan would depend largely on being able to get weapons and support services to the US troops headed to the land-locked country, which he described as "the last place where you would like to be fighting a war."
>
> – "Pentagon Boosting Afghanistan 'Eyes in the Sky'," Reuters, April 3, 2010 (https://www.reuters.com/article/afghanistan-usa/update-1-pentagon-boosting-afghanistan-eyes-in-the-sky-idUSN0214793820100403).

---

[41] "Landlocked Countries: Higher Transport Costs, Delays, Less Trade," World Bank, June 16, 2008 (https://www.worldbank.org/en/news/feature/2008/06/16/landlocked-countries-higher-transport-costs-delays-less-trade).

3.3.1 US Government and Public Limitations on OE

The US military functions under the command of the President of the United States and thus is subordinate to civilian executive agencies. The US military forms OE policies within the constraints of its civilian oversight and US public expectations. Policy constraints and public attitudes regarding US energy policies periodically change, especially with the change of US administrations. Thus, the US military needs to conduct its OE plans in a changing civilian environment. The US DOD reviews and revises OE strategy periodically to "align with the guidance and priorities" of new administrations.[42]

The DOD is the largest consumer of energy within the US government. Consequently, when civilian bodies aim to reduce energy consumption in the government or to change the fuel mix consumed, such as higher use of renewable energy versus fossil fuels, they often turn their attention to the US military. Under the Biden administration, for example, OE goals have focused on: (1) Energy Demand Reduction; (2) Energy Substitution and Diversification; (3) Supply Chain Resilience; and (4) Enterprise-Wide Energy Visibility.[43]

These policies are more likely to affect installation use of energy than OE, since generally US administrations and Congress support ensuring the greatest lethality and operational effectiveness of the US military, and thus have allowed the military to choose the fuel mix that best suits its missions.

Several US presidential administrations over recent decades have issued Executive Orders and Congress has adopted legislation that aims for reduction of use of fossil fuels and climate altering emissions. However, as stated in the 2016 OE Strategy: "The Department recognizes that while reducing the demand for energy is an essential component of any energy strategy, this may not always be an option. Instead, the department should remain focused on achieving increased warfighter capability as the salient outcome while advocating for programs and initiatives that both reduce energy demand and enhance energy supportability as a means to achieve increased capability."[44]

However, different US administrations have enacted different approaches to the US military's fuel sources. During the Biden administration, the 2023 *US Department of Defense Operational Energy Strategy* states that "In alignment with the National Defense

---

[42] Office of the Undersecretary of Defense for Acquisition and Sustainment, *Fiscal Year 2020 Operational Energy Annual Report*, May 2021, page 3 (https://www.acq.osd.mil/eie/Downloads/OE/FY20%20OE%20Annual%20Report.pdf).
[43] Department of Defense, *2023 Operational Energy Strategy*, May 2023 (https://www.acq.osd.mil/eie/Downloads/OE/2023%20Operational%20Energy%20Strategy.pdf).
[44] Department of Defense, *2016 Operational Energy Strategy*, December 3, 2015, page 10 (https://www.acq.osd.mil/eie/Downloads/OE/2016%20OE%20Strategy_WEBd.pdf).

Strategy, the Department is prioritizing energy demand reduction and seeking to adopt more efficient and clean energy technologies that reduce logistics requirements in contested environments."[45] Moreover, according to the 2022 US law governing the DOD, DOD is required to conduct "An assessment of how industry trends transitioning from the production of internal combustion engines to the development and production of alternative propulsion systems may affect the long-term availability of parts for military equipment, the fuel costs for such equipment, and the sustainability of such equipment"; and "An assessment of any technologies, including electric, hydrogen, or other sustainable fuel technologies, that may reduce operational energy demand in the near-term or long-term."[46]

The 2023 *Department of Defense Operational Energy Strategy* recognizes the challenge for the US military due to its need for energy-dense liquid fuels that today are provided chiefly by petroleum: "This energy transition will have profound implications for the Department, particularly given the military's requirement for energy-dense, liquid fuels for mobile applications."[47] The 2023 Strategy concludes: "The current state of the market and the Department's need for high performance capabilities in austere environments suggests continued reliance on liquid fuels in the near- to mid-term. However, industry and the Department continue to explore and develop alternatives to fossil fuels that maintain or enhance operational effectiveness while also improving supply chain resilience."[48]

US presidential administrations and the US Congress often promote certain technologies for energy production and consumption, and generally expect the US military to adopt those promoted technologies. For instance, in the 1990s, Congress widely subsidized biofuels, in efforts to replace oil, and support American farmers, and expected that the US military would develop use of biofuels. In the 2020s, the Biden administration widely promoted electrification of transportation and home heating in attempts to replace oil and natural gas use and in parallel expects the US military to adopt electrification of the battlefield, or at least of military transportation. In contrast to this approach, some assess that governments should not pick the technologies, but rather remain technology neutral and that scientists, the commercial sector, and the military should be free to develop technological advances.

---

[45] Department of Defense, *2023 Operational Energy Strategy*, May 2023, page 1 (https://www.acq.osd.mil/eie/Downloads/OE/2023%20Operational%20Energy%20Strategy.pdf).
[46] Office of the Law Revision Counsel, "United States Code: 10 USC 2926: Operational Energy" (https://uscode.house.gov/view.xhtml?req=granuleid:USC-prelim-title10-section2926&num=0&edition=prelim).
[47] Department of Defense, *2023 Operational Energy Strategy*, May 2023, page 2 (https://www.acq.osd.mil/eie/Downloads/OE/2023%20Operational%20Energy%20Strategy.pdf).
[48] Department of Defense, *2023 Operational Energy Strategy*, May 2023, page 7 (https://www.acq.osd.mil/eie/Downloads/OE/2023%20Operational%20Energy%20Strategy.pdf).

Some US states have enacted laws related to energy use which may affect OE options for US military units operating from bases in the US. For instance, several regions in the United States have enacted legislation prohibiting the use of natural gas in new buildings. If there is not an exemption for federal buildings, this can restrict the militaries' access to natural gas in installations, for instance. However, natural gas supply or other energy source infrastructure may not be available in certain locations. Thus, in the United States and abroad, installation location choices need to take into consideration the policies and legal limits on different fuel options.

In addition to policies that affect the fuel mix of the US military, the US government and public also expect the US military to be a source of innovation in many spheres, including energy, which can generate useful spillover technologies for the civilian sphere and/or to generate new energy transitions.

3.3.2 Hybrid Warfare: OE Threats

With the increase in hybrid warfare, American adversaries will likely increasingly target US domestic critical energy infrastructure and that of US allies and partners during conflict. US enemies will conduct attacks on domestic energy infrastructure through a variety of methods, including cyberattacks. As pointed out in the 2016 *Operational Energy Strategy:* "A2/AD and hybrid threats pose escalating risks to the assured delivery of operational energy and, by extension, the ability to project and sustain power worldwide."[49]

US domestic energy infrastructure is quite vulnerable to attacks. Energy supply disruptions could undermine American public morale and support for the war effort. Energy disruptions in the United States also have direct impact on OE. The military relies on civilian supply lines for its energy supplies. Electricity and fuel disruptions could complicate the ability of combatants to arrive at their missions. Furthermore, elements of combat operations taking place outside the United States are often operated from US territory. US drone strikes abroad, for instance, are often operated from bases in the United States.[50] Thus, the energy security of the US directly affects the operational ability of the US military.

As part of hybrid warfare, US adversaries are likely to target energy supplies and infrastructure that are sources of US OE supplies. These include fuel depots and companies, pipelines, grids, and ports. Hybrid threats to OE are especially likely to target civilian

---

[49] Department of Defense, *2016 Operational Energy Strategy*, December 3, 2015, page 9 (https://www.acq.osd.mil/eie/Downloads/OE/2016%20OE%20Strategy_WEBd.pdf).
[50] Andrew Craft, "Drone Pilots Fight Foreign Wars from Remote Nevada Desert," *Fox News*, June 20, 2018 (https://www.foxnews.com/us/drone-pilots-fight-foreign-wars-from-remote-nevada-desert).

infrastructure and supply lines since they are likely to have a much lower level of protection than military and government installations and infrastructure.

3.3.3 Reliance on Civilian Energy Supply Lines

As the US military relies on civilian American energy supply lines and energy infrastructure, such as electrical and natural gas grids, power plants, and ports, the security of US domestic energy infrastructure and the security of supply of energy in the US has direct consequences for US OE capabilities. Thus, US domestic energy infrastructure security and energy security of supply are issues of concern for the US military as part of its OE activity. Disruption of power supply in the US can spill over and disrupt functioning of additional critical infrastructure: "The reality is if you take away power, none of the other 15 officially designated critical infrastructure are going to work."[51]

> "Russia has the ability to execute cyber attacks in the United States that generate localized, temporary disruptive effects on critical infrastructure – such as disrupting an electrical distribution network for at least a few hours."
>
> – US intelligence community's *Worldwide Threat Assessment*, 2019

In addition, supply insecurity in the US domestic electricity sector also creates national security vulnerabilities that America's adversaries can exploit. Three out of the four biggest population centers in the United States – California, Texas, and New York – suffer from chronic electricity shortfalls. Florida, the third largest state in the US, receives all its natural gas via a single pipeline and its disruption could cause a massive electricity outage.

> General James Mattis reported in 2003, regarding the frequency with which he outran fuel resupply lines, calling upon the Department of Defense to "unleash us from the tether of fuel."
>
> – Quoted in Naval Research Advisory Committee Future Fuels Study Panel, "Breaking the Tether of Fuel," *Military Review*, January-February 2007 (https://www.armyupress.army.mil/Portals/7/military-review/Archives/English/MilitaryReview_20070228_art013.pdf).

As part of the military's reliance on civilian fuel supply lines, changes in civilian energy use can limit military equipment and fuel access. For instance, as pointed out in the 2023 OE Strategy, if civilian transportation transfers primarily to electric vehicles, the military will face a challenge of availability of internal combustion engine components. Moreover, the 2023 OE Strategy points out that if the civilian sector transfers away from use of fossil fuels, it "will have profound implications for the Department

---

51 Maggie Miller, "The Hard Truth behind Biden's Cyber Warnings," *Politico*, March 27, 2022.

(of Defense), particularly given the military's requirement for energy-dense, liquid fuels for mobile applications."[52]

The dependence on civilian energy supply lines is particularly challenging to provide OE needs for the US military abroad. As noted in the 2023 OE Strategy, "As a globally deployed force, the Department depends on fuel infrastructure owned by commercial companies and host countries around the globe. The Department purchases much of its fuel overseas (nearly 50 percent in FY2022) and is concerned about the shift in investments in upstream and downstream petroleum infrastructure to national oil companies (NOCs) in China and the Middle East. The Department needs to assess the potential rise of political-economic influence on the availability of jet fuel that may come with greater NOC market share and the shifts in refining capacity."[53]

3.3.4 International Legal Conventions Affecting OE

The US government is a signatory or supporter of several international treaties, agreements, and declarations that can place limitations on the activity of the US military. For instance, international agreements on maritime pollutants can limit US Navy fuel use practices. International climate change agreements obligations can create reporting requirements for US military units regarding their energy usage. OE planners may need to take these conventions into consideration.

3.3.5 OE and Sea Chokepoints

As pointed out in this chapter, most internationally traded oil and LNG supplies transit major sea trade lanes. Several of these transit major sea chokepoints, such as the Malacca Straits, the Red Sea, the Strait of Hormuz, and the Bosporus Strait, are also major energy transit waterways. Accordingly, strategic OE planners need to regularly study the threats to these chokepoints and assess how the state of their vulnerability affects the US military's access to necessary energy supplies.

3.3.6 OE Implications of the "Pivot to Asia"

In recent years, several US administrations have stated that it is a US strategic goal to "pivot" to the Asia-Pacific. This pivot creates new OE challenges:

---

[52] Department of Defense, *2023 Operational Energy Strategy*, May 2023 (https://www.acq.osd.mil/eie/Downloads/OE/2023%20Operational%20Energy%20Strategy.pdf).
[53] Department of Defense, *2023 Operational Energy Strategy*, May 2023 (https://www.acq.osd.mil/eie/Downloads/OE/2023%20Operational%20Energy%20Strategy.pdf), page 3.

- Operations will be conducted across longer distances, creating more demand for fuel, and increased supply line vulnerability.
- China has control and influence over many commercial and other entities in the energy sectors in states in Asia, such as ports, power plants, and fuel companies, and thus can disrupt access to fuels and energy during military operations. China will not need military means to do this, but can use bribery, cyber attacks, and/or recruitment of local operatives in Asia.
- Several US allies and partners and allies in Asia inhabit islands. Accordingly, energy supplies cannot be easily transported between the allies and partners to meet changing American OE needs, in contrast to the situation in the European theater.

To support operations in the European theater, the US can rely on access to the NATO alliance and Europe's dedicated network of oil pipelines and storage facilities. Various states are connected in this infrastructure and can quickly dispatch supplies as needed in wartime. This type of access and support infrastructure is lacking in Asia. With the US pivot to Asia, ensuring stable energy supplies for the US military has become even more challenging, as the US military's energy supply lines in East Asia are much longer and less supported by local alliances and dedicated infrastructure than those required for missions in Europe.

> "Multiple analysis and wargames suggest that the tyranny of distance will challenge the projection of power into and around the Asia-Pacific region. Additionally, Asia-Pacific operations will rely on energy to power the airbases, ports, and sea bases needed to employ air and sea capabilities."
>
> – Department of Defense, *2016 Operational Energy Strategy*, December 3, 2015 (https://www.acq.osd.mil/eie/Downloads/OE/2016%20OE%20Strategy_WEBd.pdf).

3.4 Protection of Energy Infrastructure of US Allies and Partners

Access to energy supplies and infrastructure abroad is an important element of OE. Accordingly, American adversaries are likely to target energy infrastructure in states friendly to the US, especially during active military operations. Therefore, OE planners should include protection of energy supplies and infrastructure in relevant friendly countries in operational plans.

The US Congress has mandated DOD to conduct every five years "An assessment of any infrastructure investments of allied and partner countries that may affect operational energy availability in the event of a conflict with a near-peer adversary."[54]

---

54 Office of the Law Revision Counsel, "United States Code: 10 USC 2926: Operational Energy," June 15, 2023 (https://uscode.house.gov/view.xhtml?req=granuleid:USC-prelim-title10-section2926&num=0&edition=prelim).

3.4 Protection of Energy Infrastructure of US Allies and Partners — 49

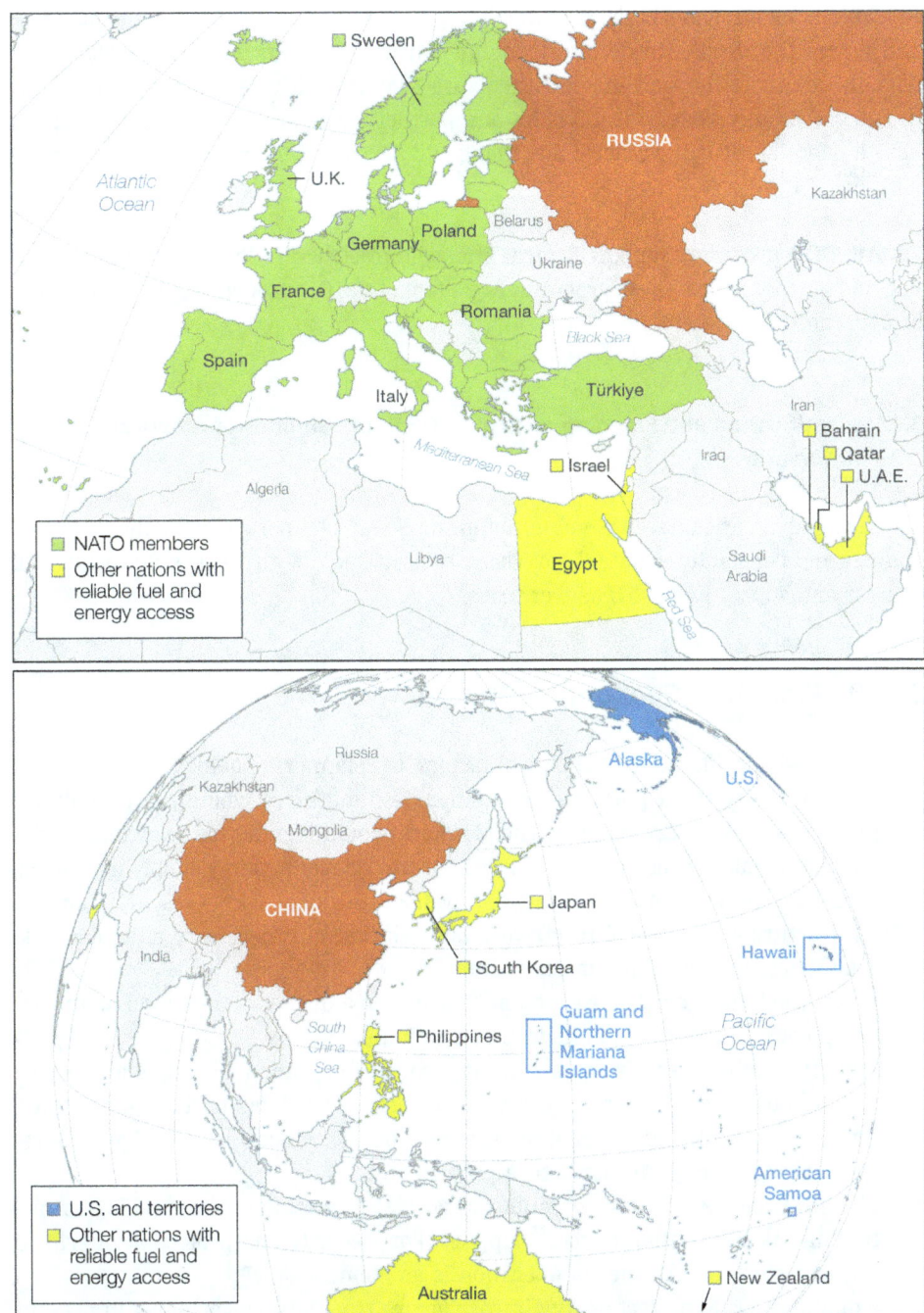

Figure 3.5: Operational Energy in European versus Asian Theaters. Map: John Fleming.

In addition, on a regular basis, the US military and DOD should go beyond the mandate and assess the threats to domestic energy infrastructure in the US and allies and friendly countries, beyond the infrastructure that explicitly serves US OE needs. If the overall energy systems in US allies and partner states are not secure, these states have a national security vulnerability that could also affect their capacity to cooperate with the US.

Several DOD programs support Critical Energy Infrastructure Protection (CEIP) in allied and partner states. These programs are a tool of the OE strategy in specific theaters of operation.

3.4.1 Identification and Planning to Exploit OE Vulnerabilities of American Adversaries

American adversaries have OE vulnerabilities. US war planners identify these vulnerabilities and constantly update them. The American bank of targets should include OE sources and supply lines of US adversaries.

3.5 OE Planning: Geopolitical Factors

In taking into consideration geopolitical factors, OE planners should:
- Identify the relevant ports, depots, companies, and more where the US military plans to access energy supplies. The planners should identify the relevant individuals, companies, local agencies etc. that control relevant energy supply infrastructure. Operational plans should identify local and regional energy resources and infrastructure and the legal framework and relationships necessary to access local fuels, energy sources, and infrastructure.
- Assess the impact of unique geographic factors in a theater of operation on the energy needs and supply options in that location.
- Identify reliable energy suppliers in the theater of operation, including identifying if they cooperate with foreign actors or domestic opponents to the United States.
- Include in planning identifying the agencies and individuals in a foreign state responsible for energy infrastructure protection.
- Plan for protection during operations of necessary energy supplies and infrastructure and transportation of these supplies. Port security and protection of critical infrastructure in a theater of operation is an element of OE.
- Examine ways to protect energy infrastructure from attacks, including to prevent weaponization of energy infrastructure.
- Establish a legal framework for use and protection of energy supplies and infrastructure. This may include concluding a legal agreement before an operation.

- Verify appropriate insurance coverage. Sometimes energy supplies are blocked from entering a conflict zone, despite no concrete threat, due to limitations imposed by insurance companies. This has been evident in the Black Sea during the Russia-Ukraine War and in 2023 during the Israel-Hamas war. In a theater of operation, the insurance framework should not have restrictions on energy supplies during operations. If so, an alternative insurance framework may need to be provided, including by US government agencies.
- Identify vulnerabilities to energy supplies in a theater that can be exploited by US adversaries.
- Identify enemy energy supply vulnerabilities.

3.6 Necessary Intelligence on Geopolitics of Energy for OE

DOD and US military intelligence assessments should include potential threats globally to US military energy supply access. These should include:
- Analysis of activity of US adversaries such as Russia, Iran, and China aimed at threatening US access to energy supplies in various operational theaters. Accordingly, US intelligence agencies should collect and analyze the control and influence of US adversaries, especially Russia and China, over energy infrastructure globally.
- US intelligence should also collect and analyze on a regular basis how US adversaries assess US OE vulnerabilities. These identified vulnerabilities are likely to be targeted by US adversaries.
- The US should identify and analyze disinformation campaigns of US adversaries related to energy, environment, and climate.
- Basic energy data should be included in portfolios on operation locations. This should include information on energy consumption and production trends in a country and/or region of operations.
- Establish an OE counterintelligence plan to protect energy supply chains.
- Complete an adversary OE intelligence assessment that can serve to support attacks on enemy OE capability.

3.6.1 Cross-Agency Cooperation: OE Supplies and Infrastructure

DOD cooperates with several other US government departments and agencies in determining its energy policies. These include the Department of State, Department of Energy, and Department of Transportation. The DOD, US military, and various US military units in foreign countries cooperate on energy policies with NATO and NATO member countries, other allies and partners, and US embassies abroad.

As part of OE, US forces should establish and maintain cooperative relations with the energy power brokers on the ground. This is likely to be improved by cooperation with

US civilian agencies, such as embassies in the foreign country where an operation is occurring, or neighboring state. Accordingly, senior DOD officials and commanders, in cooperation with the US Department of State and US embassies abroad, need to contribute to the establishment and maintenance of good alliances and partnerships in countries where the US military can procure secure energy supplies close to operation locations.

US military cooperation with allied and friendly countries on improving CEIP establishes and maintains relationships with important elements in energy sectors abroad, which can become critical in procuring energy supplies during operations.

US embassies and defense attachés, and cooperation officers should be encouraged to regularly identify key energy sector individuals, agencies, institutions, and companies in the country of their service abroad and maintain good relations with them. These may become relevant if US military engagements take place in these or nearby countries and fuel supplies need to be procured.

3.7 International and Regional Institutions

The United States is a member of and/or cooperates with several treaties and organizations that can provide information and cooperation useful for OE missions. OE planners should consider that these organizations can provide data and assistance to further their missions.

These organizations include:
- International Maritime Organization
- NATO
- NATO Centers of Excellence, including the NATO Energy Security Center of Excellence (Lithuania) and the NATO Maritime Security Center of Excellence (Istanbul)
- International Atomic Energy Agency
- International Energy Agency
- Australia, United Kingdom, United States Security Pact (AUKUS)
- Southeast Asia Treaty Organization (SEATO).

3.8 For Study

- Which fuels are the major sources of energy consumed in the United States, globally and by the US military? In 2030, what percentage of energy use is estimated to come from renewable energy?
- Memorize the three elements of energy security.

- Explain the potential limitation of a refinery on its ability to process certain types of crude and produce specific refined products.
- Study the differences between renewable energy, green energy, and clean energy.

3.9 Topics for Discussion and Research

- What are the two main reasons natural gas trade is more vulnerable to foreign political influence and more easily disrupted than oil and coal trade?
- How do geographic factors affect OE needs? Give some examples.
- Can renewable energy deliver electricity supplies without fossil fuels? Explain.
- How does the "pivot to Asia" affect OE needs?
- Name four main intelligence topics for collection as part of OE planning.
- What are the main spheres of information necessary for OE planning in an operations theater?
- How does hybrid warfare affect OE?
- Name three institutions that can provide information and cooperation on OE planning by the US military.

3.10 Case Study: Energy in Conflict – the 2020 Armenia-Azerbaijan War

The 2020 Armenia-Azerbaijan War encompassed many of the characteristic elements of twenty-first-century wars: hybrid warfare, extensive use of unmanned vehicles, targeting of civilian populations outside the battle zone, and integrated social and traditional media campaigns. OE also featured prominently.[55]

First, the trigger to the war was a threat to new international energy infrastructure: the war broke out just before the Southern Gas Corridor was scheduled to begin operations. The corridor, running from Azerbaijan to Europe, was slated to carry the first new natural gas volumes to Europe in decades. These gas supplies would help European countries to lower their dependence on Russian gas supplies. The pipeline project also provided Azerbaijan, Armenia's rival, with additional revenue and strategic influence. Thus, Moscow and its ally Armenia wanted to disrupt their arrival. In addition, Armenia targeted Azerbaijan's energy infrastructure during the war. During the war, Armenia attempted to "weaponize" Azerbaijan's energy infrastructure during the fighting.

---

55 This case study draws significantly on the article: Brenda Shaffer, "Energy in Conflict: The Case of the 2020 Armenia-Azerbaijan War," *CTX Journal* (special issue hybrid threats and energy security), April 2022.

This case study will examine the energy factor in the 2020 Armenia-Azerbaijan War and discuss the implications for energy in future warfare. It will open with a short discussion on the conflict and the role of Azerbaijan's energy exports in European energy security. This case study illustrates how Russia's goal of energy dominance in Europe affected a conflict outside of Europe, the goal of disrupting an adversaries' energy supplies during war, and the weaponization of energy infrastructure.

3.10.1 Background: The Armenia-Azerbaijan Conflict

The struggle between Armenia and Azerbaijan created one of the most lethal post-Soviet conflicts. The first war between the two newly independent states in 1992–1994 led to nearly 30,000 deaths and created over a million refugees, mostly from Azerbaijan.

While formally centered over control of the region of "Nagorno-Karabakh," Russia lies behind the escalation to full-scale war between Armenia and Azerbaijan in the 1990s and for sustaining the conflict for decades. Russia has played a central role in the emergence of the conflict and its preservation. Moscow benefited greatly from the standoff. The first war, following the Soviet breakup, left the region economically shattered for years after the independence of the two states and maintained Moscow's power over the South Caucasus region.[56]

In particular, it cemented Yerevan's dependence on Moscow. Armenia is a close ally of Russia and Moscow exerts strong control over the country. Russia maintains three military bases in Armenia and controls Armenian airspace and air defense; Russian companies own almost all of Armenia's energy and other strategic infrastructure as well as major commercial enterprises; and Armenia is a member of the Russian-led mutual defense pact – the CSTO (Collective Security Treaty Organization).

When the Soviet Union collapsed in late 1991, all the new states except Russia and Armenia recognized the previously set Soviet borders between the republics as their new international borders. In this initial post-Soviet period, Russia occupied two regions of Georgia (Abkhazia and South Ossetia) and a region of Moldova (Transnistria), and Armenia invaded Azerbaijan and captured the Nagorno-Karabakh region and seven additional regions of Azerbaijan. Yerevan expelled all the non-Armenian population from the occupied territories, creating close to 800,000 Azerbaijani refugees, in addition to the close to 300,000 Azerbaijanis that Yerevan evicted from Armenia prior to the Soviet breakup.

---

56 On the Armenia-Azerbaijan conflict, see Svante E. Cornell, *Small Nations and Great Powers* (London: Routledge Curzon, 2001); Thomas De Waal, *Black Garden* (New York: New York University Press, 2013); Svante E. Cornell (ed.), *The International Politics of the Armenia-Azerbaijan Conflict* (New York: Palgrave, 2017).

During the Soviet period, Moscow categorized Nagorno-Karabakh as an autonomous region within Soviet Azerbaijan. Following the Soviet breakup, the international community, including the United States, recognized Nagorno-Karabakh and surrounding areas as part of Azerbaijan. The USSR had carved out the borders of the autonomous region, so it had an ethnic Armenian majority within Azerbaijan. Moscow used this same policy to create division in many places in the USSR. Following the collapse of the USSR, no countries, including Russia and Armenia, recognized Nagorno-Karabakh as an independent country nor as the legal territory of Armenia.

After independence, Armenia took a page from Moscow's playbook and claimed that these regions were not under its occupation, but controlled by independent Armenian entities.[57] Thus, Yerevan referred to the areas it controlled as the "Nagorno-Karabakh Republic" even though Armenian military forces occupied the regions, Yerevan provided their budgets, and all the local officials were citizens of Armenia and many had served as senior Armenian officials.[58]

During the period of Armenian occupation, Yerevan established settlements and provided financial and other incentives to ethnic Armenians, especially from Lebanon and Syria, to move to the occupied territories. Officials in Armenia, local authorities in Nagorno-Karabakh, and diaspora organizations flaunted their efforts to bring settlers to the occupied territories.[59]

In the period following the first war, the line of contact between the forces of Armenia and Azerbaijan remained tense, with an average of more than a dozen soldiers killed each year. From time to time, the conflict flared up into full battles, including the one in April 2016, known as the "Four-Day War," which led to more than 200 deaths.

3.10.2 Energy Export

Azerbaijan is a major oil and gas producer and exporter, mostly supplied to Europe and Turkey. Azerbaijan's major oil and natural gas pipelines do not transit Russia (or Iran)

---

[57] For more on Russia and Armenia's use of proxies in attempts to evade responsibility for occupation, see: Svante E. Cornell and Brenda Shaffer, "The United States Need to Declare War on Proxies," *Foreign Policy*, February 27, 2020 (https://foreignpolicy.com/2020/02/27/russia-iran-suleimani-the-united-states-needs-to-declare-war-on-proxies/).
[58] Svante E. Cornell and Brenda Shaffer, "Occupied Elsewhere," Foundation for Defense of Democracies, 2020, pages 22–23 (https://www.fdd.org/analysis/2020/01/27/occupied-elsewhere/).
[59] Edik Baghdasaryan, "Repopulation Is an Essential Question for All Armenians," *Hetq* (Armenia), June 25, 2007 (https://hetq.am/en/article/6744); Melania Harutyunyan, "Deputy Prime Minister of Artsakh Spoke about the Resettlement of Artsakh," *Aravot* (Armenia), July 27, 2013 (https://www.aravot-en.am/2013/07/27/155729).

and thus contribute to reducing European dependence on energy supplies from Russia. Beginning in 2013, Baku began development of the Southern Gas Corridor, which aimed to bring the first new gas volumes in decades to Europe (versus rerouting existing supplies).[60] This gas megaproject aimed to transit not only Azerbaijani gas to Europe, but also created a route for supplies from other sources, such as Central Asia and Israel, to reach multiple markets in Europe. The Southern Gas Corridor served as a catalyst for the establishment of several gas interconnectors in southern Europe, which improved European energy security.

3.10.3 Energy – the Catalyst for Reignition of War

Like Japan's entry into World War II, energy access was a major factor in the outbreak of the 2020 Armenia-Azerbaijan War. Unlike Japan, however, it was not a lack of access to energy, but rather Russia and Armenia's aim to prevent or at least disrupt initiation of significant additional international energy trade, which would challenge Russia's market dominance in Europe.

The first phase of the 2020 Armenia-Azerbaijan War began on July 12 in the Azerbaijani region of Tovuz along the northern section of the international border between Armenia and Azerbaijan. This region is located 300 kilometers north of what was the line of contact between Armenia and Azerbaijan's forces in the occupied territories. Armenia launched a surprise attack several weeks before Azerbaijan planned to begin commercial operation of the Southern Gas Corridor.[61] The project commencement was poised to turn Azerbaijan into a major supplier of energy to Europe and provide a new revenue stream, wholly improving Azerbaijan's strategic position. These supplies would also challenge Russia's dominance of gas supply in several key countries in Europe, including Italy, Greece, and Bulgaria.

In the July 2020 attacks, Armenian troops attempted to gain control of the Qaraqaya Heights in Azerbaijan. The heights are perched above the energy and transit corridor that runs from the Caspian Sea to Europe and includes the Southern Gas Corridor. Ar-

---

[60] For more on the significance of Caspian energy, see Brenda Shaffer, "In the Era of US Energy Abundance: The Role of the Caspian Region in US Policy," *The Brown Journal of World Affairs*, vol. 26, no. 2, Spring/Summer 2020 (https://www.fdd.org/wp-content/uploads/2020/08/Shaffer-In-the-Era-of-US-Energy-Abundance-1.pdf); Brenda Shaffer, "Gas Politics after Ukraine: Azerbaijan, Shah Deniz, and Europe's Newest Energy Partner," *Foreign Affairs*, December 17, 2013 (https://www.foreignaffairs.com/articles/russia-fsu/2013-12-17/gas-politics-after-ukraine).
[61] Brenda Shaffer, "Armenia-Azerbaijan Conflict Poses Threat to European Energy Security," Foundation for Defense of Democracies, July 17, 2020 (https://www.fdd.org/analysis/2020/07/17/armenia-azerbaijan-conflict-energy-security/).

menian control of the heights would have enabled Yerevan to threaten the energy and transit corridor and thus the attacks posed a strategic threat to Azerbaijan.

An Armenian Special Forces member stated that his unit was ordered to attack the Azerbaijani section of the Baku-Tbilisi-Ceyhan oil pipeline during the July 2020 battles: "During the Tovuz battles, there was such a combat mission. The Central Command ordered us to explore the protected areas in that area. In connection with the order to blow up the oil pipeline, I marked the positions of the Azerbaijani Army on the map and calculated the protected areas. I made notes on maps and documents and handed them over to the relevant authorities."[62]

The July 2020 surprise attacks on Azerbaijani forces was facilitated by Armenia having established tunnels that enabled Yerevan to deploy forces in Azerbaijani territory without detection. Armenia likely received technical assistance from Iran's IRGC forces to establish these tunnels, which are used by Iranian proxies such as Hamas and Hezbollah. One of the uncovered tunnels connected Iranian territory with territory occupied by Armenia in Jabrayil.

Following the July 2020 attacks in Tovuz, senior Armenian officials stated that Armenia's goal was to make it clear to the EU that "Armenia is the guarantor" of Europe's energy security.[63] In August 2020, Armenian representatives stated that considering the July clashes, it had plans to coordinate with the EU's Directorate General for Energy on the security of the supplies to Europe, and that Yerevan planned to claim that the security of the corridor is now in Armenia's hands. Armenia sought to raise its importance in Brussels through its ability to disrupt gas supplies to Europe, and to threaten Azerbaijan's extensive investment adding an element of security risk. Amid such threats to the energy corridor, new investments in its expansion were unlikely. Thus, the July 2020 Armenian attacks risked devaluing the corridor. Yerevan also sought to undermine Azerbaijan receiving strategic benefits as a gas supplier to Europe.

Yerevan chose the timing and location of the attacks to create the impression that Armenia has the capacity to disrupt this strategic energy and transit corridor. At the time of these attacks, Elshad Nasirov, Vice-President of SOCAR, stated that "it is not by

---

62 APA Group, "Armenian Citizen Accused of Terrorism: 'We Were Instructed to Explode Baku-Tbilisi-Ceyhan Pipeline'," January 10, 2022 (https://apa.az/en/incident/armenian-citizen-accused-of-terrorism-we-were-instructed-to-explode-baku-tbilisi-jeyhan-pipeline-365617).
63 Briefing of an advisor to Armenian President Nikolai Pashinyan, August 2020; "Armenia Denies Plans to Attack Azerbaijan's Oil and Gas Infrastructure," Lenta.ru, July 19, 2020 (https://lenta.ru/news/2020/07/19/armenia/).

chance that Armenia launched a military operation against Azerbaijan three months before the start of Azerbaijani gas supplies to Europe."[64]

Azerbaijan's foreign policy adviser to President Aliyev, Hikmet Hajiyev referred also to the link between the location of the attacks and the planned commencement of the major gas exports to Europe:

> It was not coincidental why Tovuz was chosen as a venue to carry out military provocation against Azerbaijan in July 12 – 16, 2020. Tovuz is situated on the international border between Armenia and Azerbaijan, not along the Line of Contact, and hosts energy and infrastructure projects nearby. The Baku-Tbilisi-Supsa and BTC oil pipelines, and the Southern Caucasus pipeline, an important chain in the multimillion megaproject the Southern Gas Corridor (SGC), pass close by the Tovuz area. The intention of Armenia to engage third parties in the war against Azerbaijan and demolish the latter's critical energy infrastructure was also present in July.[65]

In parallel with the attacks at Tovuz, Armenian troops shelled Nakhchivan, an Azerbaijani exclave. The attempt to open new fronts in the conflict was in line with then Armenian Defense Minister David Tonoyan's doctrine of "New Wars for New Territories."[66] According to Tonoyan's doctrine, Armenia sought to expand the arenas of fighting between Armenia and Azerbaijan to deter Azerbaijan from retaking control of occupied Nagorno-Karabakh and surrounding territories.

Armenia's attempt to gain control of the hills above the Southern Gas Corridor is in line with its longstanding strategy that viewed Azerbaijan's energy production and export infrastructure as key military targets. Over the three decades of conflict, Armenian leaders had threatened to attack Azerbaijan's oil and gas production and export pipelines and Armenian military exercises frequently simulated such attacks.[67]

The energy aspects of the Armenia-Azerbaijan conflict are exceptional since traditionally belligerents target energy supplies to deny one's adversary access to energy. However, in this conflict, the energy export infrastructure was targeted, to deny Azerbaijan the strategic benefits of serving as an export state to Europe. In addition, Armenia as

---

[64] AZƏRBAYCAN 24, "Elshad Nasirov: Armenian Provocation Is a Threat to Azerbaijan's Energy Infrastructure," July 17, 2020 (https://www.azerbaycan24.com/en/elshad-nasirov-armenian-provocation-is-a-threat-to-azerbaijan-s-energy-infrastructure/).
[65] Hikmet Hajiyev, "Attacks by Armenia against Azerbaijani Civilians and Critical Infrastructure Should Not Be Overlooked," *Euractiv*, October 30, 2020 (https://www.euractiv.com/section/azerbaijan/opinion/attacks-by-armenia-against-azerbaijani-civilians-and-critical-infrastructure-should-not-be-overlooked/).
[66] Lragir.am, "We Do the Opposite – New War for New Territories: Minister Tonoyan's Tough Statement," March 30, 2019 (https://www.lragir.am/en/2019/03/30/71511); The Armenian Mirror-Spectator, "Pashinyan Backs Defense Chief's Tough on Karabakh," *Mirror-Spectator*, April 2, 2019 (https://mirrorspectator.com/2019/04/02/pashinyan-backs-defense-chiefs-tough-talk-on-karabakh/).
[67] Sargis Harutyunyan, "Missile Strikes on Oil Facilities Simulated in Armenian War Games," *Azatutyun*, October 15, 2012 (https://www.azatutyun.am/a/24740508.html).

an ally of Russia, was also operating to prevent new energy resources from arriving to Europe that could challenge Moscow's energy dominance.

By opening a new front and attempting to neutralize Azerbaijan's emerging role as an energy provider to Europe and deny new revenues to Baku, Armenia set the stage for full-scale war in late September 2020. Through the attacks in Tovuz, Yerevan had created a *casus belli*. The new strategic reality that emerged with the opening of two additional fronts and a threat overhanging its strategically important energy and transport corridor to the West was unsustainable for Baku.

3.10.4 Attacks on International Pipelines during the War

In retrospect, the July 2020 Tovuz attacks were the first phase of the Second Armenia-Azerbaijan War. In the second phase of the war, beginning September 27, 2020, Armenian threats to energy pipelines continued. In October 2020, Armenia fired missiles that landed within 10 meters of the Baku-Tbilisi-Ceyhan (BTC) oil pipeline, near the Azerbaijani city of Yevlax.[68] Despite the attempts, the missile attacks did not disrupt the operations of the BTC and other nearby pipelines.[69]

The 2020 Armenia-Azerbaijan War was not the first time that Armenia threatened or attempted to attack Azerbaijan's energy production and export infrastructure. Former Armenian president Serzh Sargsyan criticized Prime Minister Nikol Pashinyan for not using sophisticated Russian Iskandar missiles in Armenia's arsenal to attack the pipelines, saying "in the end, why did we buy these missiles? Not to use them at the right time? The Iskanders are ours, and we are the only ones to whom the ally [Russia] gave such weapons. And we didn't use them."[70] While they were not used to attack the pipeline corridor, Armenia did fire the Iskandar missiles on Azerbaijani troops in Shusha toward the end of the fall 2020 war.[71] Similar threats were made, for instance, during the April 2016 clashes between Armenia and Azerbaijan.[72]

---

[68] S&P Global, "Major Caucasus Oil, Gas Pipelines Unaffected by Rocket Attack: Azerbaijan's Socar," S&P Global/Commodity Insights, October 7, 2020 (https://www.spglobal.com/platts/en/market-insights/latest-news/natural-gas/100720-major-caucasus-oil-gas-pipelines-unaffected-by-rocket-attack-azerbaijans-socar).
[69] Reuters Staff, "BP Works on Reinforcing Security at Azerbaijan Facilities," Reuters, October 7, 2020 (https://www.reuters.com/article/armenia-azerbaijan-bp-int/bp-works-on-reinforcing-security-at-azerbaijan-facilities-idUSKBN26S27U).
[70] JAMnews, "Ex. Armenian Pres. Sargsyan Hurls New Accusations at Pashinyan Govt.," February 17, 2021 (https://jam-news.net/ex-armenian-pres-sargsyan-hurls-new-accusations-at-pashinyan-govt/).
[71] Mushvig Mehdiyev, "Fragments of Iskander Missile Found in Azerbaijan's Karabakh Region Raise Serious Questions," *Caspian News*, April 4, 2021 (https://caspiannews.com/news-detail/fragments-of-iskander-missile-found-in-azerbaijans-karabakh-region-raise-serious-questions-2021-4-4-0/).

Azerbaijan did not attempt to attack energy infrastructure in Armenia, which would have contributed to slowing down Armenia's war effort. Armenia is a member of the Russian-led CSTO defense pact and if Azerbaijan had attacked Armenian territory during the war, this would have risked Russia joining in the war to defend Armenia. The war took place entirely on the territory of Azerbaijan, aside from an unmanned aerial vehicle (UAV) attack on a line of Scud missiles at Armenia's border with Azerbaijan.

3.10.5 Weaponization of Energy Infrastructure

The Second Armenia-Azerbaijan War featured several elements of hybrid warfare, including the intentional targeting of civilian populations (such as the Armenian missile attacks on the Azerbaijani cities of Barda and Ganja), and extensive media and disinformation campaigns. As part of this hybrid warfare, Armenia and Azerbaijan both threatened to "weaponize" energy infrastructure in each other's state and unleash mass civilian casualties. In weaponizing energy infrastructure, the goal is not just to disrupt energy supplies but to create widespread damage and potential loss of life through attacks on pipelines, power plants, grids, and other energy infrastructure elements. Prior to the full emergence of the war in September 2020, Armenia threatened to attack the Mingachevir Hydropower Station. Baku, in turn, threatened that if the Mingachevir plant was attacked, it could respond by attacking Armenia's Metsamor Nuclear Power Plant, although a senior Azerbaijani official later walked back this threat.

3.10.5.1 Armenia's Threats to the Mingachevir Hydropower Station
Historically, there have been several cases of armies using intentional flooding as a military tactic, including both the Allied and Axis powers during World War II.[73] Chinese forces intentionally flooded the Yellow River in their war with Japan in 1938, leading to hundreds of thousands of deaths and the displacement of millions more. In the Iran-Iraq War, each side used intentional flooding to deny access to the battle zones. Russia likely damaged the Kakhova Dam in Ukraine in 2023 to unleash mass flooding. Concerns continue that ISIS and other terrorist groups could attack the Mosul Dam to flood areas in Iraq. For decades, Armenia has threatened to attack the Mingachevir Hydropower Station in Azerbaijan not only to disable Azerbaijan's primary source of elec-

---

72 Novosti-Armenia AMI, "URGENTLY! Karabakh Is Ready to Strike at Azerbaijan's Oil Communications," *AMI*, April 5, 2016 (https://newsarmenia.am/news/nagorno_karabakh/srochno-karabakh-gotov-na nesti-udar-po-neftyanym-kommunikatsiyam-azerbaydzhana-/).
73 Stanley W. Dziuban, "Implications of Artificial Flooding in Military Operations," *The Military Engineer*, vol. 42, no. 285 (January-February 1950), pages 13–15 (https://www.jstor.org/stable/44561030?seq= 3#metadata_info_tab_contents).

tricity, but also to cause massive flooding. A successful attack on the facility that released high volumes of water would result in significant casualties and ruin large areas of farmland. It would also hinder operation of the east-west energy and transportation corridor that runs close to the Mingachevir region and could disrupt troop movements and supplies to the battle zone with Armenia.

Following clashes between Armenia and Azerbaijan in 2014, Armenian Defense Minister Seyran Oganyan threatened an attack on the Mingachevir Dam. These threats were renewed in July 2020: a representative of Armenia's Ministry of Defense threatened to use SU-30 fighter jets and Iskander ballistic missiles to attack the dam.[74] During the 2020 war, Armenia made good on its threat and fired four "Tochka U" short-range missiles at the Mingachevir Dam.[75] The missiles missed the dam, but the shots made clear that Armenia was willing to attack the dam and potentially cause massive flooding in Azerbaijan. Accordingly, during the war the Azerbaijani government lowered the water level at Mingachevir and several other hydropower plants in Azerbaijan, to reduce flooding should the dam be hit.

3.10.5.2 Azerbaijan's Threat to the Metsamor Nuclear Power Plant

During the July 2020 clashes before the full-scale war, Azerbaijani Deputy Defense Ministry Spokesman Colonel Vagif Dargahli said in response to the Armenian threat to attack the Mingachevir Dam:

> This attack [on the Mingachevir Dam] is impossible due to the relief of the territory where [...] this strategic facility is located, the fortifications, as well as the Azerbaijani Air Forces' modern air defence systems [...] Armenia must not forget that the latest missile systems in the arsenal of the Azerbaijani army can target and launch an attack on its Metsamor nuclear power plant, which may lead to a major disaster for Armenia.[76]

Armenia's nuclear power plant is located only 35 kilometers from Yerevan, and 16 kilometers from the Turkish city Iğdır. An attack on Metsamor would expose not only the people of Armenia to danger, but also the wider region, including Turkey, Georgia, and Azerbaijan itself.[77] Thus, this was not a credible threat. Presidential adviser Hikmet Ha-

---

74 Hikmet Hajiyev, "Attacks by Armenia against Azerbaijani Civilians and Critical Infrastructure Should Not Be Overlooked," *Euractiv*, October 30, 2020 (https://www.euractiv.com/section/azerbaijan/opinion/attacks-by-armenia-against-azerbaijani-civilians-and-critical-infrastructure-should-not-be-overlooked/).
75 Hikmet Hajiyev, "Attacks by Armenia against Azerbaijani Civilians and Critical Infrastructure Should Not Be Overlooked," *Euractiv*, October 30, 2020 (https://www.euractiv.com/section/azerbaijan/opinion/attacks-by-armenia-against-azerbaijani-civilians-and-critical-infrastructure-should-not-be-overlooked/).
76 Trend News Agency, "Azerbaijan Responds to News on Armenia Targeting to Hit Mingachevir Reservoir," Trend.Az, July 16, 2020 (https://en.trend.az/azerbaijan/politics/3270655.html).
77 Brenda Shaffer, "Armenia's Nuclear Power Plant Is Dangerous: Time to Close It," *Bulletin of the Atomic Scientists*, March 5, 2021 (https://thebulletin.org/2021/03/armenias-nuclear-power-plant-is-dangerous-time-to-close-it/).

jiyev later walked back the threat to Metsamor, stating that the defense ministry spokesman had made an unauthorized statement and that Azerbaijan had no intention of attacking the Metsamor Nuclear Power Plant or any other civilian infrastructure in Armenia: "During the latest provocations different misinformation was spread [...] Azerbaijan does not have the policy to target any critical strategical facilities."[78] However, it was clear in the 2020 Armenia-Azerbaijan War that energy infrastructure was viewed not only as a potential target but as potential weapons where threatened attacks could be leveraged to deter the adversary. Azerbaijan drew lessons and Baku has undertaken steps to strengthen the defense of the country's energy infrastructure, including the Mingachevir Dam.

3.10.6 Energy Post-war

The war's outcome has affected energy flows in the wider Caspian region. First, the results of the war strengthened the security of Azerbaijan's energy export pipelines. Armenia's defeat removed Armenia's military threat to Azerbaijan's oil and natural gas pipelines and full operation of the Southern Gas Corridor commenced on schedule in December 2020 following the war. In fact, Azerbaijan's energy exports to Europe are likely to increase: in light of the 2022 energy crisis in Europe, Azerbaijan's President Ilham Aliyev announced Baku's intention to double its natural gas exports to Europe.[79]

3.10.7 Conclusions

Several strategists and military planners have studied the 2020 Armenia-Azerbaijan War, which was an arena for the use of new weapons and new uses of existing weapons such as UAVs. As discussed, some of the energy aspects of the war were also novel and thus generated new understanding of the potential impact of energy in war.

Students of war and war planners have also studied Armenia's tunnels, which were uncovered during the war. These tunnels gave Armenia the ability to conduct the surprise attack on Azerbaijani troops in Azerbaijani territory on July 12, 2020 and retreat safely back into Armenian territory.

---

78 Hikmat Hajiyev, "Armenia Has Deliberately Turned Metsamor Issue Which Poses Serious Threat for Region, into Show," *APA*, July 21, 2020 (https://apa.az/en/nagorno_garabagh/Hikmat-Hajiyev:-%22Armenia-has-deliberately-turned-Metsamor-issue-which-poses-serious-threat-for-region-into-show%22-326277).
79 Marine Straus and Jan Strupczewski, "EU Signs Deal with Azerbaijan to Double Gas Imports by 2027," Reuters, July 18, 2022 (https://www.reuters.com/business/energy/eu-signs-deal-with-azerbaijan-double-gas-imports-by-2027-2022-07-18/).

The hybrid aspects of the Second Armenia-Azerbaijan War, and especially the attacks on Azerbaijan's domestic energy infrastructure, are reminders that in conflict the boundaries between non-combatant areas, civilians and domestic energy infrastructure, blur. War planners need to continue to plan for protection of the domestic arena during time of war.

With the rise in frequency of hybrid warfare, combatants in various conflicts are increasingly targeting domestic energy infrastructure and energy supply flows. Both sides also threatened to turn parts of their respective power generation systems against the other. While targeting power generation and intentional flooding are not new to warfare, threats and attacks on major energy infrastructure pieces – such as dams and nuclear power plants (see next case study) – are an indication that weaponization of energy infrastructure is likely to play a major role in contemporary hybrid warfare and should be studied in detail. Moreover, the threats and attacks on the Mingachevir Dam are a reminder to military planners and strategists that intentional flooding is still a threat and that, consequently, they need to continue to devise mechanisms to neutralize these threats.

The threats to Mingachevir Dam are likely to generate interest in development and deployment of air defense systems for dams and other critical energy infrastructure. Military planners will continue to develop doctrine and means to protect major energy infrastructure, which may serve as a target in future wars. Azerbaijan seems likely in the future to acquire Israel's Iron Dome or other air defense system for the protection of its energy infrastructure. Deployment of systems of this type to protect energy infrastructure is likely to become more prevalent in combat zones around the globe. In future warfare, the attacks on domestic energy infrastructure will not be limited to attacks but will likely include cyberattacks, as modern energy infrastructure is all managed by cyber systems.

3.10.8 Questions for Discussion

- Discuss the geopolitical goals that led to the first stage of war between Armenia and Azerbaijan in July 2020. Why did Russia want to disrupt new Azerbaijani gas supplies to Europe? Why did Armenia want to do so? Name other conflicts where disruption or enabling of energy flows contributed to the emergence of war.
- What is the role of attacks on energy infrastructure in hybrid warfare? What are the goals?
- Discuss the need for protection of domestic energy infrastructure during warfare due to hybrid warfare. What are the consequences for OE of attacks on domestic US energy infrastructure?
- How can security of critical energy infrastructure be improved?

- Discuss historic use of weaponization of energy infrastructure during war. Where will belligerents likely weaponize energy infrastructure in the future? What are the threats to the United States and its forces through the weaponization of energy infrastructure?
- Analyze how Armenia's attacks on domestic energy infrastructure during the 2020 war could have affected Azerbaijan's OE supplies.
- Was OE superiority attained by either nation in the 2020 Armenia-Azerbaijan war?

3.11 Case Study: Nuclear Power Plants in War – The Case of Ukraine

Nuclear reactors are located around the world, including in several active war zones. During hostilities, combatants may target reactors or accidentally damage them. Intentional or accidental attacks on nuclear power plants (NPPs) can cause large-scale casualties, long-term disruption of electricity supplies, and radioactive contamination of areas. These electricity supplies may be necessary to meet the OE needs of belligerents and therefore serve as tempting targets for adversaries. However, the unique nature of NPPs, where an attack could lead to the release of radioactivity that could threaten all combatants, means that belligerents may also be inclined to cooperate during war to prevent such a release. In addition, US government agencies, and cooperation with allies and international organizations, such as the International Atomic Energy Agency (IAEA), may be able to play a role in defusing threats in these situations. Moreover, US DOD and NATO guidelines should offer guidance for operations related to NPPs located in combat theaters. This case study will examine the threats from nuclear reactors in war zones. It will discuss the ZNPP case during the Russia-Ukraine War and the role of the IAEA in potentially lowering risks from NPPs during warfare.

In the past, concerns have been raised regarding the safety of NPPs during wartime in several locations, including India/Pakistan and Armenia.[80] However, the Russia-Ukraine War that began in 2022 marked the first time that NPPs were concretely part of a battle: Russia purposely captured the Zaporizhzhya Nuclear Power Plant early in the war.

In the 2020s, concern over climate change and security of supply of energy has renewed interest in nuclear power potentially leading to the spread of nuclear power to additional volatile regions and war zones. However, little concrete guidance and policies are in place to reduce the dangers from nuclear power plants during war.

---

80 Brenda Shaffer, "Energy in Conflict: The Case of the 2020 Armenia-Azerbaijan War," *CTX Journal* (special issue hybrid threats and energy security), April 2022; Brenda Shaffer, "Armenia's Nuclear Power Plant Is Dangerous: Time to Close It," *Bulletin of the Atomic Scientists*, March 5, 2021 (https://thebulletin.org/2021/03/armenias-nuclear-power-plant-is-dangerous-time-to-close-it/).

3.11.1 The Russia-Ukraine War and the Zaporizhzhya Nuclear Power Plant

On the eve of the Russian 2022 invasion, Ukraine operated fifteen NPPs, which normally provided over half of the country's electricity. Throughout the first year of the conflict, Ukraine supplied data transmissions to the IAEA from all the monitoring systems of NPPs under its control,[81] reported on rotations of Chernobyl NPP workers even while the facility was under Russian control,[82] and proceeded with scheduled maintenance of NPPs when possible.[83] During the 2022 invasion of Ukraine, Russian forces captured the Zaporizhzhya Nuclear Power Plant (ZNPP), the largest nuclear power plant in Ukraine and in all of Europe.

On March 1, 2022, as Russian tanks moved in on ZNPP, Russia's delegation to the IAEA provided official notification that Russian military forces had taken control of the territory, and that the personnel at the plant continued their "work on providing nuclear safety and monitoring radiation in normal modes of operation."[84] It should be noted that Russia is one of the more influential powers at the IAEA, given the prominent role of nuclear energy in Russia's fuel mix, the role of Russia's Rosatom state-owned nuclear company in building new NPPs globally, and Russia's status as a nuclear-weapon superpower, a permanent member of the UN Security Council, and a leading supplier of enriched uranium and nuclear fuel. Because of its large nuclear energy sector, Russia has always ranked among the ten countries with the most advanced nuclear energy sectors that automatically qualify for seats on the IAEA's thirty-five-member Board of Governors, the body which provides regular policy direction to the IAEA Secretariat and chooses the director-general.

Despite Russia's assertions to the IAEA, it failed to take full control of the plant until several days later – as late as March 4, Russian forces were reported to be shelling

---

81 International Atomic Energy Agency (IAEA), "Update 23 – IAEA Director General Statement on Situation in Ukraine," March 16, 2022 (https://www.iaea.org/newscenter/pressreleases/update-23-iaea-director-general-statement-on-situation-in-ukraine).
82 International Atomic Energy Agency (IAEA), "Update 27 – IAEA Director General Statement on Situation in Ukraine," March 27, 2022 (https://www.iaea.org/newscenter/pressreleases/update-27-iaea-director-general-statement-on-situation-in-ukraine).
83 International Atomic Energy Agency (IAEA), "Update 48 – IAEA Director General Statement on Situation in Ukraine," April 10, 2022 (https://www.iaea.org/newscenter/pressreleases/update-48-iaea-director-general-statement-on-situation-in-ukraine); International Atomic Energy Agency (IAEA), "Update 57 – IAEA Director General Statement on Situation in Ukraine," April 19, 2022 (https://www.iaea.org/newscenter/pressreleases/update-57-iaea-director-general-statement-on-situation-in-ukraine).
84 International Atomic Energy Agency (IAEA), "Update 6 – IAEA Director General Statement on Situation in Ukraine," March 2, 2022 (https://www.iaea.org/newscenter/pressreleases/update-6-iaea-director-general-statement-on-situation-in-ukraine).

the perimeter around the facility.[85] Indeed, ZNPP lay close to the fighting throughout the first part of the war between Russia and Ukraine (between March and May 2022) with Russia's troops ultimately establishing control of much of the surrounding region.[86] When fighting in the region escalated again in late summer 2022, Russian troops fired on the front from their location inside the nuclear facility's perimeter, reportedly confident that Ukraine would be hesitant to return fire.[87]

However, growing fighting in nearby towns eventually extended to the nuclear power plant. On July 22, Ukrainian forces reportedly launched a drone attack on Russian forces deployed at ZNPP.[88] Ukraine informed the IAEA of shelling-related damage to the exterior power supply system of ZNPP on August 6, 2022.[89] Shelling continued intermittently in August and through September. Attacks damaged high-voltage power lines connecting ZNPP to the grid, contributing to regular crises at the facility and power disruptions in Ukraine.

By early September, the facility was no longer producing electricity for the grid, but attacks on power lines continued. In addition to air attacks, mines, which had been laid near a water channel that supplied the NPP cooling system, were detonated, likely by animals. At least eight explosions were reported outside the ZNPP perimeter fence between September 21 and October 1, 2022.[90]

During this period of intense attacks, Russia consolidated its control of ZNPP operations, reporting on October 18 that it was fully in control of ZNPP and its operational decisions.[91] Attacks on the facility ceased, and for several weeks there were no attacks on the related power lines.

---

85 International Atomic Energy Agency (IAEA), "Update 12 – IAEA Director General Statement on Situation in Ukraine," March 5, 2022 (https://www.iaea.org/newscenter/pressreleases/update-12-iaea-director-general-statement-on-situation-in-ukraine).
86 For details of fighting and civilian casualties in the region, see ACLED, "War in Ukraine One Year On, Nowhere Safe," March 1, 2023 (https://acleddata.com/2023/03/01/war-in-ukraine-one-year-on-nowhere-safe/).
87 Andrew E. Kramer, "Nuclear Inspectors Are in Ukraine for a High Stakes Visit to the Zaporizhzhia Plant," *New York Times*, August 30, 2022.
88 "Ukraine: Russia-Ukraine War and Nuclear Energy," World Nuclear Association (https://www.world-nuclear.org/ukraine-information/ukraine-russia-war-and-nuclear-energy.aspx).
89 International Atomic Energy Agency (IAEA), "Update 88 – IAEA Director General Statement on Situation in Ukraine," August 6, 2022 (https://www.iaea.org/newscenter/pressreleases/update-88-iaea-director-general-statement-on-situation-in-ukraine).
90 International Atomic Energy Agency (IAEA), "Update 108 – IAEA Director General Statement on Situation in Ukraine," September 29, 2022 (https://www.iaea.org/newscenter/pressreleases/update-108-iaea-director-general-statement-on-situation-in-ukraine).
91 International Atomic Energy Agency (IAEA), "Update 120 – IAEA Director General Statement on Situation in Ukraine," October 18, 2022 (https://www.iaea.org/newscenter/pressreleases/update-120-iaea-director-general-statement-on-situation-in-ukraine).

3.11.2 IAEA Plays a Role

A 2009 IAEA General Conference resolution prohibits armed attacks or threats to NPPs. However, the resolution does not provide detailed guidance. On March 2, as Russian forces were consolidating control of the territory around ZNPP, IAEA Director-General Rafael Grossi convened the IAEA Board of Governors, and provided a statement to them regarding the situation in Ukraine. In this statement, he noted the unprecedented situation of military activity against nuclear facilities and sought to establish clear parameters for nuclear safety in a situation of war. He asserted that nuclear safety systems have three functions: containment, control, and cooling. He also identified seven "indispensable pillars" of nuclear safety:[92]

- Physical integrity of the facilities (including reactors, fuel ponds, and waste storage) must be maintained.
- All safety and security systems and the equipment that supports them must remain fully functional.
- Operating staff must be able to fulfill safety and security duties and must be allowed to make decisions free of undue pressure.
- There must be secure off-site power supply from the grid for all nuclear sites.
- There must be uninterrupted logistical supply chains and transportation to and from nuclear sites.
- There must be effective on and off-site radiation monitoring systems as well as emergency preparedness and response measures.
- There must be reliable communication between the facilities and the regulator.

These criteria had a clear basis in IAEA practice but had not previously been articulated as a coherent policy. The seven "indispensable pillars" emerged to serve as the framework for reporting of concerns and violations.

From early March 2022 forward, the IAEA remained a highly visible player in reporting on all aspects of the safety and security of nuclear material and facilities in Ukraine, with Grossi personally traveling several times to the plant and to meet with Ukrainian and Russian officials. Grossi visited the South Ukraine NPP in March,[93] and the closed Chernobyl facility for the first time in April 2022.[94] His April visit was combined with a

---

[92] International Atomic Energy Agency (IAEA), "Update 6 – IAEA Director General Statement on Situation in Ukraine," March 2, 2022 (https://www.iaea.org/newscenter/pressreleases/update-6-iaea-director-general-statement-on-situation-in-ukraine).

[93] Grossi was in Ukraine March 29–30, and then met with Russian officials in Kaliningrad. See International Atomic Energy Agency (IAEA), "Update 37 – IAEA Director General Statement on Situation in Ukraine," March 30, 2022 (https://www.iaea.org/newscenter/pressreleases/update-37-iaea-director-general-statement-on-situation-in-ukraine).

[94] Grossi was at the facility on April 26, returning to IAEA headquarters on April 28. See International Atomic Energy Agency (IAEA), "Update 64 – IAEA Director General Statement on Situation in Ukraine,"

meeting with Russian officials in Kaliningrad to discuss the situation, culminating in a Russian announcement that it had returned to Ukraine control of both the closed Chernobyl NPP, occupied early in the war, and the nearby town of Slavutych, where most Chernobyl operators lived.

After months of negotiations, on September 1, 2022, Grossi visited the ZNPP with a team from the IAEA, amid a ceasefire. Grossi recommended closure of the facility. At the time of his departure, only one of the reactors remained in operation, functioning at a low level, supplying power only to the plant itself.[95] Two IAEA experts remained behind. IAEA designated them as the core of the IAEA Support and Assistance Mission to Zaporizhzhya (ISAMZ). Their role was to provide neutral observers to monitor the plant's safe operation.[96]

In mid-September, Russian forces launched attacks on the perimeter outside the facility even as it used its control inside the perimeter to change the management of the plant. The ZNPP Plant Director and subsequently the Deputy Plant Director were reportedly abducted and detained.[97] Both were released after resigning their positions. Meanwhile, Russian nuclear state company Rosatom, which then took charge of the facility, forced the Ukrainian operators to sign contracts with the company. Russia informed the IAEA on October 27 that it had assumed control of ZNPP.

The international community continues to recognize Ukraine as the legal owner of the facility, in compliance with the UN General Assembly's October 12, 2022, resolution declaring Russia's annexation of four regions as illegal under international law.[98] Some

---

April 26, 2022 (https://www.iaea.org/newscenter/pressreleases/update-64-iaea-director-general-statement-on-situation-in-ukraine-0). Russia seized the shuttered power plant and the surrounding Exclusion Zone on February 24, 2022, the first day of the invasion. It withdrew from the plant in late March, and early April 2022, after Ukrainian forces launched a successful counteroffensive to recapture occupied territory between Kyiv and the Belarus border.

95 International Atomic Energy Agency (IAEA), "Update 97 – IAEA Director General Statement on Situation in Ukraine," September 3, 2022 (https://www.iaea.org/newscenter/pressreleases/update-97-iaea-director-general-statement-on-situation-in-ukraine).

96 International Atomic Energy Agency (IAEA), "Update 98 – IAEA Director General Statement on Situation in Ukraine," September 5, 2022 (https://www.iaea.org/newscenter/pressreleases/update-98-iaea-director-general-statement-on-situation-in-ukraine).

97 Director of the facility, Ihor Musharov, was abducted on October 1 and released on October 4. Deputy Director Valeriy Martynuyk was subsequently detained for over five days and released on October 19. See International Atomic Energy Agency (IAEA), "Update 120 – IAEA Director General Statement on Situation in Ukraine," October 18, 2022 (https://www.iaea.org/newscenter/pressreleases/update-120-iaea-director-general-statement-on-situation-in-ukraine).

98 See UN General Assembly Resolution A/RES/ES-11/47. Reference: International Atomic Energy Agency (IAEA), "Nuclear Safety, Security and Safeguards in Ukraine," February 2022-February 2023, page 3 (https://www.iaea.org/sites/default/files/23/02/nuclear-safety-security-and-safeguards-in-ukraine-feb-2023.pdf).

level of cooperation with Russia regarding ZNPP had been essential, however. In late 2022 and early 2023 Grossi began to engage in shuttle diplomacy regarding the safety and security of ZNPP, and Russia has allowed the continued presence and rotation of the IAEA Support and Assistance Mission (ISAMZ) team. By the end of the first year of the conflict, the seventh ISAMZ team was in place. Russia allowed the team to continue to observe operations and provided the IAEA regular technical details of the plant operation, including the details of plans for improvements.[99]

As of mid-2023, the plant remained essentially shut down. A particularly persistent problem at ZNPP has been the inability to maintain reliable off-site power. The need for power to ensure cooling and monitoring of fuel at the plant necessitates connection to a grid. Russian fire has, however, frequently interrupted grid connections, even while Russia runs the plant. Emergency diesel generators were needed six times to power the plant during the first year of the war.[100]

New concerns arose in June 2023 with the destruction of the Kahkovka Dam. The dam had held back a reservoir with cooling water for the plant and spent nuclear fuel. While the IAEA stressed there was no "immediate danger", experts have raised concerns about the safety of the facility in the medium to long term.[101]

Other states, including the US, have supported the role of IAEA as a lead actor in ensuring the safety of ZNPP. The IAEA's aim in the conflict has been to reduce the likelihood of accident and ensure containment, control, and cooling of nuclear material as well as safeguarding the nuclear material. The IAEA also sought to assert its right to constant external monitoring of safety and security, even during war.

Grossi also continually raised the issue of the health and safety of power plant operators – including the need to rotate them regularly. Although this was only one of the seven pillars he established early in the war, it was the pillar to which he returned continuously.[102]

---

[99] International Atomic Energy Agency (IAEA), "Update 121 – IAEA Director General Statement on Situation in Ukraine," October 27, 2022 (https://www.iaea.org/newscenter/pressreleases/update-121-iaea-director-general-statement-on-situation-in-ukraine).
[100] International Atomic Energy Agency (IAEA), "Director General Statement to the Board of Governors 9 March 2023" (https://www.iaea.org/newscenter/pressreleases/director-general-statement-to-the-board-of-governors-9-march-2023).
[101] Matthew Mpoke Bigg and Andrew E. Kramer, "The Dam's Breach Does Not Pose an Immediate Risk to the Zaporizhzhia Nuclear Power Plant, Experts Say," *New York Times*, June 6, 2023 (https://www.nytimes.com/live/2023/06/06/world/russia-ukraine-news#the-dams-breach-does-not-pose-an-immediate-risk-to-the-zaporizhzhia-nuclear-power-plant-experts-say).
[102] International Atomic Energy Agency (IAEA), "Update 15 – IAEA Director General Statement on Situation in Ukraine," March 8, 2022 (https://www.iaea.org/newscenter/pressreleases/update-15-iaea-director-general-statement-on-situation-in-ukraine).

Grossi's original goal had been to establish a protection zone around the plant, but he did not succeed in attaining this, as both Ukraine and Russia opposed it: Ukraine demanded that the facility and surrounding territory be returned; Russia claimed its forces served to prevent a nuclear disaster.[103]

After several months of the conflict, Russia, Ukraine, and the IAEA appeared to have reached a *modus vivendi* regarding the operation of the ZNPP. This unofficial agreement assumed Russian control of the territory surrounding the plant. As of early 2024, it was not clear how Russia would react if Ukraine recaptured or came close to recapturing the plant.

3.11.3 Russian and Ukrainian Aims

Russia's top goal regarding ZNPP was to ensure electricity supply to Russian-controlled territories in Ukraine, including providing electricity to its troops. Given the proximity of ZNPP to Russian-controlled territory, Moscow did not want to relinquish control of a facility capable of producing significant amounts of electricity during and after the war. Hence, surrounding the facility but allowing it to remain in operation was a logical choice for Russia.

Preventing a radioactive incident was Ukraine's highest priority both at ZNPP (and the closed Chernobyl site). Constant engagement with the IAEA was a key element in this effort. Restoring Ukraine's prewar electricity supply was also a vital interest.

3.11.4 Case Conclusions

The standoff over ZNPP was a global wake-up call about the dangers surrounding NPPs in current or potential war zones. Even the threat of widespread contamination will not necessarily stop determined combatants from taking actions that might cause it.

The US military may find itself battling on territory that encompasses NPPs. It is incumbent on military planners and commanders to take this risk into account both in their general war planning and in planning focused on OE. Moreover, the US military will likely need electricity output during operations and may choose to continue operation of NPPs in occupied territories, or need to have contingency plans for alternative electricity supplies. Deployment of properly trained and skilled officers and professionals will be necessary in war zones where there are NPPs. DOD needs to consider training

---

103 United Nations, "IAEA Chief Outlines Five Principles to Avert Nuclear 'Catastrophe' in Ukraine," May 30, 2023 (https://news.un.org/en/story/2023/05/1137172).

those charged with this responsibility. This includes understanding possible contamination patterns, preventive measures, and post-contamination reactions.

Military officers likely will also need to liaise with relevant international agencies such as the IAEA in such a crisis. Training and designation of proper liaisons is necessary in preparation.

3.11.5 Topics for Discussion and Research

- Identify NPPs and reactors located in actual or likely zones of hostilities.
- Identify zones of hostilities where the US is likely to engage adversaries, where NPPs are located.
- Discuss how to replace nuclear power-produced electricity supplies that are likely to be taken offline during hostilities.
- In the case of the ZNPP, Russia wanted to maintain electricity output in the NPPs in areas of Ukraine that it occupied. What is the US DOD protocol toward operation of NPPs in zones of conflict? Will US forces want to maintain electricity output or safely shutdown nuclear power plant operations?
- Do DOD and NATO guidelines and regulations provide guidance for operations in combat theaters where NPPs are located?
- What should be added to DOD and NATO guidelines and regulations to provide guidance for operations in combat theaters where NPPs are located?
- Examine the topic of the status of nuclear power plants under occupation during military conflicts.
- Which military units are charged with dealing with nuclear threats in combat theaters?
- Discuss the training and appointments necessary to deal with NPPs in zones of conflict where the US may engage.

4 Military Threats to Operational Energy

Lawrence M. Waltzer

This chapter focuses on threats to OE, as adversaries will likely seek to disrupt energy supplies and potentially destroy critical energy infrastructure. First, it will begin with a look at the term "threat" followed by a discussion on the role of threats to energy in military planning. Next, the chapter will present the two overarching categories of threats: deliberate threats and non-deliberate threats. Finally, the chapter will examine the specific threats to OE from within each category and from key US adversaries. It is important to note that threats are posed to both friendly and enemy OE systems. Indeed, "OE superiority is the ability to fully exploit one's own energy capabilities while preventing the adversary from doing the same." Examples that highlight threats to OE are addressed in the chapter.

4.1 What Is a Threat?

As the US DOD does not explicitly define threat in its *Dictionary of Military and Associated Terms*, several other sources set the definition. The Department of Homeland Security (DHS) provides a useful starting point for the term: "A natural or manmade occurrence, an individual, an entity, or an action having or indicating the potential to harm life, information, operations, the environment and/or property."[104]

For the military, each command faces different threats based on its geographic location and current operations, whether those involve training in a peacetime environment or conducting military operations anywhere across the spectrum of conflict. Clearly, the threats to OE are different when conducting training operations on the East Coast during hurricane season versus conducting maritime security operations in the Arab Gulf. Planners also must conduct a fresh analysis of threats each time conditions change, and operators should continuously monitor threats even when operating for prolonged periods against the same adversary – planners and operators must assume a dynamic operational environment.

The following chapter discusses the threats that are most relevant to military planners and operators.

---

[104] US Department of Homeland Security (FEMA), *National Incident Management System*, October 2017, page 71 (https://www.fema.gov/sites/default/files/2020-07/fema_nims_doctrine-2017.pdf).

> "The focus of national strategy has transitioned from one on counter-insurgency operations to global deterrence and competition with peer and near-peer competitors. In order to be successful, the Chief of Naval Operations and the Commandant of the Marine Corps have asked the Services to focus on concepts like Distributed Maritime Operations and Littoral Operations in Contested Environments. The impact on the Naval Operational Energy challenges has been significant. Meeting those challenges requires the Department of the Navy (DoN) to enhance the lethality and effectiveness of forces through energy resilience, operational reach, and time on station of forward presence naval forces."
>
> – James C. Caley Director of Operational Energy, US Navy.

4.2 Thinking About Threats

Before examining the details of some specific threats to OE, it is worth reviewing a few approaches to identifying and understanding general military threats.

Writing about intelligence preparation for the battlefield, the military decision-making process, targeting, and combat assessments, former chief warrant officer and artilleryman Jimmy Gomez noted, "All must be focused on the environment, not the enemy. Focusing on the enemy networks limits your thinking and often ignores the real problem: the threat."[105] Further, it is important to note that our enemies and adversaries will go through similar processes. So, when thinking about threats to military OE, it is important to keep in mind both threats to American OE, as well as threats to the enemy's OE in various operating environments.

While not often explicitly stated in many documents, energy is a topic in the early intelligence process or Joint Intelligence Preparation of the Operational Environment (JIPOE). Planners uses this process to "analyze all relevant aspects of this environment, including the adversary and other actors; the physical domains (air, land, maritime, and space); the information environment (which includes cyberspace); and political, military, economic, social, information, and infrastructure (PMESII) systems and subsystems."[106]

---

[105] Jimmy A. Gomes, "The Targeting Process: D3 A and F3EAD," *Small Wars Journal*, July 16, 2011, page 7 (https://smallwarsjournal.com/jrnl/art/the-targeting-process-d3a-and-f3ead).
[106] Joint Chiefs of Staff, *Joint Intelligence Preparation of the Operational Environment (JP2 – 01.3)*, page I-1 (https://irp.fas.org/doddir/dod/jp2-01-3.pdf).

4.3 Center of Gravity Analysis

JIPOE assesses the operational environment[107] to gain a better understanding of threats and vulnerabilities, which can both include OE. Specifically, "The primary purpose of JIPOE is to support joint operation planning, execution, and assessment by identifying, analyzing, and assessing the adversary's COGs [Centers of Gravity], critical vulnerabilities, capabilities, decisive points, limitations, intentions, COAs [Courses of Action], and reactions to friendly operations based on a holistic view of the operational environment."[108]

Center of Gravity (COG) analysis can be particularly important in such analysis. The strategist Carl von Clausewitz introduced this term in his book *On War:* "the hub of all power and movement, on which everything depends […] the point against which all our energies should be directed."[109] The DOD builds upon this definition and defines COG as "the source of power that provides moral or physical strength, freedom of action, or will to act."[110]

According to the Joint Publication on Planning, COG analysis "supports achieving objective(s) and attaining end state(s) and helps determine the missions and tasks required to generate the desired effects."[111] With this type of analysis, it is valuable to look at the adversary through this model and to use the model to examine one's own nation and/or command at all levels of war planning.

When thinking about the United States, it is often noted that the US COG is the will of its people. According to the COG analysis model then, should an adversary carry out a campaign that significantly degrades the will of the American people to fight, its politicians may move to conclude a military operation before achieving its objectives – take a loss. Clear examples of this point are the US withdrawal from Vietnam in 1973, as well as when the US withdrew military forces from Lebanon in the aftermath of the Beirut Barracks bombing in October 1983.

---

107 The DOD *Dictionary of Military and Associated Terms* defines operational environment as, "a composite of the conditions, circumstances, and influences that affect the employment of capabilities and bear on the decisions of the commander. Also called OE." Joint Chiefs of Staff, *DOD Dictionary of Military and Associated Terms*, March 2017, page 175 (https://apps.dtic.mil/sti/pdfs/AD1029823.pdf).
108 Joint Chiefs of Staff, *Joint Intelligence Preparation of the Operational Environment (JP2 – 01.3)*, page I-1 (https://irp.fas.org/doddir/dod/jp2-01-3.pdf).
109 Carl von Clausewitz, *On War*, translated by Michael Howard and Peter Paret, Princeton, NJ: Princeton University Press, 1983.
110 Joint Chiefs of Staff, *DOD Dictionary of Military and Associated Terms*, March 2017, page 33 (https://apps.dtic.mil/sti/pdfs/AD1029823.pdf).
111 Joint Chiefs of Staff, *Joint Planning (JP 5 – 0)*, December 1, 2020, page IV-25 (https://irp.fas.org/doddir/dod/jp5_0.pdf).

After thinking through what the COG is, or even COGs are, it is necessary as part of the COG analysis in the JIPOE to identify critical capabilities, critical requirements, and critical vulnerabilities.

The DOD dictionary defines these terms:
- **Critical capability** – A means that is considered a crucial enabler for a COG to function as such and is essential to the accomplishment of the specified or assumed objectives(s).
- **Critical requirement** – An essential condition, resource, and means for a critical capability to be fully operational.
- **Critical vulnerability** – An aspect of a critical requirement which is deficient or vulnerable to direct or indirect attack that will create decisive or significant effects.[112]

During operational design, planners conduct COG analysis to design a campaign that will attack an adversary's critical vulnerabilities to achieve conflict objectives.

It is important to consider the US COG at the strategic level and understand the relevance of energy. If the US COG is indeed the will of the people, a critical capability is the strength of the US economy. The critical requirements for a strong economy include a steady supply of electricity – i.e., a well-functioning electrical grid. Threats to the US grid highlight a critical vulnerability. One such vulnerability lies in the grid's high-voltage transformers. These transformers are very large, very expensive, built to tight specifications (not interchangeable parts), and take six months to a year and a half to replace. Their vulnerability is illustrated by a 2013 attack on the Metcalf Transmission site in Silicon Valley – the largest in the region, providing a third of the area's electricity (see the case study in this chapter). This critical infrastructure site was completely shut down after a rifle attack led to $15 million in damage.[113] The destruction of several similar facilities throughout the US could severely damage the nation's electrical grids and potentially affect the economy and the national will. As pointed out, the US military relies primarily on civilian energy supply lines to meet its energy needs. Thus, disruption of civilian energy infrastructure in the US and abroad can affect American OE success.

---

[112] Joint Chiefs of Staff, *DOD Dictionary of Military and Associated Terms*, June 16, 2017, pages 58–59 (https://apps.dtic.mil/sti/pdfs/AD1029823.pdf).
[113] Peter Skurkiss, "The Metcalf Incident," American Thinker (blog), February 10, 2014 (https://www.americanthinker.com/articles/2014/02/the_metcalf_incident.html).

Warfighter's Look

Primary sources of moral or physical; strength, power and resistance.

Primary abilities which merits a CoG to be identified as such in the context of a given situation or mission.

Essential conditions, resources and means for a critical capability to be fully operative.

Critical requirements or components thereof which are deficient, or vulnerable to neutralization, interdiction or attack in a manner achieving decisive results.

Figure 4.1: Warfighter's Look.

4.4 Connecting the JIPOE with Planning and Targeting

The JIPOE applies a systems approach regarding the operating environment that requires cross-functional headquarters staff elements to collaborate with organizations and other relevant government departments – such as the Department of Energy – as well as nongovernmental entities in order to ensure leverage of a wide range of expertise to guarantee a proper level of understanding.[114] Each PMESII system and subsystems (such as critical energy infrastructure) should be diagrammed to highlight its nodes and links in such a manner that "the capabilities of US instruments of national power (diplomatic, informational, military, and economic) can be employed against selected key nodes to create operational and strategic effects."[115]

The US military combines all the aspects of the operating environment developed from the systems perspective into a single integrated assessment to focus how the operating environment affects friendly and adversary courses of action.[116] Importantly, "Once a

---

[114] Joint Chiefs of Staff, *Joint Intelligence Preparation of the Operational Environment (JP2 – 01.3)*, page xiv (https://irp.fas.org/doddir/dod/jp2-01-3.pdf).

[115] Joint Chiefs of Staff, *Joint Targeting (JP 3 – 60)*, January 2013, page III-46 (https://jfsc.ndu.edu/Portals/72/Documents/JC2IOS/Additional_Reading/1F4_jp3-60.pdf).

[116] Joint Chiefs of Staff, *Joint Intelligence Preparation of the Operational Environment (JP2 – 01.3)*, page xiv (https://irp.fas.org/doddir/dod/jp2-01-3.pdf).

systems perspective of the operating environment has been developed (and appropriate links and nodes have been identified), the linkage and relationship between COGs, LOOs [lines of operation], and decisive points can become more obvious."[117]

The US military then targets these decisive points and – by their nature – targets related to OE regularly make the list. The staff can then provide an analysis of the enemy and any adversary capabilities and intentions to determine the potential effects to friendly forces.[118]

4.5 Control and Weaponization of Energy

Throughout history, militaries have sought to gain energy supplies and deny them to their adversaries. During war and other active conflicts, control of energy (oil, gas grids, power plants, coal supplies, oil and coal ports, LNG facilities, and coal mines) becomes a goal. Governments and militaries aim to retain control over energy sources and infrastructure to supply energy to their own forces, while denying their adversaries access to energy supplies.

> Governments and militaries aim to retain control over energy sources and infrastructure to supply energy to their own forces, while denying their adversaries access to energy.

In addition, the US military plans for potential "weaponization of energy infrastructure" during a military engagement. Many military strategists have also "weaponized" energy infrastructure – not just attempting to disrupt energy supplies, but to create significant damage and potentially loss of life through attacks on pipelines, power plants, grids, and other energy infrastructure elements. Historically, several militaries have used intentional flooding as a military tactic, including both Allied and Axis powers in World War II.[119] During the Russia-Ukraine War, in June 2023 Moscow broke the massive Kakhovka Dam to cause significant flooding in Ukraine and undermine Kyiv's anticipated counteroffensive.

---

117 Joint Chiefs of Staff, *Joint Planning (JP 5–0)*, December 1, 2020, page IV-28 (https://irp.fas.org/doddir/dod/jp5_0.pdf).
118 Joint Chiefs of Staff, *Joint Planning (JP 5–0)*, December 1, 2020, page C-6 (https://irp.fas.org/doddir/dod/jp5_0.pdf).
119 Stanley W. Dziuban, "Implications of Artificial Flooding in Military Operations," *The Military Engineer*, vol. 42, no. 285, January-February 1950, pages 13–15 (https://www.jstor.org/stable/44561030?seq=3#metadata_info_tab_contents).

4.6 Deliberate versus Non-deliberate Threats to OE

There are two main categories of threats in the operating environment: deliberate and non-deliberate threats, each of which can be catastrophic to OE.

Non-deliberate threats to OE are those threats that are not planned or intended. They can include geography, weather, accidents, unintended consequences, and even wildlife. Unintended consequences may also stem from cascading effects resulting from deliberate actions or poor policy/decision making.

Deliberate threats are manmade, with planning and intent.

Given the challenges posed by today's adversaries, "the (Defense) Department needs to assess risks to energy in resource and planning processes; prepare and develop mitigations for energy disruptions across the battlespace; and foster the ability of installations and the Joint Force to sustain critical missions in energy-constrained environments."[120] To assess the risk to OE, it is imperative to understand the threats – non-deliberate and deliberate – outlined below.

4.7 Non-deliberate Threats to OE

While deliberate threats to OE rightfully get more attention during combat operations, the potential for non-deliberate threats to affect military operations can be significant.

4.7.1 Geography

Geography can be a hazard to OE (and of course to other aspects of military operations from communications to maneuvers) and planners must consider it seriously to avoid miscalculation and overcome any potential challenges. With geography being the understanding of physical locations and the relationships between people and their environments,[121] planners can highlight geographic factors that directly impact military operations, including weather, terrain, climate, and even animals.

In recent years, many US missions have occurred in landlocked (Afghanistan) and semi-landlocked countries (such as Iraq, which has a very small coastline). The US military relies heavily on sea-based platforms to move fuels. Thus, missions in landlocked coun-

---

[120] Office of the Law Revision Counsel, "United States Code: 110 USC. § 2911, 2925, and 2926" (https://uscode.house.gov/).
[121] *National Geographic*, "What Is Geography" (https://www.nationalgeographic.org/education/what-is-geography/).

tries pose a particular OE challenge. In strategic logistical planning at the Joint Staff and US Central Command, providing critical fuels to combatants in Afghanistan, a landlocked country with rugged terrain surrounded by adversaries, partners, and unreliable partners, was a constant concern and challenge.

For military planners, terrain is likely the first thing to come to mind when assessing geography and operational planning. Next, weather is one of the first considerations when assessing geography and OE. In the United States, military commands located on the East Coast contend with hurricanes, while those on the plains are well acquainted with tornadoes, and those on the West Coast have encountered earthquakes. The potential degradation of energy infrastructure after such destructive events may have a significant impact on the availability of OE in a given theater.

Multiple threats or hazards may combine to degrade or negatively affect OE and, therefore, military operations as well. This applies to both enemy and friendly forces in a manner that may pose challenges and opportunities.

During a World War II German air-ground offensive in 1941, terrain combined with heavy rains significantly disrupted operations in several ways including OE. German motorized and mechanized vehicles were brought to a standstill on the water saturated sand roads. As Richard Overy stated, "The supply of fuel and lubricants for the front broke down; tanks that could cruise on a pint of oil for 60 miles on flat summer roads now consumed over 4 gallons to cover the same distance."[122]

This situation compelled the German forces to revert to greater use of an earlier form of energy, horsepower – literally horses. While the necessity for horses stemmed from several factors such as supply chains and industrial capacity, such challenges also physically decimated the horses (more than 250,000 suffered from frostbite and malnutrition in the first months).[123] As noted in Chapter 2, horses, like vehicles, require fuel.

It is important to note that in a resource-constrained environment, it can be difficult to adequately prepare for worst-case scenarios. In such cases, some risk is common and must be accepted.

Another aspect of geography is human interaction with other creatures, which can also affect OE. For example, the number one cause of power outages in the US – beyond destructive weather – is squirrels. Indeed, with squirrels leading the charge in the US, "Wildlife near power equipment is the most common cause of outages at public

---
[122] Richard Overy, *Why the Allies Won*, New York: W. W. Norton & Company, 1997, page 216.
[123] Richard Overy, *Why the Allies Won*, New York: W. W. Norton & Company, 1997, page 216.

power utilities."[124] It is important that those responsible for energy, and other aspects of military operations where animals can wreak havoc, plan for such contingencies.

4.7.2 Accidents/Safety

It is also important to recognize that many elements of energy are inherently dangerous, where accidents and safety incidents can threaten OE. Beyond the potential loss of life, such incidents can also jeopardize the availability of OE. As increasing amounts of electricity are required for the operation of new and emerging military platforms, the risk increases that high-voltage electricity systems will produce deadly accidents. Beyond accidents, there is also the potential for human error or miscalculations that can result from employing ever more complex and energy-hungry systems.

One example of a known safety issue with OE involves Lithium-ion batteries. As one author noted, "Current Lithium-ion (Li-ion) batteries, well known for their widespread use in commercial items such as laptops, are virtually indispensable to the military; they are used for a wide range of combat essential technologies, including computers, night vision, laptops, laser illuminators, radios, gun sights, night versions of gun sights, GPS units and navigation systems. However, despite their utility and crucial role supporting our operating forces, existing Lithium-Ion batteries are extremely heat-sensitive and subject to explosion in certain circumstances."[125]

In September 2022, a large battery storage facility had a battery burn that resulted in the shutdown of California's Highway 1 for more than twelve hours. The battery that ignited was one of the 256 Tesla Megapacks.[126] In addition to the highway closure, businesses closed and officials issued a shelter-in-place order due to the possible release of dangerous toxins into the air.[127] While researchers are investigating ways to safeguard such batteries from this threat, the example highlights that emerging energy technology will likely remain hazardous as it develops. These challenges have also impacted American adversaries. In one example, "Russia says the main cause of the deadly in-

---

[124] Jeannine Anderson, "Squirrels, Other Wildlife Are Most Common Cause of Outages, Survey Finds," American Public Power Association, April 27, 2016 (https://www.publicpower.org/periodical/article/squirrels-other-wildlife-are-most-common-cause-outages-survey-finds).
[125] Warrior Maven, "Why the Army Requires Purpose-Built Battery Packs," *The National Interest*, January 14, 2022 (https://nationalinterest.org/blog/reboot/why-army-requires-purpose-built-battery-packs-199440).
[126] Ariel Cohen, "Tesla Begins Construction of World's Largest Battery Storage Facility," *Forbes*, August 13, 2020 (https://www.forbes.com/sites/arielcohen/2020/08/13/tesla-begins-construction-of-worlds-largest-energy-storage-facility/?sh=2abeb8554fde).
[127] Felix Cortez, "Highway 1 Reopened Near Moss Landing, Shelter-in-Place Lifted," *KSBW*, September 21, 2022 (https://www.ksbw.com/article/highway-1-reopened-near-moss-landing-shelter-in-place-lifted/41302918).

cident on board a submersible which killed 14 [...] was a fire in the battery compartment."[128]

4.7.3 Aging or Poorly Constructed, Maintained, and/or Operated Infrastructure

Aging infrastructure also poses a threat to OE. As one of the first nations to industrialize, much of the US energy infrastructure is now aging and in many cases its capacity is being stretched beyond planned limits. There have been several catastrophes in the United States due to aging and over-stressed energy infrastructure, leading to loss of life and significant costs that could have been avoided with better management and increased resources. Such events often also include a loss of power. When deployed, US forces regularly leverage the power and fuel infrastructure of the local operating area, much of which cannot be assumed to have been developed to adequate standards.

4.7.4 Poor Decision-Making and Policies

Poor decision-making also affects OE. In the years leading up to the Ukraine War, Germany's overreliance on Russian gas may have been, from a geopolitical perspective, short-sighted. To be sure, such interdependent relations are often sustainable[129] right up to the point when they are not. Germany discovered this when Russia invaded Ukraine in early 2022. A second lesson learned at the strategic level was Germany's decision to close its nuclear power plants before an alternative was put in place. Similar poor analysis can take place at the operational and tactical levels of conflict.

4.7.5 Theft

Theft is a major threat to OE. Globally, the United Nations University World Institute for Development Economics Research assessed the annual theft of $133 billion (US) per year (equivalent to 5–7 percent of the global market for crude oil and petroleum fuel).[130] In 2018, during US operations in Afghanistan, the Special Inspector General for Afghanistan reconstruction reported the "disappearance of at least $154.4 million worth of stolen fuel that was meant for coalition and Afghan troops." The sale of

---

128 Steve Rosenberg, "Russia Submersible Fire Was in Battery Compartment," *BBC*, July 4, 2019 (https://www.bbc.com/news/world-europe-48865332).
129 For examples of different natural gas supply relations and impact on national security, see Brenda Shaffer, "Natural Gas Supply Stability and Foreign Policy," *Energy Policy*, vol. 56, May 2013, pages 114–125.
130 Etienne Romsom, *Global Oil Theft: Impact and Policy Responses*, WIDER Working Paper 16/2022, United Nations University, 2022, page 1.

the stolen products likely funded the Taliban and other insurgent forces, according to federal auditors.[131] In 2021, the United States filed a theft complaint with Romanian prosecutors.

US adversaries can also use criminal networks in US partner and other countries to disrupt fuel supplies to American forces.

4.8 Deliberate Threats to OE

There are several types of attacks that threaten OE for the military. The threats listed below begin with asymmetric and unconventional measures and then progress to those present in conventional warfare.

4.8.1 Terrorism

The US DOD definition of terrorism is, "The unlawful use of violence or threat of violence, often motivated by religious, political, or ideological beliefs, to instill fear and coerce governments or societies in pursuit of goals that are usually political."[132] Much of the US's critical infrastructure – and that of many other countries for that matter – was built with safety in mind rather than security against attacks. Following the 9/11 attacks, American officials have recognized the vulnerability of such systems and increased efforts to further the resilience of energy systems against deliberate attacks.

A common terrorist tactic involves planting bombs to disrupt energy systems and OE. While few bomb attacks have occurred on US soil in the first quarter of the twenty-first century, this has not always been the case. Some will recall the alarming period of the early 1970s when American domestic terrorist groups frequently laid pipe bombs. Historian and author Eric Alterman stated, "According to FBI statistics, the United States experienced more than 2,500 domestic bombings in just 18 months in 1971 and 1972, with virtually no solved crimes and barely any significant prosecutions."[133] In the 1970s, several Leftist groups actively engaged in domestic terrorism in the US: "the Black Panthers, the Black Liberation Army, the Symbionese Liberation

---

[131] JP Lawrence, "At Least $154.4 Million in Fuel Stolen in Afghanistan," *Stars and Stripes*, April 16, 2018.
[132] Joint Chiefs of Staff, *DOD Dictionary of Military and Associated Terms*, March 2017, page 234 (https://apps.dtic.mil/sti/pdfs/AD1029823.pdf).
[133] Eric Alterman, "Remembering the Left-Wing Terrorism of the 1970s," *The Nation*, April 14, 2015 (https://www.thenation.com/article/archive/remembering-left-wing-terrorism-1970s/).

Army, the New World Liberation Front, the FALN, the 'family' and the United Freedom Front."[134]

These groups targeted critical infrastructure. Erin Miller highlighted that from 1970 to 2015 the US endured 2723 terror attacks – mostly by left-wing organizations. Approximately 75 percent of the attacks targeted critical infrastructure and 109 of those 2055 attacks involved the energy sector.[135] Such attacks can jeopardize the readiness of military forces and OE.

As mentioned earlier, there was a shooting at the California Metcalf Transmission site in the early hours of April 16, 2013, and to this day, authorities reportedly do not have either leads or suspects. At the time, Jon Wellinghoff, a former Chairman of the Federal Energy Regulatory Commission, toured the site with US Navy Seals and was convinced it was a "professional job" and "the most significant incident of domestic terrorism involving the grid that has ever occurred" in the United States.[136] Such an attack near a major military facility could jeopardize installation power and OE. The infrastructure was not built with such potential attacks in mind.[137]

Environmental extremists have attacked US critical energy infrastructure in the first quarter of the twenty-first century. These groups conducted several attacks on the Dakota Access Pipelines and in October 2016 groups broke into locked enclosures to turn off manual valves to five pipelines operating in four states.[138] In February 2017, law enforcement shot and killed a terrorist after the subject used a rifle to attack the Sabal Train Pipeline, a natural gas pipeline under construction at the time in Florida.[139]

---

134 Eric Alterman, "Remembering the Left-Wing Terrorism of the 1970s," *The Nation*, April 14, 2015 (https://www.thenation.com/article/archive/remembering-left-wing-terrorism-1970s/).
135 Erin Miller, "Terrorist Attacks Targeting Critical Infrastructure in the United States, 1970–2015," College Park, MD: START, 2016 (https://www.start.umd.edu/pubs/START_DHS_GTD_Targeting%20Critical%20Infrastructure%20in%20the%20US_June2016.pdf).
136 Peter Skurkiss, "The Metcalf Incident," American Thinker (blog), February 10, 2014 (https://www.americanthinker.com/articles/2014/02/the_metcalf_incident.html).
137 Altered Dimensions, "PG&E Metcalf Substation Attack" (https://www.youtube.com/watch?v=7N-4tynUMJo).
138 Paul W. Parfomak, "Pipeline Security: Recent Attacks," *Congressional Research Services (CRS) Insight*, March 21, 2017 (https://sgp.fas.org/crs/homesec/IN10603.pdf#:~:text=Recent%20acts%20of%20sabotage%20against%20US%20pipelines%20have,from%20fossil%20fuels%22%20to%20avert%20a%20%22climate%20catastrophe.%22).
139 Paul W. Parfomak, "Pipeline Security: Recent Attacks," *Congressional Research Services (CRS) Insight*, March 21, 2017 (https://sgp.fas.org/crs/homesec/IN10603.pdf#:~:text=Recent%20acts%20of%20sabotage%20against%20US%20pipelines%20have,from%20fossil%20fuels%22%20to%20avert%20a%20%22climate%20catastrophe.%22).

Another attack method that may threaten OE is a small boat attack. The attack on the *USS Cole* in 2000 is a model. For if a warship can be successfully attacked in such a manner, petroleum tankers are even more vulnerable. Like vehicle bombs, small boat attacks can threaten infrastructure too. As Daniel Yergin noted during the early insurgency in Iraq after the US 2003 invasion, "In what could have been a disaster, two suicide bombers in a motorized dinghy came close to blowing up part of the critically important offshore oil export terminal, but the craft exploded short of its target."[140]

Oil tankers have been held for ransom, and one could imagine such a tanker potentially weaponized as an explosive device as well. In one such attack in October 2002, Al Qaeda operatives in the Gulf of Aden off Yemen bombed the French oil tanker *MV Limburg*, which caused oil prices to increase by 1.3 percent within hours.[141] Chia-ya Lee shows that terrorists conducted twenty-three attacks on oil tankers between 1970 and 2018, and that attacks on wider energy facilities and infrastructure were extensive:

Table 4.1: Terrorist Attacks on Energy Facilities, 1970–2018.

Target Type	# of Terrorist Incidents	Average Property Loss (estimated in US dollars)
Electricity facilities	4282	$45,731
Oil facilities	1230	$234,551
Gas/oil/electricity companies	1100	$61,709
Gas facilities	581	$10,976
Oil tankers	23	$1,956,522
All other attacks		$43,653

Sources: Calculated from the Global Terrorism Database; Chia-yi Lee, "Why Do Terrorists Target the Energy Industry? A Review of Kidnapping, Violence and Attacks against Energy Infrastructure," *Energy Research & Social Science*, vol. 87, 2022, page 4 (https://doi.org/10.1016/j.erss.2021.102459).

Lee further surmises that attacks on tankers are less of a threat than hijacking due to the difficulty of detonating or sinking a tanker because of their compartmentalization and double hulls.[142] Hijackings, whether of petroleum tankers or fuel trucks, pose risks

---

140 Daniel Yergin, *The Quest: Energy, Security, and the Remaking of the Modern World*, New York: Penguin Books, 2011, page 158.
141 Chia-yi Lee, "Why Do Terrorists Target the Energy Industry? A Review of Kidnapping, Violence and Attacks against Energy Infrastructure," *Energy Research & Social Science*, vol. 87, 2022, page 5 (https://doi.org/10.1016/j.erss.2021.102459).
142 Chia-yi Lee, "Why Do Terrorists Target the Energy Industry? A Review of Kidnapping, Violence and Attacks against Energy Infrastructure," *Energy Research & Social Science*, vol. 87, 2022, page 6 (https://doi.org/10.1016/j.erss.2021.102459); US Naval War College Professor Kevin Delamer describes compartmentalization in ships as, "a series of compartments that can be completely sealed, rendering them water-tight, [which] allows a ship to survive damage, where in combat or from other causes." Double hulls in tank-

to military operations as well. This tactic can be used to seek ransoms from oil companies, or adversaries may steal fuel trucks for their own operations. This was a problem with logistics routed through Pakistan to support US forces in Afghanistan – fuel and supply trucks would be hijacked or "taxed" regularly.

On January 16, 2013, Islamist militants seized the Amenas Natural Gas Plant in Algeria. Thirty-two terrorists overran the facility's perimeter in minutes leading to the seizure of the entire plant. The terrorists killed forty victims from ten different nations, many of them employees of international oil companies, as the terrorists targeted foreign workers, sparing those from Algeria. Additionally, the attackers sought to damage the infrastructure and after the three-day seizure, it took nearly six months to restart operations, with losses reported at $12 billion dollars. Twenty-nine of the thirty-two terrorists were killed, and the others were captured. These terrorists knew this mission would likely result in their deaths. Such an ideological foe is a danger on the battlefield as suicide missions can be directed at critical OE nodes.

Terrorist groups also use kidnappings as a tactic against energy companies. They target workers or senior company officials to extort ransoms or possibly seek to shut down operations in an effort to weaken the host government of the energy production site. Terrorist groups view kidnapping of energy workers as a lucrative business: they have targeted Western multinational oil companies regularly, and energy companies have increasingly purchased kidnap and ransom insurance for their employees working in risky areas.[143]

Terrorist attacks have increasingly used drone attacks. Perhaps one of the earlier uses of drones by terrorists occurred with, "Hezbollah's first flight of an unmanned aerial vehicle (UAV) or drone, into Israeli airspace for reconnaissance [...] in November 2004, catching Israeli intelligence off guard."[144] Since then, and notably in the summer of 2021, Lebanon's Hezbollah has attempted drone attacks on Israeli offshore energy platforms. The use of drones by militaries around the world has become more and more

---

ers have, "double layers of the watertight surface. The inner and outer layers of the hull are on the bottom as well as the sides of the tanker ships. The double-layer construction helps in reducing the risks of maritime pollution during a collision, grounding, any other form of ship's hull damage." Source: Anish, "*Single Hull vs. Double Hull Tankers,*" January 8, 2021 (https://www.marineinsight.com/naval-architecture/single-hull-vs-double-hull-tankers/).
143 Chia-yi Lee, "Why Do Terrorists Target the Energy Industry? A Review of Kidnapping, Violence and Attacks against Energy Infrastructure," *Energy Research & Social Science*, vol. 87, 2022, page 4 (https://doi.org/10.1016/j.erss.2021.102459).
144 Milton Hoenig, "Hezbollah and the Use of Drones as a Weapon of Terrorism," Federation of American Scientists, June 5, 2014 (https://fas.org/publication/hezbollah-use-drones-weapon-terrorism/).

common with today's drones featuring increasing capabilities as seen in the wars in Ukraine (2022), Azerbaijan (2020),[145] and Israel-Hamas (beginning 2023).

Various actors have targeted energy infrastructure in conflict taking place in the first quarter of the twenty-first century. Via its proxy, the Yemeni Houthis, Iran has attacked energy and other infrastructure in Saudi Arabia, the world's largest exporter of oil, and in the United Arab Emirates (UAE) hundreds of times. As part of these attacks, Saudi Arabia has experienced several hundred drone attacks against its critical energy infrastructure. The most significant took place on September 14, 2019, when "dozens of cruise missiles and over 20 drones attacked the Khurais oil field and the Abqaiq oil processing facility – the world's largest – in what one expert declared was, an attack on '… the heart of the system and they just had a heart attack.'"[146] Despite the successful attack that included a corresponding – but temporary – price spike, the facilities were brought completely back online within weeks. The case of this incident illustrates both the system vulnerabilities and impressive resilience. This attack combined a swarm drone attack with a more conventional means of attack, cruise missiles.

Given the high volatility of global energy prices, this event turned out to be just one of many, many blips in oil prices and was far from consequential, though likely frustrating to the attackers. Iran's former Quds Force Commander, Qassem Soleimani openly praised the attack, which he likely directed. A few months later, the US assassinated Soleimani.

Unmanned Underwater Vehicle (UUV) attacks require attention. They have an advantage over UAVs in lurking undetected. US strategic competitors – Russia and China – possess UUVs. China's reported capability includes the ability to attack submarines autonomously with UUVs that, "have the ability to recognize, follow, and attack enemy submarines without human instruction, and was developed by Harbin Engineering University, Beijing's top submarine research institute."[147] Furthermore, China appears to have developed a large UUV that was first displayed in an October 2019 parade. One assessment judged that its features likely include the capability to mount mines and torpedoes as well as advanced sonar and mast technology to provide intelligence on

---

145 Brenda Shaffer, "Energy in Conflict: The Case of the 2020 Armenia-Azerbaijan War," *CTX Journal* (special issue hybrid threats and energy security), April 2022.
146 Martha Raddatz, "Iran Fired Cruise Missiles in Attack on Saudi Oil Facility: Senior US Official," *ABC News*, September 15, 2019; Gulf News, "Saudi Arabia: Attacks on Aramco, Largest Oil Processing Facility, Explained," *Saudi – Gulf News*, September 15, 2019 (https://gulfnews.com/world/gulf/saudi/saudi-arabia-attacks-on-aramco-largest-oil-processing-facility-explained-1.1568522843716#).
147 Military+Aerospace Electronics, "China Reportedly Developed Unmanned Underwater Vehicle (UUV) Able to Attack Enemy Submarines Autonomously," July 20, 2021 (https://www.militaryaerospace.com/computers/article/14207024/unmanned-underwater-vehicle-uuv-attack-enemy-submarines-autonomously).

surface, shore, and aerial targets; to swarm with like-UUVs; and conduct seabed warfare sitting on the bottom of the ocean for potentially greater than thirty days observing movements and noises. Potentially they can carry up to six maritime special forces personnel.[148] Such capabilities could be positioned to threaten far more than potential OE supply chains.

4.8.2 Looting

Military planners must assess the likelihood of looting and any potential it may have on energy infrastructure. Yergin noted that Iraq has a history of looting during civilian strife and so it was predictable that some would occur after the 2003 US invasion. He notes that critical energy infrastructure was not spared as, "The oil industry was a prime target for [...] stripping [...][as] all the water pumps, critical to its operation, were stolen from the giant Rumalia oil field. Only by mustering his workers with their private arm did the head of the Daura Refinery succeed in standing off an army of looters at the refinery gate."[149]

Yergin further highlighted that Iraqi looters also targeted the electrical grid: "Vandals took down the electric wires and pulled down the transmission towers and carted their booty off to Iran or Kuwait to sell as scrap. Even the computerized control room of the power station that controlled Baghdad's electric grid was looted."[150] Toward the end of the 2020 Armenia-Azerbaijan War, Armenian forces took parts of and destroyed hydroelectric plants and electricity transmission wires as their defeat became imminent.[151] Clearly, the looting threat to critical energy infrastructure must be a planning factor in military operations.

4.8.3 Sabotage

Sabotage is an age-old military tactic. Sabotage is a destructive or obstructive action carried on by a civilian or enemy agent to hinder a nation's war effort. There were sig-

---

[148] Lyle J. Goldstein, "China's Underwater Unmanned Vehicles: How They'll Dominate Undersea Combat," *The National Interest*, January 29, 2022 (https://nationalinterest.org/blog/reboot/chinas-underwater-unmanned-vehicles-how-theyll-dominate-undersea-combat-200098).
[149] Daniel Yergin, *The Quest: Energy, Security, and the Remaking of the Modern World*, New York: Penguin Books, 2011, pages 157–158.
[150] Daniel Yergin, *The Quest: Energy, Security, and the Remaking of the Modern World*, New York: Penguin Books, 2011, pages 157–158.
[151] "Azerbaijan Reclaims Second District Returned by Armenia under Ceasefire Deal," *France24*, November 26, 2021 (https://www.france24.com/en/europe/20201126-azeris-celebrate-as-troops-enter-second-district-returned-by-armenia).

nificant acts of sabotage throughout WWI and WWII – including some on the US homeland – with some 200,000 anti-German partisans in 1942 attacking different types of targets to thwart German operations. These included an advanced team known as Groupe G, "headed by scientists and engineers at the University of Brussels" that attacked critical energy infrastructure to include electricity supply.[152]

While never implemented, the Soviet Union reportedly had many plans during the Cold War to conduct sabotage throughout the US and North America that included targeting specific electrical power grids and pipelines, as highlighted in the so-called "Mitrokhin Archive" – a collection of classified documents provided to MI6 by a defector who had worked in the KGB as a senior archivist.[153] These plans included several named operations (such as Operation Doris, Target Granit, Operation Kedr – "Cedar") where reconnaissance provided intelligence and targeting details on critical energy infrastructure, to include the US Kerr Dam, reportedly the largest power production system in the world at the time.[154]

4.8.4 Cyberattack

While many cyberattacks also fit the description of sabotage, the method of attack deserves a category of its own. Indeed, NATO's Energy Security Centre of Excellence (ENSEC COE) relates to cyberattacks as a modern form of sabotage warfare that takes advantage of: the reliance of critical energy infrastructure on information and communication technologies (ICT); the difficulty of attributing such attacks; and the ever-increasing vulnerability of increasingly interconnected systems.[155] One challenge with the realm of the cyber world and threats is that it "is notoriously secretive, and much is classified."[156]

Russia has been a major player in conducting cyberattacks internationally, including attacks on critical energy infrastructure that provide insights on its likely capabilities to negatively affect OE. Moscow's arsenal, "has deployed sophisticated cyber capabili-

---

[152] Oregon Public Broadcasting (PBS), "Wartime Acts of Sabotage" (https://www.pbs.org/opb/historydetectives/feature/wartime-acts-of-sabotage/).
[153] NATO Energy Security Centre of Excellence (NATO ENSEC COE), *Energy in Irregular Warfare*, 2017, page 24 (https://enseccoe.org/data/public/uploads/2017/05/irregular_warfare_176x250mm_20170526.pdf).
[154] NATO Energy Security Centre of Excellence (NATO ENSEC COE), *Energy in Irregular Warfare*, 2017, pages 24–26 (https://enseccoe.org/data/public/uploads/2017/05/irregular_warfare_176x250mm_20170526.pdf).
[155] NATO Energy Security Centre of Excellence (NATO ENSEC COE), *Energy in Irregular Warfare*, 2017, pages 26–27 (https://enseccoe.org/data/public/uploads/2017/05/irregular_warfare_176x250mm_20170526.pdf).
[156] James Di Pane, "Cyber Warfare and US Cyber Command," The Heritage Foundation, October 18, 2022.

ties to conduct disinformation, propaganda, espionage, and destructive cyberattacks globally," with Russia's military intelligence agency having, "been implicated in some of Russia's most notorious and damaging cyber operations."[157]

Russian cyberattacks have enjoyed significant success in damaging critical energy infrastructure, causing the loss of essential services, and/or disrupting national economies. In August 2008 a section of the Baku-Tbilisi-Ceyhan (BTC) pipeline exploded in Turkey. Russia was a vocal opponent of the pipeline for it enabled oil to flow from Azerbaijan to world markets, circumventing Russia's control. Investigations conducted after the event revealed that , "The cause of the explosion was not a physical attack but a cyberattack: hackers had shut down crude alarms, and cut off communication systems, and super-pressurized the crude oil in the line, provoking an explosion."[158] Several Western intelligence services and international oil companies view Russia as the culprit.[159] Moscow sought to disable the pipeline in the run-up to its 2008 invasion of the Republic of Georgia.

Electrical systems are also vulnerable to cyberattack, with Russia demonstrating sophisticated capabilities in planning and executing attacks against electrical grids. Most notably, Russia cyberattacks against Ukraine's electrical systems led to the first known power outages due to cyberwarfare. In 2015, "As many as 80,000 residents in western Ukraine lost power for six hours [...][and] Cybersecurity firms SANS ICS and iSight Partners have attributed the blackout to Russian hacking group Sandworm and its malicious software, BlackEnergy 3."[160] Sandworm is one of several alleged Russian military intelligence cyber units with others including APT (Advanced Persistent Threat) 28, Voodoo Bear, Fancy Bear, and Tsar Team.[161]

While Russia has been actively conducting cyberattacks since its 2007 attacks on Estonia, most governments and commercial entities have increased cybersecurity defenses as quickly as possible. Since the war in Ukraine began in February 2022, Russian cyber units have conducted constant attacks on Ukraine. However, Ukrainian defenses have had some successes including halting an attack that would have resulted in 2 million

---

157 Andrew S. Bowen, "Russian Cyber Units," Congressional Research Service, February 2, 2022 (https://crsreports.congress.gov/product/pdf/IF/IF11718).
158 NATO Energy Security Centre of Excellence (NATO ENSEC COE), *Energy in Irregular Warfare*, 2017, pages 28–29 (https://enseccoe.org/data/public/uploads/2017/05/irregular_warfare_176x250mm_20170526.pdf).
159 Jordan Robertson and Michael Riley, "Mysterious '08 Turkey Pipeline Blast Opened New Cyberwar," *Bloomberg*, December 10, 2014 (https://www.bloomberg.com/news/articles/2014-12-10/mysterious-08-turkey-pipeline-blast-opened-new-cyberwar?sref=qmS8rGlM); and author's interviews.
160 Riley Walters, "Russian Hackers Shut Down Ukraine's Power Grid," *Newsweek*, January 14, 2016 (https://www.newsweek.com/russian-hackers-shut-ukraine-power-grid-415751).
161 Andrew S. Bowen, "Russian Cyber Units," Congressional Research Service, February 2, 2022, page 1 (https://crsreports.congress.gov/product/pdf/IF/IF11718).

people without power.[162] This attack too is thought to be the work of the Sandworm hacking group that, "attempted to destroy computers at a Ukrainian energy company using a wiper, malware specifically designed to destroy targeted systems by erasing key data and rendering them useless."[163]

Russian cyber units have been heavily engaged in the 2022 war in Ukraine that has at times expanded to hit cyber targets outside of Ukraine that are involved in providing it with energy. Indeed, "The Russians targeted Viasat, an American satellite communications company that provided support to the Ukrainian military, with malware designed to erase its data before disabling it [...] and it ended up affecting other ground satellite components, causing hundreds of thousands of people outside of Ukraine to lose electrical power and their connection to the internet."[164]

China has also conducted cyber attacks on American critical infrastructure. It has also targeted the US DOD and defense industries significantly with one Senate report highlighting, "the Chinese government-linked hackers had breached contractors for US Transportation Command 20 times in one year. The command, which is responsible for the global movement of US troops and military equipment, had been aware of only two of those breaches."[165] The cyber threat is persistent and requires constant vigilance and resources to combat.

For nearly two decades, there has been frustration among security professionals that adversaries were seemingly attacking Western targets on the cyber front uninhibited. In the late 2010s, the US began to go on the offensive with great effectiveness reportedly responding to the Iranian downing of a US drone with a cyber response by the US, "Reaching into the enemy's most secure networks – seemingly at will – to frustrate operational capability [that] carries terrifying implications."[166]

---

[162] Patrick H. O'Neill, "Russian Hackers Tried to Bring Down Ukraine's Power Grid to Help the Invasion," *MIT Technology Review*, April 12, 2022 (https://www.technologyreview.com/2022/04/12/1049586/russian-hackers-tried-to-bring-down-ukraines-power-grid-to-help-the-invasion/).
[163] Patrick H. O'Neill, "Russian Hackers Tried to Bring Down Ukraine's Power Grid to Help the Invasion," *MIT Technology Review*, April 12, 2022 (https://www.technologyreview.com/2022/04/12/1049586/russian-hackers-tried-to-bring-down-ukraines-power-grid-to-help-the-invasion/).
[164] James Di Pane, "Cyber Warfare and US Cyber Command," The Heritage Foundation, October 18, 2022.
[165] Sean Lyngaas, "Suspected Chinese Hackers Breach More US Defense and Tech Firms," *CNN*, December 3, 2021 (https://www.cnn.com/2021/12/02/politics/china-hackers-espionage-defense-contractors/index.html).
[166] Zak Doffman, "Cyber Warfare: US Military Admits Immediate Danger Is 'Keeping Us Up at Night'," *Forbes*, July 21, 2019 (https://www.forbes.com/sites/zakdoffman/2019/07/21/cyber-warfare-u-s-military-admits-immediate-danger-is-keeping-us-up-at-night/?sh=5c8b0f9c1061).

On another front, Israel displayed a game-changing response to Hamas cyberattacks – devastating force. The multi-domain conflict was highlighted in social media as Israel tweeted its response to announce that it targeted a building where Hamas cyber operatives had worked – including an overhead photo with the unit's former building highlighted – stating, "HamasCyberHQ.exe has been removed."[167] Clearly, this is a response that will resonate with some would-be hackers.

The Pentagon is increasing not only its cyber defenses but developing a strong offense. However, as Lt. Gen. Robert Ashley, as the Director of the Defense Intelligence Agency, stated to one cyber group: out of all the threats in the world, it is indeed the cyber threat that keeps him up, for the internet of things leads to a vulnerability for all systems that are connected to it.[168] For the US military, even its most sensitive communications are vulnerable because, "top secret military and diplomatic dispatches are created, transmitted, and received, and read in the '0s' and '1s' of computer code."[169]

While there are many bad actors on the cyber front, as one expert has noted, "There are only four problems in cybersecurity [...] They're called China, Russia, Iran, and North Korea."[170] The threat from cyberattacks is highly likely to remain, indefinitely, with vulnerabilities to both US defense systems and energy systems essential for OE.

US Cyber Command is charged with both offensive and defensive cyber capabilities and will be constantly challenged to monitor DOD networks and support critical infrastructure defense while focusing on its three lines of operation, "Provide mission assurance for the Department of Defense (DOD) by directing the operation and defense of the Department of Defense Information Networks (i.e. the DODIN) and its key terrain and capabilities; Defeat strategic threats to the United States and its national interests; and Assist Combatant Commands to achieve their missions in and through cyberspace."[171] The importance of OE to friendly and adversary military operations will ensure that cyber vulnerabilities will be targeted continuously.

---

[167] Zak Doffman, "Israel Responds to Cyberattack with Air Strike on Cyber-Attackers in World First," Forbes, May 6, 2019 (https://www.forbes.com/sites/zakdoffman/2019/05/06/israeli-military-strikes-and-destroys-hamas-cyber-hq-in-world-first/?sh=45ac3e7dafb5).
[168] Zak Doffman, "Cyber Warfare: US Military Admits Immediate Danger Is 'Keeping Us Up at Night'," Forbes, July 21, 2019 (https://www.forbes.com/sites/zakdoffman/2019/07/21/cyber-warfare-u-s-military-admits-immediate-danger-is-keeping-us-up-at-night/?sh=5c8b0f9c1061).
[169] Gray Analytics, "Military Cyber Security: Threats and Solutions," July 13, 2020 (https://grayanalytics.com/in-the-news/military-cyber-security-threats-and-solutions/).
[170] Zak Doffman, "Cyber Warfare: US Military Admits Immediate Danger Is 'Keeping Us Up at Night'," Forbes, July 21, 2019 (https://www.forbes.com/sites/zakdoffman/2019/07/21/cyber-warfare-u-s-military-admits-immediate-danger-is-keeping-us-up-at-night/?sh=5c8b0f9c1061).
[171] James Di Pane, "Cyber Warfare and US Cyber Command," The Heritage Foundation, October 18, 2022.

4.8.5 Blockade

For energy import-dependent countries, adversaries' blockages threaten energy security. During WWI, Germany used U-boats to block Britain from oil, iron ore, and food. In October 1914, German U-boats began attacking merchant ships, with Admiral Henning von Holtzendorff, the Imperial German Navy's Chief of Admiralty, believing that a German U-boat blockade could force the British government to its knees in five months.[172] The campaign did lead to dangerous oil shortages by the summer of 1914 that highlighted Britain's new dependence on Middle East supplies.[173]

The Houthi attacks on Red Sea shipping beginning in 2019, and increasing significantly in 2023–2024, illustrate the ability of a low-tech militia, backed by a state – Iran, to disrupt international shipping. The Houthis disruptions had a large impact on global energy supplies, energy prices, and insurance rates. Accordingly, not only have the attacks disrupted energy supplies, they serve as an economic instrument. The US has not succeeded in deterring Iran from launching these attacks via its proxy in Yemen. The Houthi attacks highlight the importance of preventive action and planning that ensure the freedom of shipping upheld in a handful of key global strategic waterways.

With China widely seen as a growing threat, should there be a significant military conflict one can anticipate serious efforts to blockade shipping traffic to Beijing. However, there are differing assessments regarding the feasibility of shutting China off from global trade that go beyond concerns regarding economic interdependencies.

US Chief of Naval Operations Admiral Michael Gilday highlighted the importance of a blockade strategy in the US 2020 *Naval Doctrine Publication 1*, noting, "naval forces exist [in part to] prevent an adversary's seaborne movement of commerce and military forces."[174] In other regions of conflict as well, there are states whose dependence on foreign energy sources make them vulnerable to a blockade strategy. Of course, US forces must also ensure their own supply lines cannot be blockaded.

---

172 NATO Energy Security Centre of Excellence (NATO ENSEC COE), *Energy in Irregular Warfare*, 2017, page 14 (https://enseccoe.org/data/public/uploads/2017/05/irregular_warfare_176x250mm_20170526.pdf).
173 NATO Energy Security Centre of Excellence (NATO ENSEC COE), *Energy in Irregular Warfare*, 2017, page 14 (https://enseccoe.org/data/public/uploads/2017/05/irregular_warfare_176x250mm_20170526.pdf).
174 David Axe, "To Defeat China in War, Strangle Its Economy: Expert," *Forbes*, August 24, 2020 (https://www.forbes.com/sites/davidaxe/2020/08/24/to-defeat-china-in-war-strangle-its-economy/?sh=545b1eb531a9).

4.8.6 Aerial Bombings / Indirect Military Fires

Whether surface-to-surface missiles from the sea, air-to-surface missiles, or artillery, or gravity bombs, such attacks will remain a significant threat to energy systems and the military's OE.

As is illustrated in the case study in Chapter 2, access to oil and coal was a strategic factor in the outcome of WWII. For example, "The German command recognized the potential of Caspian oil reserves in the USSR. Securing these oil supplies played a decisive factor in the decision to invade the USSR."[175] Indeed, one of Hitler's key concerns regarding OE for its forces was that the entry of the US, a major oil producer, into the war in 1941 made a short-term victory unlikely and would also make the potential for problematic petroleum shortfalls even more of a strategic concern – thus the push for seizing all the regional oil fields.[176] Had Germany captured the Caspian oil fields and succeeded in transporting the oil to its troops, it could have obtained four times the amount of oil its forces had in 1941.[177]

Operation Desert Storm provides a good case study on energy infrastructure during combat. US and Coalition bombings decimated Iraqi energy infrastructure beginning with the very first Coalition airstrikes. "Eighteen Tomahawks were directed against electrical facilities in and around Baghdad. Many of the missiles carried a highly classified special carbon filament designed to short the electrical grid systems. In Riyadh, then Major David Deptula (Central Air Forces air planner) let out a cheer when the CNN telecast from Baghdad went off the air. The allies turned out the lights."[178] After just two days, eleven major power plants were down with some bombed and others shut off by the Iraqis to avoid them being targeted.[179]

NATO forces again turned out the lights during Operation Allied Force in the former Yugoslavia in 1999, which contributed to increasing public pressure on Serbia to capitulate and thus terminate the conflict.

---

175 NATO Energy Security Centre of Excellence (NATO ENSEC COE), *Energy in Irregular Warfare*, 2017, page 16 (https://enseccoe.org/data/public/uploads/2017/05/irregular_warfare_176x250mm_20170526.pdf).
176 Jeremy Black, *Military Strategy: A Global History*, New Haven, CT: Yale University Press, 2020, pages 203–204.
177 Richard Overy, *Why the Allies Won*, New York: W. W. Norton & Company, 1997, page 228.
178 Michael R. Gordon and Bernard E. Trainor, *The General's War*, Boston: Back Bay Books, Little, Brown and Company, 1995, page, 216.
179 Michael R. Gordon and Bernard E. Trainor, *The General's War*, Boston: Back Bay Books, Little, Brown and Company, 1995, page 224.

4.9 US Adversaries' Views on Disruption of Opponents' OE Supplies

This section discusses the approaches of the US's main adversaries – China, Russia, and Iran – to attacking the OE systems of their enemies and particularly American OE systems.

4.9.1 China

The Chinese military has long maintained an overarching doctrine of "active defense." This means employing an offensive doctrine of using "long range, precision-guided munitions [...] to keep a potential enemy as far as possible from the economically fast-developing Chinese coastal areas"[180] at the onset of war. The initial strike, meant to achieve de-escalation by "seizing the initiative," is envisioned to feature cyberattacks targeting not only command and control systems, but also "logistics" and "commercial activities,"[181] which include both energy supplies and energy infrastructure. In parallel, China plans to use kinetic weapons to cripple enemy electrical grids and electronic systems.

In Chinese military doctrine, support systems, including energy supplies, are integral to every operational system and are therefore viewed as legitimate targets in warfare.[182] In using cyber and kinetic weapons to paralyze enemy energy systems, the PLA can accomplish a core task in its doctrine of "system warfare," paralyzing the enemy's operational system without eliminating most physical enemy assets. Insofar as the system warfare doctrine calls for "bypassing enemy systems' areas of strength" and striking elsewhere to offset those advantages, the PLA is likely to focus on strikes on American logistical support systems, including energy, in a conflict with the US military, which it perceives as having advantages in weapons technologies.[183]

---

[180] Defense Intelligence Agency, "China Military Power: Modernizing a Force to Fight and Win," 2019, page 3 (https://www.dia.mil/Portals/110/Images/News/Military_Powers_Publications/China_Military_Power_FINAL_5MB_20190103.pdf).
[181] Defense Intelligence Agency, "China Military Power: Modernizing a Force to Fight and Win," 2019, pages 23 and 46 (https://www.dia.mil/Portals/110/Images/News/Military_Powers_Publications/China_Military_Power_FINAL_5MB_20190103.pdf).
[182] Defense Intelligence Agency, "China Military Power: Modernizing a Force to Fight and Win," 2019, page 8 (https://www.dia.mil/Portals/110/Images/News/Military_Powers_Publications/China_Military_Power_FINAL_5MB_20190103.pdf); Wei Jun and Zheng Zhengbing, "How to Choose the Main Direction of Attack under the Condition of Informatization," *PLA Daily*, July 2, 2019 (http://www.mod.gov.cn/jmsd/2019-07/02/content_4845005.htm).
[183] Department of the Army, "Chinese Tactics," August 2021, pages 1–17 (https://armypubs.army.mil/epubs/DR_pubs/DR_a/ARN34236-ATP_7-100.3-001-WEB-3.pdf).

Chinese military (PLA) publications emphasize that advanced weapons systems, whether mechanized or digitized, are particularly reliant on energy supply, and an energy cutoff can quickly paralyze the enemy fighting system.[184]

A US military intelligence report from 2005 which cited Chinese sources assessed that China plans to use high-altitude electromagnetic pulse and graphite-fiber bombs in a potential conflict with Taiwan, both against Taiwanese infrastructure and against US carrier groups.[185] Both types of weapons are designed to paralyze electronic devices and electrical grids. The People's Liberation Army's (PLA) establishment of a Strategic Support Force – parallel to the Ground Force, Navy, Air Force, and Rocket Force – with the responsibility of "integrating cyber data and capabilities with electromagnetic and space warfare information and operations,"[186] highlights the importance attached to these vectors of activity.

Chinese strategic writings view the United States as being more energy secure than China given its lack of dependence on energy imports. Specifically, Chinese strategic writings point to the "Malacca problem" as a strategic Chinese vulnerability. This Chinese vulnerability is the US's ability to block the Malacca Straits – which connect the Pacific and Indian Oceans – during a crisis.[187] Most of China's energy imports transit the strategically important Malacca Straits. Over the last decade, China has increased its oil storage capacity, which can help offset this vulnerability.

In addition, to balance China's need for energy imports in contrast to the United States, Beijing will likely seek to disrupt domestic American energy supplies. According to US official assessments, China possesses both the will and the capability to disrupt US energy supply systems, including American domestic energy supply systems and infrastructure. A US intelligence assessment from 2019 claims that "China has the ability to launch cyberattacks that cause localized, temporary disruptive effects on critical infrastructure – such as disruption of a natural gas pipeline for days to weeks – in the

---

184 Wang Yang and Zuo Wentao, "Clearly Recognizing the Key Factors of Victory in Intelligent Warfare," *PLA Daily*, June 18, 2020 (http://www.81.cn/jfjbmap/content/2020-06/18/node_8.htm); Yuan Yi, Gao Dongming, and Cao Shixin, "What Are the Differences between Mechanization, Informatization, and Intelligence?," *PLA Daily*, August 1, 2019 (http://www.81.cn/jfjbmap/content/2019-08/01/content_239773.htm).
185 National Ground Intelligence Center, "China: Medical Research on Bio-Effects of Electromagnetic Pulse and High-Power Microwave Radiation," 2005 (https://nsarchive2.gwu.edu/NSAEBB/NSAEBB351/Doc011.PDF).
186 Edmund J. Burke, Kristen Gunness, Cortez A. Cooper III, and Mark Cozad, "People's Liberation Army Operational Concepts," 2020, page 1 (https://www.rand.org/content/dam/rand/pubs/research_reports/RRA300/RRA394-1/RAND_RRA394-1.pdf).
187 Christopher Bassler and Ben Noon, "Mind the Power Gap: The American Energy Arsenal and Chinese Insecurity," Center for Strategic and Budgetary Assessments (https://csbaonline.org/uploads/documents/CSBA8274_(Mind_the_Power_Gap)_FINAL_web.pdf).

United States."[188] In 2021, the Cybersecurity and Infrastructure Security Agency (CISA) and Federal Bureau of Investigation (FBI) released a joint cybersecurity advisory that attributed to "Chinese state-sponsored actors" a range of cyberattacks targeting "23 US natural gas pipeline operators" between 2011 and 2013. Of these, "13 were confirmed compromises, 3 were near misses, and 8 had an unknown depth of intrusion."[189] According to the US Department of Energy, the Chinese government is also "equipped and actively planning to undermine the electric power system in the United States," prompting concerns over Chinese-manufactured equipment in US electrical infrastructure.[190]

Following Xi Jinping's military reforms launched in 2015, the Chinese government and PLA released a series of top-level documents outlining new warfighting principles, which include the "Chinese Military Strategy" white paper in 2015[191] and the "Guidelines on Joint Operations" in 2020. These documents detail China's strategy, including plans to target adversaries' energy systems. According to the Chinese Military Strategy, China's initial strike will aim at those targets with "the strongest supporting function in the enemy's operational system, the largest impact on the enemy's political situation and public psychology, and the highest threat to [friendly forces'] subsequent operations." Attacks on American domestic energy supply systems are likely to have a huge psychological impact on the American public and its attitude toward sustaining a war effort with China, without even one fatality.

According to the Chinese doctrine, its initial strike will focus on "core targets," with follow-on strikes aimed at "important targets" and "ordinary targets" to "deprive or restrict the enemy's warfighting potential from the source."[192] This would likely include energy supplies. Moreover, the Chinese explicitly mention "forces ensuring resource logistics" as an initial strike target intended to achieve "system-level paralysis through

---

188 Daniel R. Coats, "Statement for the Record: Worldwide Threat Assessment of the US Intelligence Community," January 29, 2019 (https://www.dni.gov/files/ODNI/documents/2019-ATA-SFR--SSCI.pdf).
189 Cybersecurity and Infrastructure Security Agency (CISA) and Federal Bureau of Investigation (FBI), "Joint Cybersecurity Advisory: Chinese Gas Pipeline Intrusion Campaign, 2011 to 2013" (https://www.cisa.gov/sites/default/files/publications/AA21-201A_Chinese_Gas_Pipeline_Intrusion_Campaign_2011_to_2013%20(1).pdf).
190 Office of Electricity, Department of Energy (DOE), "Notice of Request for Information (RFI) on Ensuring the Continued Security of the United States Critical Electric Infrastructure," April 22, 2021 (https://www.federalregister.gov/documents/2021/04/22/2021-08482/notice-of-request-for-information-rfi-on-ensuring-the-continued-security-of-the-united-states).
191 *China Daily*, "2015 China National Defense White Paper 'China's Military Strategy'," May 26, 2015 (http://www.chinadaily.com.cn/interface/toutiao/1138561/2015-5-26/cd_20821000.html).
192 Xu Shiyong and Xuan Bangdong, "Pay Attention to the Research and Analysis of the 'Decisive' First Battle," *PLA Daily*, December 27, 2022 (http://www.mod.gov.cn/jmsd/2022-12/27/content_4929277.htm).

destruction at a single point."[193] According to such doctrine, the PLA will target energy supplies in an initial strike if the PLA assesses that they are crucial to the functioning of the adversary's operational system.

4.9.2 Russia

Russia's military doctrine targets energy infrastructure. Russia's "non-linear warfare" theory, which was articulated in the mid-2010s, included the use of asymmetrical "military-political measures" such as cyber attacks, covert operative missions, and the use of proxy forces.[194] These measures include focusing cyberattacks on the disruption of US OE supplies.

From 2017 until 2021, Russian-linked elements have reportedly engaged in three landmark cyber hacks on companies and infrastructure that are central to US energy supplies, including US OE: the Maersk shipping company, SolarWinds software, and the Colonial Pipeline (see case study in this chapter). The Solar Winds hack affected the Departments of Energy and Defense, and the Maersk Shipping Company is an important energy shipper.[195] The May 2021 Colonial Pipeline ransomware attack was a direct blow to US domestic fuel supply and caused widespread disruption. The pipeline runs from refineries near Houston, Texas to carry gasoline, jet fuel, and home heating oil to the US East Coast, providing nearly half of the fuel needed for the East Coast, including the locations of the DOD and the Department of Homeland Security.

4.9.3 Iran

Like Russia's non-linear approach, Iran's doctrine of asymmetric warfare "focuses on exploiting weaknesses in enemy capabilities and creating a credible deterrence despite

---

193 Wei Jun and Zheng Zhengbing, "How to Choose the Main Direction of Attack under the Condition of Informatization," *PLA Daily*, July 2, 2019 (http://www.mod.gov.cn/jmsd/2019-07/02/content_4845005.htm).
194 Michael Kofman, "Russian Hybrid Warfare and Other Dark Arts," War on the Rocks, 2016 (https://warontherocks.com/2016/03/russian-hybrid-warfare-and-other-dark-arts/); Pavel Felgengauer, "To Attain Superiority over the Whole Mankind," *Novaya Gazeta* [orig. from Russian: "Dobitsya prevoskhodstva nad vsem chelovechestvom"], no. 26, March 11, 2019 (https://novayagazeta.ru/articles/2019/03/09/79808-dobitsya-prevoshodstva-nad-ostalnym-chelovechestvom); A. Greenberg, "The Untold Story of NotPetya, the Most Devastating Cyberattack in History," *Wired*, 2018 (https://www.wired.com/story/notpetya-cyberattack-ukraine-russia-code-crashed-the-world/).
195 D. Temple-Raston, "A 'Worst Nightmare' Cyberattack: The Untold Story of the SolarWinds Hack," *NPR*, 2021 (https://www.npr.org/2021/04/16/985439655/a-worst-nightmare-cyberattack-the-untold-story-of-the-solarwinds-hack).

constraints on Iranian military power."[196] In this doctrine, UAV and missile strikes, as well as cyberattacks, play an important role. Tehran perceives the last of these as "a weapon of first choice due to its perceived low risk/high reward" ratio and the plausible deniability it affords. According to a US military assessment, Iranian cyberattacks are particularly likely to target "critical infrastructure such as energy and transportation, financial institutions and military command and control networks."[197] Such attacks fit well with Iran's asymmetric warfare doctrine given Iranian perceptions of the US military's technological superiority and "overreliance on technology."[198]

In addition to its doctrine, Iran has a concrete history of directly targeting the energy infrastructure of its adversaries through cyber, proxy, and various military means. Iran has launched repeated cyberattacks against Gulf energy companies, most notably Saudi Aramco. Moreover, as pointed out earlier in the chapter, Iran and its proxies have conducted attacks on energy infrastructure in Saudi Arabia and the UAE, including a 2019 drone and cruise missile attack against the Abqaiq oil facility – the key Saudi crude oil processing installation. In addition, Yemeni Houthis – Iran's proxy force – have also conducted drone and missile strikes on regional energy infrastructure in the Arab Gulf.[199] Iran also maintains the ability to threaten shipping in the Straits of Hormuz, the world's most important energy transit waterway.[200] Additionally, Iran-backed Hezbollah regularly threatens to target Israel's electricity production and transmission.

Since its establishment in 1979, the Islamic Republic of Iran has frequently used naval guerilla warfare to target oil tankers in the Hormuz Strait and Arab Gulf. As part of this activity, small vessels, supported by land-based anti-ship missiles and aircraft, drop sea mines, or attack and quickly maneuver away from the target. In the 1980s, Tehran attacked multiple civilian oil tankers transiting the Hormuz Straight and Arab Gulf.[201]

To counter the US Navy, Iran has employed covert and asymmetric tools. Iran has anti-surface warfare capabilities, including naval mining (e.g., moored contact, drifting con-

---

[196] US Army Asymmetric Warfare Group, *Iran Quick Reference Guide*, Version 1.1, page 14 (https://www.moore.army.mil/armor/316thcav/DCT-MT/Content/PDF/Iran%20Quick%20Reference%20Guide.pdf).
[197] US Army Asymmetric Warfare Group, *Iran Quick Reference Guide*, Version 1.1, page 17 (https://www.moore.army.mil/armor/316thcav/DCT-MT/Content/PDF/Iran%20Quick%20Reference%20Guide.pdf).
[198] Defense Intelligence Agency, "Iran Military Power: Ensuring Regime Survival and Securing Regional Dominance," 2019, pages 22–23 (https://www.dia.mil/Portals/110/Images/News/Military_Powers_Publications/Iran_Military_Power_LR.pdf).
[199] Ilan Goldenber, Jessica Schwed, and Kaleigh Thomas, "In Dire Straits? Implications of US-Iran Tensions for the Global Oil Market," Columbia Center on Global Energy Policy, November 2019, pages 21–24 (https://www.energypolicy.columbia.edu/wp-content/uploads/2019/11/SOH-CGEP_Report_111722.pdf).
[200] Alireza Nader, "Iran after the Bomb: How Would a Nuclear-Armed Tehran Behave?," RAND Corporation (National Security Research Division), page 18 (https://apps.dtic.mil/sti/pdfs/ADA580454.pdf).
[201] Michael Connell, "Iran's Military Doctrine," *The Iran Primer*, October 11, 2010 (http://iranprimer.usip.org/resource/irans-military-doctrine).

tact, and limpet mines), UAVs, small-boat swarming tactics, and coastal defenses that can be readily deployed close to the sea and on the Iranian-claimed islands in the Gulf.

Tehran has demonstrated a capacity to attack energy tankers as well as US naval forces which engage in protection of the right of passage in international waterways. For instance, in 2016, Iran detained ten US sailors. Also, in June 2019 Iranian forces took down a US Global Hawk drone over the Strait of Hormuz; less than a month later US ship *USS Boxer* retaliated by downing an Iranian UAV which threatened the vessel's safety.[202]

Iranian proxy forces in the form of Yemeni Houthis have frequently attacked Saudi and UAE energy infrastructure. Saudis claim to have downed a vast majority of incoming aerial targets (up to 90 percent),[203] however, Saudi Arabia and the UAE have not succeeded in maintaining a complete defense from these attacks. Houthi forces have launched their assaults without significant expenses – it is the Saudis who have had to counter with highly expensive Patriot anti-missiles. Houthis have leveraged UAV, missile technology, as well as naval mine warfare.

Iran has sought to expand its naval presence beyond the neighboring waters of the Arabian Gulf, Gulf of Oman, and Arabian Sea. If Iran can reach a critical chokepoint for the United States, it could pose an additional threat to US OE. In January 2023, Iranian Navy commander Rear Admiral Shahram Irani announced that Iran had for the first time sent its ships to the Panama Canal.[204] In spring 2024, Iran's Houthi proxy made threats to the shipping in the Indian Ocean, with Iran-supplied missiles.

4.9.4 Conclusions on US Adversaries' Views of American Operational Energy Vulnerabilities

It is clear from this examination of the views of the main US adversaries – China, Russia, and Iran – that they view US OE and domestic energy supplies and infrastructure as key targets in conflicts with the United States. All three states see focusing on US energy supply systems as a key tool to overcoming American weapon and platform superiority. Moreover, all three states engage in planning on how to disrupt American OE and domestic energy supplies.

---

202 International Crisis Group, "Strait of Hormuz," June 7, 2023 (https://www.crisisgroup.org/trigger-list/iran-us-trigger-list/flashpoints/hormuz).
203 International Crisis Group, "Strait of Hormuz," June 7, 2023 (https://www.crisisgroup.org/trigger-list/iran-us-trigger-list/flashpoints/hormuz).
204 Heather Mongilio, "Iranian Navy Sending Ships to Panama Canal, Says Commander," January 13, 2023 (https://news.usni.org/2023/01/13/iranian-navy-sending-ships-to-panama-canal-says-commander).

4.10 For Study

- Understand COG analysis and how it might be used to analyze threats to OE.
- Understand deliberate and non-deliberate threats to OE.
- Learn the primary threats to US OE from key US adversaries.
- Understand the core Chinese, Russian, and Iranian doctrines toward the OE of their adversaries.

4.11 Questions for Discussion

- Which types of threats to OE are the biggest concern to military forces?
- What security issues can you identify regarding OE?
- In your last operational command, what cyber vulnerabilities – if attacked – would have affected OE?
- Can you think of a time when your unit was in an operational pause due to a lack of fuel? Why did this take place? Was it a frequent occurrence? Discuss details.
- How have you planned to target or targeted an adversary's critical energy infrastructure and/or energy supplies? Discuss these cases.
- What is the American approach toward disrupting electricity supply to civilian populations in adversary countries?
- What is the American approach toward destruction of enemy civilian energy infrastructure during warfare?
- What is the approach of Russia, China, and Iran to American OE vulnerabilities?
- What is the American approach to disrupting OE of China, Russia, and Iran?

4.12 Case study: Destroying the Enemy's Energy Supplies in the Twenty-First Century

OE strategy is two-sided: providing energy supplies for one's own war effort, while denying energy supplies to the enemy. Successful OE strategy requires both "efficient, effective and sustained energy supplies of combat power," while "enemy combat power production is disrupted, degraded, or destroyed." As pointed out by Darling and Carpenter, "OE superiority is the ability to fully exploit one's own energy capabilities while preventing the adversary from doing the same."[205] This case study examines the cases of the Russia-Ukraine War (beginning in February 2022) and the Israel-

---

[205] RuthAnne Darling and Paul Mason Carpenter, "Energy: An Essential Element for Winning Future Wars – Operational Energy Part 1," *Surge*, Summer 2020, Naval Postgraduate School (https://nps.edu/web/eag/future-wars).

4.12 Case study: Destroying the Enemy's Energy Supplies in the Twenty-First Century — 101

Hamas war (beginning October 2023), and the role that limitations on disrupting enemy fuel supplies played in the wars.

Throughout history, disrupting an enemy's energy supplies has been a major war goal and has determined the outcome of battles and wars, as illustrated by the examples in Chapter 2. During World War I, Germany determined that US oil supplies gave the Allies battlefield advantages. Thus, Berlin sent U-boats armed with torpedoes to target American boats supplying the Allies with oil and other supplies. In World War II, energy shortages affected the advances of both the Allies and Axis. From May 1944 to May 1945, the US and British air forces conducted the "Oil Plan," which targeted German refineries, oil fields, and synthetic fuel plants in order to deny Germany access to energy. The US and NATO have frequently disabled the electricity supply to the civilian population in an adversary country, to disrupt OE to the enemy but also to increase public pressure for a surrender. For instance, during Operation Allied Force in 1999 in the former territory of Yugoslavia, NATO forces turned out the lights to increase public pressure on Serbia to surrender.

Denying energy supplies to the adversary in war has been a bedrock of military strategy. However, in the Russia-Ukraine War and the Israel-Hamas War of the 2020s, the United States, Europe, and United Nations institutions have sought to limit the disruptions that Ukraine and Israel could cause to their adversaries: Russia and Hamas. In the case of Israel, the United States and Europe demanded that Israel not only desist from disrupting such supplies but actually provide energy to Hamas. In the case of Ukraine, in the early stages of the war, the United States requested that Kyiv refrain from attacking targets in Russian territory, including fuel supplies, in order to prevent the war from escalating.

4.12.1 Details of Cases

4.12.1.1 Russia – Ukraine (from February 2022)
Russia advanced its invasion of Ukraine in February 2022. In response, the United States, European Union member states, and other US allies imposed sanctions on Russia and streamed massive economic aid to Kyiv. The US and Europeans began to supply arms and other military supplies and sequentially provided more lethal and precise weapons, potentially risking a widening of the conflict beyond Ukraine. In an attempt to prevent widening and escalation, Washington requested that Ukraine not attack Russian territory, but limit its attacks to the Russian forces deployed on Ukrainian territory. Washington also required that US-supplied arms not be used against Russian targets outside Ukraine.[206] This limitation reduced Kyiv's ability to disrupt Moscow's fuel sup-

---

[206] Idrees Ali and Phil Stewart, "Ukraine Shouldn't Use US Weaponry inside Russia, US General Says,"

ply lines. The limit also put Ukraine in a difficult disadvantage, as Moscow focused on destroying Ukraine's fuel supplies and parts of Ukraine's energy infrastructure, including components of its power system, during the war.[207]

However, beginning in April 2022, Ukraine's policy shifted, and it began to attack Russian energy supplies.[208] Kyiv conducted several attacks on fuel depots and refineries in Russian territory. This shift was likely facilitated by a change in policy of some of Ukraine's Western backers to support such Ukrainian attacks. For example, The UK's Minister of Armed Forces James Heappey stated in April 2022:

> it is entirely legitimate to go after military targets in the depth of your opponent to disrupt their logistics and supply lines.[209]

Throughout 2023 and continuing into 2024, Ukraine openly and explicitly targeted fuel production on Russian territory.[210] Kyiv used multiple means to attack energy supplies in Russian territories, including missiles and drones and likely also helicopters.[211] Ukraine claimed that it launched the attacks on Russia's refineries to disrupt energy supplies to Russia's troops and also to deny revenue to Moscow from oil product ex-

---

Reuters, May 25, 2023 (https://www.reuters.com/world/europe/ukraine-shouldnt-use-us-arms-inside-russia-us-general-says-2023-05-25/).

[207] An interesting energy aspect of the war is that neither side disrupted Russia's natural gas exports via the territory of Ukraine.

[208] BBC, "War on Ukraine: Russia Accuses Ukraine of Attacking Oil Depot," April 1, 2022 (https://www.bbc.com/news/world-europe-60952125); Upstream, "Russian Fuel Depot in Flames as Attacks Switch to Energy Installations," April 1, 2022 (https://www.upstreamonline.com/production/russian-fuel-depot-in-flames-as-attacks-switch-to-energy-installations/2–1–1194826); Reuters, "Kremlin Says Ukraine Strike on Russian Fuel Depot Creates Awkward Backdrop for Talks," April 1, 2022 (https://www.reuters.com/world/europe/kremlin-says-ukraine-strike-russian-fuel-depot-creates-awkward-backdrop-talks-2022-04-01/); Bloomberg News, "Russia Blames Oil Refinery Blaze on Ukrainian Drone Strike," June 22, 2022 (https://www.bloomberg.com/news/articles/2022-06-22/russia-blames-oil-refinery-blaze-on-ukrainian-drone-strike?sref=qmS8rGlM).

[209] Deborah Haynes, "Ukraine War: 'Entirely Legitimate' for Kyiv to Hit Military Targets in Russia Using Western Weapons, Minister Says," *Sky*, April 26, 2022 (https://news.sky.com/story/ukraine-war-entirely-legitimate-for-kyiv-to-hit-military-targets-in-russia-using-western-weapons-minister-says-12599296).

[210] For example, CNBC, "Ukraine's SBU Hits Russia's Volgograd Oil Refinery in Drone Attack, Source Says," February 3, 2024 (https://www.cnbc.com/2024/02/03/ukraines-sbu-hits-russias-volgograd-oil-refinery-in-drone-attack-source-says.html); James Marson, "Ukraine Strikes Russian Fuel Terminal on Baltic Sea in Long-Range Attack," *The Wall Street Journal*, January 21, 2024 (https://www.wsj.com/world/europe/ukraine-strikes-russian-fuel-terminal-on-baltic-sea-in-long-range-attack-76692dd5); Amanda Battersby, "Ukraine Drone Attacks Russian Refinery Near Crude Export Terminal," October 30, 2023 (https://www.upstreamonline.com/safety/ukraine-drone-attacks-russian-refinery-near-crude-export-terminal/2-1-1544096).

[211] Emre Gurkan Abay, Ruslan Rehimov, and Dmitiri Chirciu, "Russia Says Ukraine Helicopters Hit Oil Refinery," February 4, 2022 (https://www.aa.com.tr/en/energy/oil/russia-says-ukrainian-helicopters-hit-oil-refinery/35021).

port.[212] It is not clear if Kyiv coordinated with or received approval from Washington to expand its warfighting to the energy supplies in Russian territory. The attacks on Russian refineries did limit Moscow's ability to export refined petroleum products in the weeks following the attacks in early 2024.[213]

During 2023 and 2024, Ukraine also initiated attacks on Russian oil tankers in the Black Sea, which disrupted Russian oil export.[214]

4.12.1.2 Israel-Hamas (from October 7, 2023)
On the morning of October 7, 2023, the Hamas militia launched a multipronged attack on Israel that included massive rocket fire on central and southern Israel, attacks on military bases and outposts, and large-scale massacres of the civilian population in southern Israel and the taking of 240 hostages. In order to prevent future Hamas attacks, destroy the Hamas militia and its military infrastructure, and attempt to rescue the hostages, Israel launched a large-scale offensive against Hamas forces in the Gaza Strip.

On October 9, Israel's Prime Minister Binyamin Netanyahu and several of his ministers announced that Israel would stop fuel supplies to the Gaza Strip.[215] However, in response to strong American pressure, on November 19, the Israeli cabinet decided to provide regular fuel supplies to Gaza.[216]

In the war, Hamas needed fuel to support its underground tunnel infrastructure and thereby protect its military capacity. Hamas had established an extensive system of underground bases linked by tunnels, to allow it to launch attacks without fear of air attacks and detection. This underground system requires liquid fuels to supply oxygen and provide cooling. Most of the tunnels were built with entrances via hospitals, schools, mosques, etc. so that the entrances were not detectable and prior to the fall

---

212 *New York Times*, "Ukraine Targets Russian Oil Plants, Aiming to Disrupt Military Operations," January 19, 2024 (https://www.nytimes.com/2024/01/19/world/europe/ukraine-russia-oil-drone-attack.html).
213 Robert Perkins, "Factbox: Russian Fuels Exports Under Fire as Drone Attacks Escalate," S&P Global Commodity Insights, January 26, 2024 (https://www.spglobal.com/commodityinsights/en/market-insights/latest-news/oil/012624-factbox-russian-fuels-exports-under-fire-as-drone-attacks-escalate).
214 Brenda Shaffer, "Insecurity in the Black Sea Puts Upward Pressure on the Global Oil Market," Real Clear Energy, September 21, 2023 (https://www.realclearenergy.org/articles/2023/09/21/insecurity_in_the_black_sea_puts_upward_pressure_on_the_global_oil_market_981150.html); Energy Intelligence Group, "Black Sea Attacks Put Russian Oil Shipments at Risk," August 9, 2023 (https://www.energyintel.com/00000189-d0b2-d8ee-a3bb-f4fb66b00000).
215 Prior to the war, Israel had provided most of the Gaza strip's water and electricity supplies free of charge, and supplied liquid fuels in theory for payment, but payments were rarely made in recent years.
216 Eichner, "Liters of Diesel, Everyday: The 60,000 Cabinet Approved the Introduction of Fuel into Gaza," Ynet, November 19, 2023 (https://www.ynet.co.il/news/article/rywshwv4t).

2023 would not be likely to be attacked by Israel due to the status of these public buildings under the Geneva Convention.

Due to the large displacement of people during the war, a humanitarian crisis emerged in the Gaza Strip. Prior to the launch of the military campaign in Gaza, Israel announced to the civilian Palestinian population that they needed to move to safe zones that were established outside the fighting zones. The US, Europe, the UN, and more called on Israel to allow aid, including fuel, to be supplied to the civilian population. In fact, the United States expected that Israel itself would provide fuel (and electricity and water) to the Gaza Strip. Israel agreed, hoping that the fuel and aid would serve as an incentive for the hostages' release. However, due to American pressure on Israel, the fuel supplies continued, after the first batch of hostages were released in late November, despite a lack of further hostage releases.

In reality, supplying the civilian population meant supplying fuel to Hamas during the war. Since Hamas controls the Gaza Strip, these supplies ended up in the hands of the Hamas fighters, especially since Hamas forces are embedded among the civilian Gaza population. Much of the liquid fuel supplied to Gaza, presumably for general electricity generation, enables Hamas to continue to supply oxygen to the tunnels and thus sustain its military campaign. The importance of these fuel supplies to Hamas is illustrated by the fact that in several rounds of negotiations on releases of Israeli hostages, Hamas requested to obtain fuel supplies. Hamas asked for diesel fuel, which could power the tunnel air and cooling systems, and not electricity, for instance, for hospitals, or for solar panels and batteries, for charging the population's cell phones. Prior to the war, Hamas prepared and stored large amounts of energy supplies to maintain its underground operations.[217] The provision of fuel to Hamas fighters clearly enabled them to continue the war from underground and thus lengthened the war.

4.12.2 Case Conclusions

In wars in the 2020s, the United States and its allies have put limitations on partner nations that prevented them from disrupting the fuel supplies of enemy armies. In the case of the 2023 Israel-Hamas War, not only did the US prevent Israel from disrupting energy supplies to the enemy, but Washington also demanded that Israel provide fuel and enable fuel delivery that ended up being supplied to Hamas. If the demands to refrain from attacking enemy fuel supply lines, or even to enable supplies to pass to the enemy become the norm, it will greatly change the nature of warfare. The cases in

---

217 Anna Schecter, "Hamas Is Hoarding Vast Amounts of Fuel as Gaza Hospitals Run Low, U.S. Officials Say," NBC News, November 1, 2023 (https://www.nbcnews.com/news/investigations/hamas-hoarding-vast-amounts-fuel-gaza-hospitals-run-low-us-officials-s-rcna122977).

this study show that in twenty-first-century warfare, powers may impose limits on states at war from destroying the enemies' energy supply lanes. The US promotes provision of aid, which can include fuel, to civilians during warfare as part of its foreign policy. This fuel can reach enemy combatants. In addition, global and regional powers often impose limits on actors in war in order to prevent widening or escalation of a conflict. Refraining from disrupting or destroying enemy fuel supplies likely contributes to the lengthening of wars.

Liquid petroleum derived fuels continue to be the prized energy source in war fighting. Ukraine disrupted production of refined petroleum products, and Hamas fighters gained access to diesel and heavy oil to run their underground installations. Liquid petroleum derived fuels remain the necessary fuel for waging war.

4.12.3 Questions for Discussion and Research

- In preparing for war and battle, what steps should be taken to successfully plan disruption and/or destruction of enemy energy supplies?
- What intelligence information is pertinent to gather on enemy energy supplies?
- Identify the main means to disrupt enemy energy supplies.
- Which energy supplies are important to the enemy's war effort? Liquid fuels, solid fuels, electricity, batteries?
- Discuss the case of Ukraine. How did the shift in Kyiv's policy toward attacking fuel supplies in Russia affect developments in the war?
- Discuss the Ukrainian attacks beginning in 2023 on Russian oil tankers in the Black Sea. How did this affect developments in the war? Global energy security? Freedom of the seas? Global oil price?
- Discuss fuel supplies to Hamas in 2023/24 in the Israel-Hamas War.
- Is a new norm emerging in warfighting to refrain from disrupting energy supplies to opponents?
- If so, how will this affect conflict and war?
- What is your opinion on this development? Should fuel supply be enabled in order to promote other geopolitical or humanitarian goals?
- Identify plans to deal with the foreign policy aspects of dealing with constraints on attacking enemy energy supply lines.

4.13 Case Study: The Attack on the Metcalf Electricity Substation

On April 16, 2013, an attack took place on the Metcalf electricity substation in northern California. The Metcalf case is a reminder that US adversaries may target US domestic energy infrastructure during warfare with the United States. It also illustrates the vulnerability of the US electrical grid, electricity supply, and critical energy infrastructure to attack from adversaries. At the same time, the case illustrates the resilience of the American electricity infrastructure, since the attack did not cause a power outage during the time that the site was offline. Finally, the Metcalf case illustrates the challenges in identifying the source of attacks, potentially diminishing the ability of the United States to deter or retaliate against such attacks.[218]

Americans are not widely familiar with the Metcalf incident. But one former federal regulator told the *Wall Street Journal* that "if it were widely replicated across the country, it could take down the US electric grid and black out much of the country."[219]

4.13.1 Background: Metcalf and the Role of Transformers in the Energy Grid

The Pacific Gas and Electric (PG&E) Metcalf Transmission Substation provides more than a quarter of the electricity supplied to the city of San Jose and part of the power provided to the Silicon Valley. The substation, like others located across the country, uses large power transformers to turn high-voltage electricity produced at generating stations and carried on high-voltage lines into lower-voltage electricity to end users, such as businesses and residences. Such transformers cost millions of dollars each and are difficult to replace. Each is custom made and weighs up to 800,000 pounds.[220]

As a 2014 US Energy Department publication, put it: "The procurement and manufacturing of LPTs [large power transformers] is a complex process that includes prequalification of manufacturers, a competitive bidding process, the purchase of raw materials, and special modes of transportation due to its size and weight. The result is the possibility of an extended lead time that could stretch beyond twenty months if the manufacturer has difficulty obtaining certain key parts or materials."[221]

---

218 This case relies in part on a detailed chronology assembled by the *Wall Street Journal* from filings PG&E made to state and federal regulators; from other documents, including a video released by the Santa Clara County Sheriff's Department; and from interviews within relevant officials. Rebecca Smith, "Assault on California Power Station Raises Alarm on Potential for Terrorism," *The Wall Street Journal*, February 4, 2014 (https://www.wsj.com/articles/assault-on-california-power-station-raises-alarm-on-potential-for-terrorism-1391570879).
219 Rebecca Smith, "Assault on California Power Station Raises Alarm on Potential for Terrorism," *The Wall Street Journal*, February 4, 2014 (https://www.wsj.com/articles/assault-on-california-power-station-raises-alarm-on-potential-for-terrorism-1391570879).
220 US Department of Energy, "Large Power Transformers and the US Electric Grid," April 2014, page vi (https://www.energy.gov/ceser/articles/large-power-transformers-and-us-electric-grid-report-update-april-2014).
221 US Department of Energy, "Large Power Transformers and the US Electric Grid," April 2014, page vi (https://www.energy.gov/ceser/articles/large-power-transformers-and-us-electric-grid-report-update-april-2014).

According to the *Wall Street Journal* report, many of the 2000 large power transformers in the United States, including Metcalf, "sit out in the open, often in remote locations, protected by little more than cameras and chain-link fences."[222] As a result, high-voltage transformers are "ordinarily easier to access than other critical electric facilities such as generation plants and control centers."

At the Metcalf substation, the transformers were housed in the facility, allowing power from generators and high-voltage transmission to flow to corporate customers like Apple and Google. Metcalf is therefore a crucial node in a region essential to the US economy, and thus a tempting critical infrastructure target for US adversaries.

4.13.2 Attack on Metcalf

The April 16, 2013 attack on the Metcalf substation began when attacker(s) first cut telecommunications and the internet cable in two underground vaults (manholes) just outside the substation. Soon thereafter, the shooter/shooters fired shots at the transformers for nearly 20 minutes; multiple individuals reportedly shot at the high-voltage transformer radiators with .30 caliber rounds, causing the transformers to shut down, and triggering motion sensors and alarms on some of the transformers.[223]

Within minutes, an operator of the nearby power plant called the 911 emergency phone line to report a problem. The shooting ceased soon thereafter and just a minute before police arrived; however, the police departed quickly after finding the gate to the facility locked. After another hour, an electrical technician arrived from the utility.

According to the *Wall Street Journal*, the attack damaged seventeen massive transformers and six circuit breakers at three plant locations and caused 52,000 gallons of cooling oil to leak: repairs cost $15 million and took nearly a month. To avoid a blackout, the electricity system rerouted automatically, illustrating its resilience. As a result, the attacks did not lead to electricity outages; however, the incident disrupted telecommunications in San Jose.[224]

---

[222] Rebecca Smith, "Assault on California Power Station Raises Alarm on Potential for Terrorism," *The Wall Street Journal*, February 4, 2014 (https://www.wsj.com/articles/assault-on-california-power-station-raises-alarm-on-potential-for-terrorism-1391570879).
[223] Rich Heidorn Jr., "Substation Saboteurs 'No Amateurs'," RTO Insider, April 2, 2014 (http://www.rtoinsider.com/pjm-grid2020-1113-03/).
[224] Rebecca Smith, "Assault on California Power Station Raises Alarm on Potential for Terrorism," *The Wall Street Journal*, February 4, 2014 (https://www.wsj.com/articles/assault-on-california-power-station-raises-alarm-on-potential-for-terrorism-1391570879).

The attackers were careful to cover their tracks. No fingerprints were found on more than 100 expended shell casings; no boot prints could be matched with those in existing databases, and no tire tracks remained from getaway vehicles. After the attacks, authorities did not receive any credible phone calls, emails, or letters claiming responsibility. Police were left without any suspects or leads and did not make any arrests. The case remains unsolved. And both suspects and motives remain a mystery.

4.13.3 Assessment of the Attack

US government officials, former PG&E officials, and other experts largely agree that knowledgeable professionals conducted the attacks, potentially even facility or company insiders. As *The Atlantic* reported "Whoever executed the maneuver knew where to shoot the transformers. They aimed at the oil-cooling systems, causing them to leak oil and eventually overheat. By the time that happened, the attackers were long gone."[225]

One former PG&E executive told a utility security conference that he feared the incident was preparation for a larger attack "This wasn't an incident where Billy-Bob and Joe decided, after a few brewskis, to come in and shoot up a substation [...] This was an event that was well thought out, well planned and they targeted certain components."[226] Suggested motives have included: diversion from another attack, financial gain, or the desire to cause a power outage in Silicon Valley.

The FBI did not label the incident a terrorist attack. Since the perpetrator or perpetrators are unknown, also the motive is unknown and thus it cannot be concluded necessarily political. However, Jon Wellinghoff, then Chairman of the Federal Energy Regulatory Commission (FERC), who toured the site with experts from the Defense Department's Joint Warfare Analysis Center, after stepping down from his post called it "the most significant incident of domestic terrorism involving the grid that has ever occurred" in this country. He noted that shots were "carefully targeted so as not to hit the parts of the equipment that would cause an explosion and attract the attention of

---

225 Alexis C. Madrigal, "Snipers Coordinated an Attack on the Power Grid, but Why?" *The Atlantic*, February 5, 2014 (https://www.theatlantic.com/technology/archive/2014/02/snipers-coordinated-an-attack-on-the-power-grid-but-why/283620/).
226 The comments by Mark Johnson, a former PG&E Vice President for Transmission Operations, came in an online video and were first cited in *Foreign Policy*, and then by numerous other publications: Shane Harris, "Military-Style Raid on California Power Station Spooks US," *Foreign Policy*, December 27, 2013 (https://foreignpolicy.com/2013/12/27/military-style-raid-on-california-power-station-spooks-u-s/).

drivers on nearby US 101. Of some 120 shots fired from at least 40 yards outside the fence, 110 of them hit transformers," Wellinghoff told the *Los Angeles Times*.[227]

A FERC analysis determined that the US could suffer a coast-to-coast blackout if saboteurs knocked out just nine of the country's 55,000 electric-transmission substations on a scorching summer day. The study concluded that coordinated attacks in each of the nation's three separate electrical grids could cause the entire power network to collapse, according to the *Wall Street Journal*.[228]

A 2018 report from the staff of the California Public Utilities Commission (CPUC) offered a more sanguine assessment of the risk of attacks on facilities like the Metcalf substation, however:

> On the issue of physical security, it has become clear that there exists a clear distinction between those issues that apply to distribution assets versus more critical assets on the high voltage transmission networks. Even a coordinated attack against distribution facilities is unlikely to result in widespread system disturbances or cascading outages, owing to the local grid's built-in redundancy and the relatively small service share typically assigned to any single distribution substation. Depending on the design of the distribution system, redundancy can be built into system such that disruptions can be limited, and an affected distribution circuit can be served by an alternative substation.[229]

Nonetheless, in 2019, CPUC approved Physical Security Decision, D.19–01–018,[230] noting California as the first state in the nation to adopt rules to safeguard its electric distribution grid against terrorist attack.[231]

---

227 Evan Halper and Marc Lifsher, "Attack on California Electric Grid Raises Alarm," *Los Angeles Times*, February 6, 2014 (https://www.latimes.com/business/la-xpm-2014-feb-06-la-fi-grid-terror-20140207-story.html).
228 Rebecca Smith, "US Risks National Blackout from Small-Scale Attack: Federal Analysis Says Sabotage of Nine Key Substations Is Sufficient for Broad Outage," *The Wall Street Journal*, March 12, 2014 (https://www.wsj.com/articles/SB10001424052702304020104579433670284061220).
229 The Executive Summary of the white paper report, titled "Physical Security Staff White Paper," by the California Public Utilities Commission – Safety and Enforcement Division, is available at https://www.cpuc.ca.gov/-/media/cpuc-website/divisions/safety-policy-division/reports/r1506009-physical-security-executive-summary.pdf.
230 California Public Utilities Commission, "D1901018 Phase I Decision on OIR Re the Physical Security of Electrical Corp.," January 22, 2019 (https://docs.cpuc.ca.gov/SearchRes.aspx?docformat=ALL&DocID=260335905).
231 California Public Utilities Commission, "Security and Resilience for California Electric Distribution Infrastructure," (https://www.cpuc.ca.gov/uploadedFiles/CPUCWebsite/Content/Safety/Risk_Assessment/physicalsecurity/Final%20CPUC_Physical_Security_White_Paper_January_2018(1).pdf).

4.13.4 Discussion

- With the increase in hybrid warfare, US adversaries are likely to attack American domestic civilian energy infrastructure, especially during military engagements. How should protection of the home front be integrated into US military planning?
- Discuss the approaches of China, Russia, and Iran to disruption of American civilian energy infrastructure.
- How can military installations improve resilience to civilian power outages?
- What are the main vulnerabilities of the US critical energy infrastructure?
- If electricity and other energy supplies are disrupted in a region of a military base in the United States, what effect will this have on its operations?
- What are the protocols for cooperation between US military and civilian authorities in prevention and response to attacks on civilian energy infrastructure that can affect US military operations in the United States?
- Are protocols in place for US military bases in the United States to receive from civilian authorities immediate notice of energy infrastructure disruptions/outages that can affect US military operations?

5 Operational Energy Policy, Strategy, and Institutions

This chapter examines the role of the US Congress and the Executive Branch in the establishment of OE policy beginning in the 2000s. It also discusses the main institutions within the US DOD that guide OE policy and implementation. The chapter explores the factors that motivated Congress to elevate the importance of OE in US defense operations.

The chapter also discusses the main strategy documents – the White House's *National Security Strategy* and the DOD's *National Defense Strategy* and *Operational Energy Strategy.* The chapter also examines the US DOD documents that direct the US military on the operational goals and how to achieve them, and the precise organization of the relevant institutions in OE.

5.1 Congressional Interest

Before 2009, the US considered OE a subset of logistics. Congress included provisions in the Duncan Hunter fiscal year 2008 National Defense Authorization Act (NDAA) mandating categorization and management of energy in the US military, and especially OE.[232] Congress took an interest in operational policy due to a combination of economic and political factors. Developments on the battlefields in Iraq and Afghanistan were especially important in shaping Congressional interest: US and partner forces had suffered increasing casualties while moving fuel and water in these conflict zones. In addition, a 2008 spike in the price of crude oil brought oil above $140 a barrel. Dramatic fluctuations in the price of oil challenged annual budgeting for the DOD. In addition to the barrel price, delivery of fuel to the battlefield also added considerable expense. Moreover, OE needs had been growing.

5.2 DOD Interest

In parallel throughout the 2000s, growing recognition emerged within the US DOD of the challenges generated by the growing energy needs of the US military. With the enlarged demands, the Defense Science Board issued an analysis already in 2001 raising concerns and suggesting that energy demand had become a vulnerability.[233] In addi-

---

[232] Rep. Ike Skelton, "National Defense Authorization Act for Fiscal Year 2008," January 28, 2008 (https://www.congress.gov/bill/110th-congress/house-bill/4986).
[233] Defense Science Board, "More Capable Warfighting through Reduced Fuel Burden," May 2001.

tion, General James Mattis in 2003, then commanding general of the 1st Marine Division in Operation Iraqi Freedom, stated in a memorandum from a DOD task force to the chairman of the Defense Science Board, that given the frequency with which his troops outran fuel resupply lines, the Pentagon needed to "unleash us from the tether of fuel."[234] Mattis' early experience of fuel supply as a vulnerability was reprised throughout the years of the Iraq war. Fuel comprised half of the tonnage supplied to the arena.[235]

Responding to persistent logistical challenges, the Under Secretary of Defense for Acquisition, Technology and Logistics directed the Defense Science Board in 2006 to establish a Task Force to examine US DOD energy strategy. In addition, DOD began in 2007 to consider energy savings in dollars per gallon of fuel based on the "fully burdened cost of fuel." That is, the cost, including force protection, of delivering the fuel to its battlefield end-user, and not just the nominal cost of the purchase price of the fuel.

The Defense Science Board's task force report was released in 2008.[236] Titled *More Fight – Less Fuel*, the report concluded that battlespace fuel demand was imposing unnecessary higher costs and risks, compromising operational capability and mission success, and requiring excessive support structures.[237] Among the report's key findings were that the DOD did not properly manage energy risks and lacked the information and governance structures to do that and that the DOD had failed to implement earlier recommendations regarding fuel efficiency. The report assessed that it was possible to reduce fuel demand without reducing effectiveness.[238]

While analysis continued in DOD, field experience led to a growing awareness of the vulnerability of supply convoys. The Marine Corps convened an Energy Summit in 2009, which set a goal of reducing the average soldier's use of fuel on the battlefield by 25 percent by 2011.

---

[234] Office of the Under Secretary of Defense for Acquisition, Technology, and Logistics, Defense Science Board Task Force Memorandum, *More Fight – Less Fuel*, February 2008 (https://apps.dtic.mil/sti/pdfs/ADA477619.pdf).
[235] Office of the Under Secretary of Defense for Acquisition, Technology, and Logistics, Defense Science Board Task Force Memorandum, *More Fight – Less Fuel*, February 2008 (https://apps.dtic.mil/sti/pdfs/ADA477619.pdf).
[236] Office of the Under Secretary of Defense for Acquisition, Technology, and Logistics, Defense Science Board Task Force Memorandum, *More Fight – Less Fuel*, February 2008 (https://apps.dtic.mil/sti/pdfs/ADA477619.pdf).
[237] Office of the Under Secretary of Defense for Acquisition, Technology, and Logistics, Defense Science Board Task Force Memorandum, *More Fight – Less Fuel*, February 2008 (https://apps.dtic.mil/sti/pdfs/ADA477619.pdf).
[238] Office of the Under Secretary of Defense for Acquisition, Technology, and Logistics, Defense Science Board Task Force Memorandum, More Fight – Less Fuel, February 2008 (https://apps.dtic.mil/sti/pdfs/ADA477619.pdf).

5.3 National Defense Authorization Legislation

Congress approves National Defense Authorization Legislation (NDAA) every fiscal year, setting overarching policy for the US DOD. The NDAA provides authorization of appropriations for the DOD, nuclear weapons programs of the Department of Energy, and other defense-related activities.[239] It does not provide the actual funding to implement the policies it sets, since that is the purview of the Appropriations Committees and their separate statutory authority.

The OE provisions of the legislation, required the establishment of a Director of Operational Energy Plans and Programs to develop and oversee implementation of a strategy for managing the energy required for moving and sustaining military forces and weapons platforms for military operations. It required the secretaries of the Army, Navy, and Air Force to designate a senior official accountable for their service's OE programs; and to conduct a "life-cycle cost analysis for new capabilities," including "the fully burdened cost of fuel during analysis of alternatives and evaluation of alternatives and acquisition program design trades."

Within the DOD, much of the legislation was crystallized in the form of a DOD Directive (DODD) 4180.01, entitled "DOD Energy Policy." Based upon this the Office of the Secretary of Defense (OSD) provides budgetary and financial recommendations to the Secretary relating to OE strategy.[240]

5.4 National Security, Defense, and OE Strategies

Beyond legal requirements, the US government produces several key documents which help to shape OE strategy. The White House issues the *US National Security Strategy* (NSS) that outlines the US government's key national security priorities. The civilian leadership of the US DOD issues the *National Defense Strategy*, which outlines the Pentagon's top defense priorities. Both documents are usually issued every four years near the start of a new administration. These documents help to frame the *Operational Energy Strategy*, which the DOD is required to submit to Congress every five years. Each US military service branch also develops and publishes OE service plans. DOD is also required to submit an annual report to Congress certifying that its budget is meeting the goals laid out in the *Operational Energy Strategy.*

---

[239] Congressional Research Service, "Defense Primer: The NDAA Process," *In Focus*, December 6, 2021 (https://sgp.fas.org/crs/natsec/IF10515.pdf).
[240] Department of Defense, *Directive 4180.01: Energy Policy*, April 16, 2014 (https://www.esd.whs.mil/Portals/54/Documents/DD/issuances/dodd/418001.pdf?ver=2018-11-07-112520-837).

Each administration's specific strategic priorities affect its directions on OE. For instance, the Trump administration placed emphasis on DOD promoting American "energy dominance." In contrast, the Biden administration has emphasized the military's potential role in "the clean energy transition."

By the late 2010s, the *National Security Strategy* began to address OE. The 2018 *National Security Strategy* tasked DOD: "There should be resilient and agile logistics [...] and that [...] [i]nvestments will prioritize prepositioned forward stocks and munitions, strategic mobility assets, partner and allied support, as well as non-commercially dependent distributed logistics and maintenance to ensure logistics sustainment while under persistent multi-domain attack."[241]

The 2022 *National Defense Strategy* referred to several energy issues. The document discussed the threat from Iran to threatened key chokepoints and to obstruct the global "free flow of energy resources."[242] It pledged research and development funds for directed energy weapons and clean energy technology[243] to leverage commercial developments in renewable energy generation and storage,[244] to "make reducing energy demand a priority, and seek to adopt more efficient and clean-energy technologies that reduce logistics requirements in contested or austere environments."[245]

The 2022 *National Defense Strategy* outlines an operational environment where "every domain is contested – air, land, sea, space, and cyberspace" and emphasizes that the "homeland is no longer a sanctuary."[246] It points out that "Preparing for the battlefield of 2025 and sustaining resilient installations necessitates the assured delivery of cyber-secure fuel and power in contested environments against near-peer competitors."[247]

The DOD's strategic guidance is further encapsulated in the DOD *Operational Energy Strategy*, which the Pentagon is required to submit to Congress every five years. The first DOD *Operational Energy Strategy* was released in 2011. The 2016 *Operational En-*

---

[241] Department of Defense, *National Defense Strategy*, 2018, page 7 (https://dod.defense.gov/Portals/1/Documents/pubs/2018-National-Defense-Strategy-Summary.pdf).
[242] Department of Defense, *National Defense Strategy*, October 27, 2022 (https://media.defense.gov/2022/Oct/27/2003103845/-1/-1/1/2022-NATIONAL-DEFENSE-STRATEGY-NPR-MDR.PDF).
[243] Department of Defense, *National Defense Strategy*, October 27, 2022 (https://media.defense.gov/2022/Oct/27/2003103845/-1/-1/1/2022-NATIONAL-DEFENSE-STRATEGY-NPR-MDR.PDF).
[244] Department of Defense, *National Defense Strategy*, October 27, 2022 (https://media.defense.gov/2022/Oct/27/2003103845/-1/-1/1/2022-NATIONAL-DEFENSE-STRATEGY-NPR-MDR.PDF).
[245] Department of Defense, *National Defense Strategy*, October 27, 2022 (https://media.defense.gov/2022/Oct/27/2003103845/-1/-1/1/2022-NATIONAL-DEFENSE-STRATEGY-NPR-MDR.PDF).
[246] Department of Defense, *National Defense Strategy*, October 27, 2022 (https://media.defense.gov/2022/Oct/27/2003103845/-1/-1/1/2022-NATIONAL-DEFENSE-STRATEGY-NPR-MDR.PDF).
[247] Department of Defense, *National Defense Strategy*, October 27, 2022 (https://media.defense.gov/2022/Oct/27/2003103845/-1/-1/1/2022-NATIONAL-DEFENSE-STRATEGY-NPR-MDR.PDF).

ergy Strategy has three broad pillars:[248] First, it calls for using OE to increase "future warfighter capability." It says that in the process of developing future military capabilities, the military should analyze the energy that would be needed to support them. It also calls for innovation to support both combat effectiveness and the ability for OE to support such tools. Secondly, it calls for DOD to "Identify and reduce logistics and operational risks" through war games, modeling, simulation, and other analytical tools. Finally, the strategy contained several near-term initiatives to improve the robustness and flexibility of the energy supply chain, enhance the ability to operate in contested environments, and support the rebalance to the Indo-Pacific region.

The 2023 *Operational Energy Strategy* states that "the Operational Energy Strategy will ensure that Joint Forces have the energy needed to fight and win in contested environments through four lines of effort: Energy Demand Reduction; Energy Substitution and Diversification; Supply Chain Resilience; and Enterprise-wide Energy Visibility."[249]

The 2023 *Operational Energy Strategy* states:

> Energy is an essential enabler of military capability, and the Department depends on energy resilient forces and weapon systems to achieve its mission. However, contested logistics, reliance on commercial technology and infrastructure, and the imperative to understand the Department's energy use each pose challenges to ensuring energy secure forces in competition, crisis, and conflict.[250]

5.5 OE Institutions

The 2009 National Defense Authorization Act mandated that DOD appoint a Director of Operational Energy Plans and Programs and that OE policy development fall under the Assistant Secretary of Defense for Energy, Installations, and Environment (ASD)(EI&E). Congress called for the Assistant Secretary to oversee OE policy; certify the budget for DOD alternative fuel activities; and, in consultation with the heads of the appropriate DOD components, prepare the annual *Report on Operational Energy Management* and implementation of the *Operational Energy Strategy*.[251] Congress also required that the

---

248 Department of Defense, *2016 Operational Energy Strategy*, December 3, 2015 (https://www.acq.osd.mil/eie/Downloads/OE/2016%20OE%20Strategy_WEBd.pdf); Department of Defense, *Fiscal Year 2022 Operational Energy Budget Certification Report*, December 2021, page 2 (https://www.acq.osd.mil/eie/Downloads/OE/FY22%20OE%20Budget%20Certification%20Report.pdf).
249 Department of Defense, *2023 Operational Energy Strategy*, May 2023 (https://www.acq.osd.mil/eie/Downloads/OE/2023%20Operational%20Energy%20Strategy.pdf).
250 Department of Defense, 2023, *Operational Energy Strategy*, May 2023 (https://www.acq.osd.mil/eie/Downloads/OE/2023%20Operational%20Energy%20Strategy.pdf).
251 Title 10, United States Code, section 2926(e)(4), requires that the Secretary of Defense submit a report on each military department's and defense agency's budget estimate for activities associated with implementing the *Operational Energy Strategy 2*, which were previously reviewed and certified by the

US Secretary of Defense consider the fully burdened cost of fuel and energy efficiency in planning, capability requirements development, and acquisition processes.

Over time, the OE mission has been housed in different parts of the DOD bureaucracy. At the time of publication, responsibilities for OE guidance development resided in the Office of the Assistant Secretary of Defense for Sustainment.[252] This Senate-confirmed individual advises and assists the Secretary of Defense, the Deputy Secretary of Defense, and the Under Secretary of Defense for Acquisition and Sustainment (USD(A&S)) with respect to the facilities, energy, infrastructure, logistics, materiel readiness, and product support needed to execute worldwide missions.

As of early 2024, the point person for OE in the US DOD is the Deputy Assistant Secretary of Defense for Energy Resilience & Optimization (ER&O), who reports to the Office of the Assistant Secretary of Defense for Energy, Installations, and Environment, which reports to the Under Secretary of Defense for Acquisition & Sustainment

5.6 Requirements of the Different Services

Congress required each of the services, through each respective secretary – Army, Navy, and Air Force – to designate a senior official accountable for OE programs.[253] Each of the services has complied with this requirement by creating an Operational Energy office. Each service already had an Assistant Secretary for Energy, Installations, and Environment (for the Navy, this is the ASN (E, I & E); for the Air Force, it is the ASAF (E, I & E), and for the Army, it is the ASA (E, I & E). Then, each service created a Deputy Assistant Secretary for Operational Energy.

Under Secretary of Defense for Acquisition and Sustainment (USD(A&S)) as either adequate or inadequate for implementing the objectives of the *Operational Energy Strategy.* Reference: Office of the Law Revision Counsel, "United States Code: 10 USC 2926: Operational Energy," June 17, 2023 (https://uscode.house.gov/view.xhtml?req=granuleid:USC-prelim-title10-section2926&num=0&edition=prelim).
252 Department of Defense, *Directive 4180.01: Energy Policy,* April 16, 2014 (https://www.esd.whs.mil/Portals/54/Documents/DD/issuances/dodd/418001.pdf?ver=2018-11-07-112520-837); Office of the Assistant Secretary of Defense for Sustainment, "Operational Energy," (https://www.acq.osd.mil/eie/OE/OE_index.html).
253 Rep. Ike Skelton, "National Defense Authorization Act for Fiscal Year 2008," January 28, 2008 (https://www.congress.gov/bill/110th-congress/house-bill/4986).

5.7 US DOD Institutions

5.7.1 US Transportation Command and the Defense Logistics Agency

The US Transportation Command serves as the single manager for global bulk fuel management and delivery.

Defense Logistics Agency-Energy (DLA-Energy) is the major logistical support in DOD for its energy needs. DLA-Energy works with the private sector and others to ensure there is enough energy of many types for operations in battle and outside of battle. It is important to know how DLA-Energy works and how to be part of and use the DLA-Energy system.[254]

DLA "manages the end-to-end global defense supply chain – from raw materials to end user disposition – for the five military services, eleven combatant commands, other federal, state, and local agencies and partner and allied nations [...] [their] mission is to "deliver readiness and lethality to the Warfighter Always and support our nation through quality, proactive global logistics."[255]

After the release of the 2022 *National Defense Strategy*, General Jacqueline Van Ovost, commander of the US Transportation Command said the command "was given the responsibility of the Department's single manager for global bulk fuel." She stated that "partnering with DLA's capability and experience, TRANSCOM will focus on the synchronization of posture, planning, execution, and advocacy for resources to meet the energy needs of the joint force in a contested environment." This is intended to ensure fuel will be transported to vital locations and can get to the warfighting units during conflict, while reducing the threat to this resource.[256]

The Military Sealift Command is critical for supply of the OE needs of the US Navy. The Military Sealift Command operates over a hundred civilian-crewed ships that supply US Navy ships, preposition combat cargo at sea around the globe, and transit US military cargo and supplies for US forces and coalitions partners.

---

[254] Mason Carpenter, Paul Sullivan, and Dan Nussbaum, "Operational Energy: Essential Knowledge for Military Officers" (https://nps.edu/web/eag/operational-energy-essential-knowledge-for-military-officers).
[255] Defense Logistics Agency, "About the Defense Logistics Agency" (https://www.dla.mil/AboutDLA/).
[256] Scott D. Ross, "US Transportation Command in 2023: An Eye to the Future," US Transportation Command, December 12, 2022 (https://www.ustranscom.mil/cmd/panewsreader.cfm?ID=414027D4-C202-2000-3D6A36F927C81FE2&yr=2022).

5.8 For Study

- Understand US law on OE.
- Read and understand the key provisions of the 2018 and 2022 *National Defense Strategy* and the full 2016 and 2023 *Operational Energy Strategy*.
- Understand the responsibilities of the Assistant Secretary of Defense for Sustainment and the Deputy Assistant Secretary of Defense for Sustainment (Energy and Energy Resilience). Names of these offices responsible for OE may change in the future.
- Learn the service offices that are responsible for the OE mission.
- Understand how US law on OE has been implemented by OSD, the services, the Defense Logistics Agency, and US Transportation Command.

5.9 Topics for Discussion and Research

- What motivated Congress to direct the DOD to develop OE policies?
- The 2018 *National Defense Strategy* states that a goal of OE policy is to "increase lethality." Discuss ways that OE policy can further this goal.
- Who is responsible for overseeing OE issues in DOD and the services?
- How does the 2023 *National Security Strategy* characterize the current challenges to the US OE mission?
- What are the roles of the Defense Logistics Agency, US Transportation Command, and the Military Sealift Command in OE?

5.10 Case Study: The Colonial Pipeline Cyberattack

The May 7, 2021 Colonial Pipeline cyberattack was one of the largest attacks on critical infrastructure in American history. The US military acquires most of its fuel supplies at home and abroad through civilian suppliers and commercial infrastructure. Thus, disruptions of civilian critical energy infrastructure can affect both civilian and military operations. This case examines the details of the Colonial Pipeline attack and analyzes ways in which the US military can reduce risks from its use of civilian suppliers. The case also examines the increased threats stemming from the digitalization of energy infrastructure.

5.10.1 Background

Approximately 2.5 million miles of pipelines transport crude and refined oil products across the United States. This pipeline network is generally able to withstand a variety of natural and manmade disasters. Yet, this sector has become increasingly vulnerable to cyber and other attacks with the addition to the system of thousands of networked devices that meter and monitor flow and pressure.[257] Digitalization improves efficiency and has other benefits but also creates increased vulnerabilities to cyber and other attacks.

5.10.2 The Colonial Pipeline

The Colonial Pipeline is the longest pipeline in the USA delivering refined oil products. The pipeline transports 100 million gallons of petroleum products per day, or roughly 45 percent of the gasoline, diesel, and jet fuel consumed on the US East Coast. Originally founded in 1962, the Colonial Pipeline Company (CPC) is privately held and headquartered in Alpharetta, Georgia. Five commercial entities own the Colonial Pipeline Company: CDPQ Colonial Partners, L.P.; IFM (US) Colonial Pipeline 2, LLC; KKR-Keats Pipeline Investors, L.P.; Koch Capital Investments Company, LLC; and Shell Midstream Operating, LLC. The pipeline extends 5500 miles from Houston to New York Harbor and includes 28 million barrels of storage capacity. It is a dual-pipe network with distribution terminals connecting more than a dozen major international airports and industrial centers. The pipeline can carry more than eighty types of products but transports mainly gasoline, diesel, heating oil, and jet fuel.[258]

Since its inception, the Colonial Pipeline has been at the forefront of systems automation, moving from a manual or paper-based management environment into a digitized one. These have included efforts to improve asset management and the use of condition-based and predictive maintenance computer tools as well as a separate operational technology (OT) network to meter, monitor, and control product flows. This technology has helped CPC maintain its system and wring economies of scale from its large and complex operations.[259]

5.10.3 Importance to US National Security

The Colonial Pipeline system is critical to the US economy and national security. It delivers fuel supplies to the nation's capital and major military facilities (including the Pentagon) located in the Mid-Atlantic region. It also provides fuel to numerous East Coast Power Projection Platforms, critical logistical and operational nodes in this coun-

---

[257] Congressional Research Service, "Colonial Pipeline: The DarkSide Strikes," *CRS Insight*, May 11, 2021 (https://crsreports.congress.gov/product/pdf/IN/IN11667).
[258] It generally takes from fourteen to twenty-four days for a batch of fuel to get from Houston, Texas to the New York Harbor, with an average of 18.5 days. Colonial Pipeline, "About Us" (https://www.colpipe.com/).
[259] Colonial Pipeline, "Assessment Management" (https://www.colpipe.com/).

try's vast overseas military network. These include Aerial Ports of Embarkation (APOE), such as Dover Air Force Base, and Sea Ports of Embarkation (SPOE), such as the massive naval facilities (Naval Station Norfolk) in the Norfolk, Virginia area, the world's largest naval complex.[260] Moreover, the Strategic Highway Network (STRAHNET)[261] and Strategic Rail Corridor Network (STRACNET),[262] key transportation assets in the event of national emergencies, are both tied into the Colonial Pipeline.

This civilian transportation network aids both homeland security and disaster relief efforts. The nation's dependence on the effectiveness and resilience of a private pipeline is typical. Most US critical energy infrastructure is owned and operated by private companies. Close cooperation is necessary between the private companies that own and operate the US critical energy infrastructure and federal, state, and local governments. In addition, the US military needs a reliable system and rules of interaction with these private companies.

5.10.4 Pipeline Performance

The Colonial Pipeline has proven resilient to extreme weather and natural disasters. It has withstood some of the most severe hurricanes to hit the US East Coast. While the pipeline itself has never been damaged by storms, operations have been curtailed or shutdown due to power outages affecting pumping stations and supply shortages to refineries, and as a preventive measure. For instance, Colonial closed its main pipeline as a precautionary measure before Hurricane Sandy made landfall in October 2012,[263] as did East Coast oil refineries, amid concern that the storm could breach plant defenses and cause damage.[264] The storm itself did not damage the pipeline; however, flooding and the loss of power at its terminus outside New York City (Linden, New Jersey) caused the CPC to shut down the segment of its mainline system serving Philadelphia,

---

260 GlobalSecurity.org, "Sea Port of Embarkation (SPOE)" (https://www.globalsecurity.org/military/facility/spoe.htm).
261 GlobalSecurity.org, "Strategic Highway Network (STRAHNET)" (https://www.globalsecurity.org/military/facility/strahnet.htm).
262 GlobalSecurity.org, "Strategic Rail Corridor Network (STRACNET)" (https://www.globalsecurity.org/military/facility/stracnet.htm).
263 Janet McGurty, "Sandy Cuts East Coast Fuel Supply; Refiners, Pipelines Shut," Reuters, October 29, 2012 (https://www.reuters.com/article/us-storm-sandy-refining/sandy-cuts-east-coast-fuel-supply-refiners-pipelines-shut-idUKBRE89S17620121029).
264 Janet McGurty, "Sandy Cuts East Coast Fuel Supply; Refiners, Pipelines Shut," *Reuters*, October 29, 2012 (https://www.reuters.com/article/us-storm-sandy-refining/sandy-cuts-east-coast-fuel-supply-refiners-pipelines-shut-idUKBRE89S17620121029).

New Jersey, and New York Harbor. Colonial brought in portable generators to power the terminus facility and restored normal operations within five days.[265]

5.10.5 IT Performance

Until the May 2021 event, there had not been any reported cyberattacks on the pipeline. Still, beginning in 2017, four independent cybersecurity assessments spotted deficiencies, prompting a 50 percent increase in IT spending in the period before the May 2021 attack.[266] A January 2018 report identified serious deficiencies, such as limited security-awareness training for employees to thwart phishing schemes, the cause of more than 90 percent of cyber-intrusions. Following the report, Colonial expanded its cybersecurity regime to include regular simulated phishing campaigns. Additionally, the 2018 report noted inadequate network security to the extent that "an eighth grader could have hacked into that system." One of the report's recommendations was that Colonial hire a chief information security officer, a position that cybersecurity experts consider essential in any company with such vital infrastructure.[267]

Colonial did implement some recommendations, such as active monitoring and overlapping threat-detection systems, which identified the DarkSide hack, as well as enhancing its data-loss-prevention capability (supported by three different software tools) to alert operators when data is removed from the network. However, deficiencies remained by the time of the May 2021 attack, perhaps most notably the lack of a chief information security officer (CISO) and weak security-awareness training. Another deficiency at the time of the ransomware attack was the lack of multifactor authentication, which could have prevented or delayed the attack. In Colonial's defense, it was in the process of advertising for the CISO position in May 2021. In fact, this position had been open for over thirty days, indicating the challenge many companies face trying to hire qualified employees in the sphere of cybersecurity.

It should also be noted that, unlike American utilities, the US government has not subjected pipelines to mandatory cyber standards.[268]

---

265 The Association for Convenience & Fuel Retailing, "When Mother Nature Strikes," May 1, 2017 (https://www.convenience.org/Topics/Fuels/When-Mother-Nature-Strikes).
266 Jamie Crawford and Veronica Stracqualursi, "Colonial Pipeline Returns to 'Normal Operations' after Restart," *CNN*, May 15, 2021 (https://www.cnn.com/2021/05/15/politics/colonial-pipeline-returns-normal-operations/index.html).
267 Spectrum Local News, "2018 Audit Found 'Glaring Deficiencies' at Pipeline Company," *Associated Press* (Boston), May 12, 2021 (https://spectrumlocalnews.com/ap-top-news/2021/05/12/2018-audit-found-glaring-deficiencies-at-pipeline-company).
268 Spectrum Local News, "2018 Audit Found 'Glaring Deficiencies' at Pipeline Company," *Associated Press* (Boston), May 12, 2021 (https://spectrumlocalnews.com/ap-top-news/2021/05/12/2018-audit-found-glaring-deficiencies-at-pipeline-company).

5.10.6 Anatomy of the Attack: Events of May 7, 2021, and After

Colonial first learned of the attack shortly before 5 AM on Friday, May 7, when an employee discovered a ransom note on the company IT network. Hackers had "exfiltrated" 100 GB of data from the company's shared internal drive and demanded approximately five million dollars in exchange for the files. The company CEO, Joseph Blount, later provided the US Senate Committee on Homeland Security and Governmental Affairs with a detailed overview of events: "At approximately 5:55 AM employees began to shutdown, which was confirmed by 6:10 AM, all 5,500 miles of pipelines had been shut down," Blount testified, adding that the decision to shut down the entire pipeline was "the imperative to isolate and contain the attack to [...] ensure the malware did not spread to the Operational Technology network, which controls our pipeline operations, if it had not already." That Colonial preemptively shut down its OT networks after its IT networks were compromised indicates its two systems could be connected.[269]

By 7 AM CPC management had hired FireEye to conduct a forensic assessment of the damage. Its investigators attributed the attack to the Russian criminal group DarkSide, responsible for forty previous ransomware attacks that included demands ranging from 200,000 to over two million dollars.[270] Also, by 7 AM CPC engaged external legal counsel and consultants to negotiate with the hackers. This external legal expertise was needed to determine that DarkSide was not under sanction, in order to allow the company to pay the ransom without violating US law.[271]

Within twenty-four hours the company paid the hackers $4.4 million in cryptocurrency (Bitcoin).[272] CEO Blount said: "I made the decision to pay, and I made the decision to keep the information about the payment as confidential as possible," Blount later said. "I kept the information closely held because we were concerned about operation-

---

[269] William Turton and Kartikay Mehrotra, "Hackers Breached Colonial Pipeline Using Compromised Password," *Bloomberg*, June 4, 2021 (https://www.bloomberg.com/news/articles/2021-06-04/hackers-breached-colonial-pipeline-using-compromised-password).

[270] Ron Brash, "Colonial Pipeline Attack: Lessons Learned for Ransomware Protection," *Verve* (blog), May 10, 2021 (https://verveindustrial.com/resources/blog/colonial-pipeline-attack-lessons-learned-for-ransomware-protection/).

[271] Geneva Sands and Brian Fung, "Colonial Pipeline CEO Defends His Handling of Ransomware Attack That Crippled East Coast Supply," *CNN*, June 8, 2021 (https://www.cnn.com/2021/06/08/politics/colonial-pipeline-ceo-on-capitol-hill-ransomware/index.html).

[272] On May 7, 2021, this amounted to 75 Bitcoins, each worth $56,508 for the total of $4.2M USD. Andrew Morse, "Colonial Pipeline CEO Tells Senate Decision to Pay Hackers Was Made Quickly," *CNET*, June 8, 2021 (https://www.cnet.com/tech/services-and-software/colonial-pipeline-ceo-tells-senate-decision-to-pay-hackers-was-made-quickly/).

al safety and security, and we wanted to stay focused on getting the pipeline back up and running."[273]

While Colonial had full data backup, it still paid the ransom. While some questioned this decision (the backup should have enabled CPC to restore the data infrastructure), the attack was a double extortion; instead of threatening to delete the data if the ransom was not paid, a double extortion attack threatens to leak proprietary or sensitive data for a failure to comply.[274]

Colonial did not have a ransomware response plan, and thus made these decisions in response to the attack. Regardless, the company succeeded in isolating the problem by disconnecting the system from the internet and brought in experts to assess the damage and recover the system. Blount said: "What we learned was, being transparent and responding quickly and not being afraid to come forward is probably one of the most important things that we did in this particular case."[275]

5.10.6.1 Pipeline Recovery Actions

Within forty-eight hours of the attack, Colonial had received the decryption key needed to access its data, although employees found the process of resuming operations slow and laborious. The pipeline restarted operations on May 13 and returned to full capacity operations ten days after the attack, on May 17. However, it took about two weeks for fuel from Houston, Texas to reach final destinations along the East Coast,[276] since it generally takes from fourteen to twenty-four days for a batch to get from Houston, Texas to the New York Harbor, with 18.5 days the average time.[277]

---

[273] Andrew Morse, "Colonial Pipeline CEO Tells Senate Decision to Pay Hackers Was Made Quickly," *CNET*, June 8, 2021 (https://www.cnet.com/tech/services-and-software/colonial-pipeline-ceo-tells-senate-decision-to-pay-hackers-was-made-quickly/).
[274] Jack M. Germain, "Dissecting the Colonial Pipeline Incident," *ECT News Network*, May 20, 2021 (https://www.technewsworld.com/story/dissecting-the-colonial-pipeline-incident-87138.html).
[275] Geneva Sands and Brian Fung, "Colonial Pipeline CEO Defends His Handling of Ransomware Attack That Crippled East Coast Supply," *CNN*, June 8, 2021 (https://www.cnn.com/2021/06/08/politics/colonial-pipeline-ceo-on-capitol-hill-ransomware/index.html).
[276] Products move through the main lines at a rate of about 3 to 5 miles per hour (4.8 to 8.0 km/h). Max Pyziur and Lucian Pugliaresi, "Colonial Pipeline Hack Highlights Growing Energy Security Risks," June 2021 (https://eprinc.org/2021/06/colonial-pipeline-hack-highlights-growing-energy-security-risks-report-by-lucian-pugliaresi-and-max-pyziur/#sthash.K79s6Mue.dpbs).
[277] Max Pyziur and Lucian Pugliaresi, "Colonial Pipeline Hack Highlights Growing Energy Security Risks," June 2021 (https://eprinc.org/2021/06/colonial-pipeline-hack-highlights-growing-energy-security-risks-report-by-lucian-pugliaresi-and-max-pyziur/#sthash.K79s6Mue.dpbs).

5.10.6.2 What Was Targeted and How?

The pipeline was hacked through an unused, though still active, single authentication virtual private network (VPN). Interestingly, the system was initially hacked in late April, after which the attackers bided their time and observed developments. A careless or disgruntled former employee divulged the password, where it ended up on the dark web.[278] During his June 8 testimony to the Senate committee, Blount said, "It was a complicated password [...] so I want to be clear on that. It was not a 'Colonial123'-type password."[279]

5.10.6.3 The Perpetrators

The US Department of Justice and the FBI both assessed that DarkSide, a Russian cybercriminal hacking group, likely conducted the attack.[280] The Russian government seems to allow DarkSide to operate without interference. The motivation was probably money. DarkSide claimed its attacks promote a professional "experience," focusing on providing "quality products" to its "consumers." The hackers only attack those who have the means to pay or are known to have cybersecurity insurance. The group also utilizes double extortion – victims pay for unencrypting their data or, failing that, the group blackmails them with the threat of public release of data exfiltrated as part of the crime.[281] Hence CPC's decision to pay the ransom.

By Monday, May 10, DarkSide, potentially under pressure from the Kremlin, international publicity, and the focused governmental and law enforcement efforts in the wake of the incident, expressed contrition for the Colonial Pipeline attack. The group stated: "We are apolitical. We do not participate in geopolitics, do not need to tie us with a defined government and look for other our motives. Our goal is to make money, and not creating problems for society." DarkSide vowed to halt further attack on utilities, such as Colonial. "From today we introduce moderation and check each company that our partners want to encrypt to avoid social consequences in the future."[282] On May 13, DarkSide claimed its servers and other equipment had

---

278 William Turton and Kartikay Mehrotra, "Hackers Breached Colonial Pipeline Using Compromised Password," *Bloomberg*, June 4, 2021 (https://www.bloomberg.com/news/articles/2021-06-04/hackers-breached-colonial-pipeline-using-compromised-password).
279 Geneva Sands and Brian Fung, "Colonial Pipeline CEO Defends His Handling of Ransomware Attack That Crippled East Coast Supply," *CNN*, June 8, 2021 (https://www.cnn.com/2021/06/08/politics/colonial-pipeline-ceo-on-capitol-hill-ransomware/index.html).
280 Max Pyziur and Lucian Pugliaresi, "Colonial Pipeline Hack Highlights Growing Energy Security Risks," June 2021 (https://eprinc.org/2021/06/colonial-pipeline-hack-highlights-growing-energy-security-risks-report-by-lucian-pugliaresi-and-max-pyziur/#sthash.K79s6Mue.dpbs).
281 Jack M. Germain, "Dissecting the Colonial Pipeline Incident," *ECT News Network*, May 20, 2021 (https://www.technewsworld.com/story/dissecting-the-colonial-pipeline-incident-87138.html).
282 Robert McMillan and Dustin Volz, "Colonial Pipeline Hacker DarkSide Says It Will Shut Operations," *Wall Street Journal*, May 14, 2021 (https://www.wsj.com/articles/web-site-of-darkside-hacking-group-linked-to-colonial-pipeline-attack-is-down-11621001688?mod=Searchresults_pos16&page=7).

been confiscated, but did not elaborate. On May 27, court records show, a sum including 63.7 bitcoins traced to the Colonial ransom landed at a final address, where the FBI seized the funds.[283]

US President Biden stated, "We do not believe the Russian government was involved in this attack, but we do have strong reason to believe the criminals who did this attack are living in Russia."[284]

5.10.7 Impact and Recovery

One of the immediate results of the attack on the Colonial Pipeline was a spike in gasoline prices in the United States. As markets opened Sunday evening May 9, gasoline futures were up about 1.6 percent at 2.16 dollars a gallon, after briefly rising more than 3 percent.[285]

On May 7, it was estimated East Coast gasoline inventories would last 26.5 days, with 64.6 million barrels stockpiled. Soon, long lines appeared at gas stations along the Eastern Seaboard amid warnings of shortages. On Wednesday, May 12, the average US price of gasoline stood above $3 a gallon for the first time in over six years.

5.10.7.1 Fuel Hoarding
The attack triggered consumer panic buying and fuel hoarding even though there was not an actual fuel shortage. The Departments of Energy and Homeland Security reported the country could afford only another three to five days without Colonial Pipeline supplies before buses and other mass transit would have to limit operations from a lack of diesel fuel. East Coast-based chemical plants and refineries would also shut down because they would not be receiving oil; flight schedules were disrupted and many flights were canceled. Alternative ways to haul gasoline and jet fuel up the East Coast were not immediately in place. There was also a shortage of truck drivers and of tanker cars for trains.[286]

---

[283] David Uberti, "How the FBI Got Colonial Pipeline's Ransom Money Back," *Wall Street Journal*, June 11, 2021 (https://www.wsj.com/articles/how-the-fbi-got-colonial-pipelines-ransom-money-back-11623403981).
[284] "Pipeline Attack Yields Urgent Lessons about U.S. Cybersecurity," *New York Times*, June 8, 2021.
[285] Collin Eaton, James Rundle, and David Uberti, "US Pipeline Shutdown Exposes Cyber Threat to Energy Sector," *Wall Street Journal*, May 9, 2021 (https://www.wsj.com/articles/u-s-pipeline-shutdown-exposes-cyber-threat-to-energy-sector-11620574464?mod=Searchresults_pos15&page=9).
[286] David E. Sanger and Nicole Perlroth, "Pipeline Attack Yields Urgent Lessons about US Cybersecurity," May 14, 2021 (https://www.nytimes.com/2021/05/14/us/politics/pipeline-hack.html).

5.10.8 US Federal and State Government Response

The initial White House response to the attack on Colonial Pipeline was standoffish, treating the attack on the pipeline and the subsequent fuel supply disruption as a commercial matter. In fact, US Secretary of Energy Jennifer Granholm used the case to promote use of electric vehicles that are not dependent on liquid fuels. At a press conference following the attack, Secretary Granholm stated: "you know, if you drive an electric car, this would not be affecting you, clearly."[287]

To alleviate the impact of the attack, the Department of Transportation temporarily halted implementation[288] of some federal regulations and issued an emergency "hours of service exemption" for transporting fuel along the East Coast.[289] Additionally, states of emergency were declared in many East Coast states in response to the shortages.[290] For example, Georgia Governor Brian Kemp temporarily suspended the state's gas tax to compensate for the increased prices, while other states enacted anti-price gouging laws.[291]

As the crisis evolved, the administration changed its approach and recognized the public implications. On May 12, President Biden issued Executive Order 14028 to strengthen national cybersecurity.[292] The order included the creation of a Cyber Safety Review Board that will convene after major incidents. Members of the Departments of Defense and Justice and several security agencies and private sector specialists will be on the board. The Executive Order also directs "threat intelligence sharing between different agencies and between providers and federal agencies; modernizing federal government IT infrastructure; enhancing software supply chain security; establishing a Federal Government plan for responding to cyber incidents and vulnerabilities; improving detection of cyber incidents; improving the Federal Government's Investigative and Re-

---

[287] Press Secretary Jen Psaki, Secretary of Energy Jennifer Granholm, and Secretary of Homeland Security Alejandro Mayorkas, "Press Briefing" (The White House), May 11, 2021 (https://www.whitehouse.gov/briefing-room/press-briefings/2021/05/11/press-briefing-by-press-secretary-jen-psaki-secretary-of-energy-jennifer-granholm-and-secretary-of-homeland-security-alejandro-mayorkas-may-11-2021/).
[288] United States Department of Transportation, Regional Emergency Declaration, Under 49 CFR § 390.23, No. 2021–002, May 9, 2021 (https://www.fmcsa.dot.gov/emergency/esc-ssc-wsc-regional-emergency-declaration-2021-002-05-09-2021).
[289] Charlie Osborne, "Colonial Pipeline Cyberattack," *Zero Day*, May 13, 2021 (https://www.zdnet.com/article/colonial-pipeline-ransomware-attack-everything-you-need-to-know/).
[290] United States Department of Transportation, Regional Emergency Declaration, Under 49 CFR § 390.23, No. 2021–002, May 9, 2021 (https://www.fmcsa.dot.gov/emergency/esc-ssc-wsc-regional-emergency-declaration-2021-002-05-09-2021).
[291] State of Georgia, Attorney General's Office, "Carr: Kemp Declares State of Emergency Due to Colonial Pipeline Cyber Incident, Invokes Price Gouging Statute," May 11, 2021 (https://law.georgia.gov/press-releases/2021-05-11/carr-kemp-declares-state-emergency-due-colonial-pipeline-cyber-incident).
[292] The White House, "Executive Order 14028: Improving the Nation's Cybersecurity," May 12, 2021 (https://www.govinfo.gov/content/pkg/FR-2021-05-17/pdf/2021-10460.pdf).

mediation Capabilities; and improving Department of Defense National Security Systems."[293]

On May 27, the DHS issued a Security Directive requiring critical pipeline owners and operators to report confirmed and potential cybersecurity incidents to the DHS Cybersecurity and Infrastructure Security Agency and to designate a Cybersecurity Coordinator, available twenty-four hours a day, seven days a week. It also required critical pipeline owners and operators to review their current practices as well as to identify gaps and related remediation measures to address cyber-related risks and report the results to the DHS within thirty days.[294] On June 7, the US Department of Justice announced that its Ransomware and Digital Extortion Task Force recovered 63.7 of the 75 bitcoins paid to DarkSide. The FBI has not divulged how it recovered the Bitcoin, but, in effect, "stole back" the ransom.[295] Following the event, the White House convened relevant government and commercial representatives to discuss cooperation and best practices to prevent and respond to future cyberattacks on critical infrastructure.[296]

5.10.8.1 Balance between Commercial and Government Oversight
The US will depend on petroleum derived liquid fuels for years to come. The US fuel pipeline network, while admittedly aging, is integrated, efficient, and generally well-managed. However, the use of advanced technologies, especially digitalization, has exposed the US pipeline network to a new set of threats. While the Colonial Pipeline is perhaps the largest and most important US pipeline network, other pipelines that transfer crude, refined products, natural gas, or electricity have similar network-based vulnerabilities.

These pipelines are owned and operated by the private sector, yet their adequate functioning has significant public and national security implications. The private sector seeks to manage these extensive infrastructure networks at maximum efficiency, while providing for adequate threat prevention and post-event resilience. This is not an easy balancing act. All levels of government have vital roles to play regarding legis-

---

[293] The White House, "Executive Order 14028: Improving the Nation's Cybersecurity," May 12, 2021 (https://www.govinfo.gov/content/pkg/FR-2021-05-17/pdf/2021-10460.pdf).
[294] Geneva Sands and Brian Fung, "Colonial Pipeline CEO Defends His Handling of Ransomware Attack That Crippled East Coast Supply," *CNN*, June 8, 2021 (https://www.cnn.com/2021/06/08/politics/colonial-pipeline-ceo-on-capitol-hill-ransomware/index.html).
[295] David Uberti, "How the FBI Got Colonial Pipeline's Ransom Money Back," *Wall Street Journal*, June 11, 2021 (https://www.wsj.com/articles/how-the-fbi-got-colonial-pipelines-ransom-money-back-11623403981).
[296] The White House, "Fact Sheet: Biden Administration and Private Sector Leaders Announce Ambitious Initiatives to Bolster the Nation's Cybersecurity," August 25, 2021 (https://www.whitehouse.gov/briefing-room/statements-releases/2021/08/25/fact-sheet-biden-administration-and-private-sector-leaders-announce-ambitious-initiatives-to-bolster-the-nations-cybersecurity/).

lative oversight for safety, revenue generation, and environmental reasons and need to determine division of responsibility between the government and commercial entities.

5.10.9 Topics for Discussion and Research

- Discuss the lessons that the military should learn from the Colonial Pipeline case regarding OE.
- Discuss the balance between government oversight and commercial management of critical energy infrastructure. Should government take a larger role in management or regulating civilian critical energy infrastructure? If so, what role?
- What are the formal channels of communication between the US military and relevant commercial companies, and local, state, and federal governments regarding stable fuel, natural gas, and electricity supplies to US military installations? How can they be improved?
- What are the formal channels of communication between the US military and relevant commercial companies, and foreign governments regarding stable fuel, natural gas, and electricity supplies to US military installations and operations abroad? How can they be improved?
- How should local, state, and federal government interface with commercial entities during attacks on critical infrastructure?
- Which emergency powers should be legislated to secure supplies to the US military during cases of disruption to commercial infrastructure and commercially supplied energy?
- Increased digitization of critical energy infrastructure improves efficiency. However, it also creates new vulnerabilities. Discuss the tradeoffs and the appropriate balance.
- Following the attack, the US Department of Transportation and several relevant state governors exempted fuel deliveries from some regulations. Discuss these exemptions and propose which exemptions should be in place during future critical energy infrastructure disruptions.
- Discuss public communications during times of attacks or other disruption of critical energy infrastructure. Which messages should the US government and relevant commercial entities disseminate to prevent hoarding of energy and other public response?
- The US military relies primarily on fuel supplies from commercial supply lines and entities. What are the lessons from the case of the Colonial Pipeline for reducing US military energy supply disruptions? Should the US military change its reliance on commercial supply lines?
- Is the US military trained and equipped to contend with a Colonial Pipeline type incident in the future?

6 Operational Energy Vulnerability and Resilience

Daniel A. Eisenberg and David L. Alderson

OE systems are vulnerable and can be seriously disrupted by accidents, failures, extreme weather, or deliberate attack. Determining where such vulnerabilities lie is an important task for the military. So is developing strategies that use new technologies to make OE systems more resilient and able to adapt and complete missions if such systems are compromised.

This chapter focuses on the concepts of *vulnerability* and *resilience* as they pertain to OE systems. It describes how to think about vulnerability and resilience for OE systems, provides key analysis techniques to identify vulnerabilities, and presents a framework to compare different resilience strategies. In the contingent case study, these methods are applied to the case of the US Virgin Islands and their local energy systems in response to the 2017 hurricane season.

Vulnerability is a broad concept that encompasses several commonly used analysis techniques, namely reliability, risk, and adversarial analysis. This chapter covers the distinctions between these techniques, including their treatment of uncertainty when modeling and identifying OE system vulnerabilities. What is rarely discussed is that these techniques tend to identify different vulnerabilities in the same system, which can create difficulties in determining an appropriate management approach.

Toward this end, this chapter provides four distinct ways in which resilience is viewed to describe the way that a system responds to stress, resilience outcomes to aim for, and examples of strategies to achieve them. All resilience outcomes are beneficial for OE systems; however, it may be difficult to achieve them. In addition, strategies to achieve each outcome can be in conflict.

6.1 Background on Vulnerability and Resilience in OE Systems

OE systems like power grids, fuel pipelines, and supply chains are generally large, complicated, diverse, and difficult to fully comprehend, even for experts. This chapter begins with a brief overview of systems concepts to help orient thinking about OE systems and their vulnerability and resilience.

The first step to taking a systems perspective is to define an OE system, i.e., define all the infrastructure, organizations, environmental factors, etc. that are "in" the system and everything "outside" the system. When it comes to OE (and other critical infrastructure), there are two common ways analysts and designers approach this task:

1. A list of assets (not recommended)
   The basic idea is to list all the relevant OE assets in inventory at the installation or command, then use some rack-and-stack scheme to prioritize the most important ones. Examples of OE assets include things like fuel storage tanks, fuel delivery trucks, electric generators, solar panels, or microgrids.
2. An interconnected *network* that works to achieve a particular function (recommended)
   The emphasis here is not so much on the assets but the functions that they provide. One of the most powerful ways to relate assets to functions is to consider how they are managed as a *network*. Examples of OE systems often represented as networks include power grids or fuel storage and distribution pipelines.

Although obtaining an inventory of the things to be managed or protected is perhaps a necessary first step, it turns out that simple lists tend to be poor tools for identifying what matters most and what to do about it. Lists tend to focus on assets in isolation, without consideration for the interactions or dependencies between them which are often critical to mission success.

Instead, it is important to recognize that *assets* are commonly organized into *systems* that work to provide a *function* which enables a *capability* and ultimately supports a *mission*.

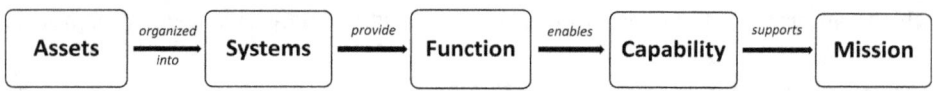

Figure 6.1: A conceptual view for the relationship between assets, function, and mission success.

Even the smallest building block of an OE system (such as circuits and logic gates in electronic hardware) can be and often are represented by a simple network to show their input-output relationships and functions. Like these building blocks of OE systems, larger infrastructure (e.g., transformers, generators, pumps, pipes, etc.) are not isolated from each other. They are always interconnected into networks that work together to provide a function (e.g., electricity, fuel distribution). Importantly, the vulnerability and resilience of an OE system depends on how it functions as a network; using a network perspective enables military planners to test and measure how the loss of an asset or sub-system impacts the overall functioning of a system.

Consider the following analogy: a traditional *kill-chain analysis* identifies the structure of an attack and reveals the ways in which an interruption at any stage in the "chain" can interrupt the entire process. In a similar manner, the breakdown of a key element in an energy system can lead to a failure in the OE mission. Viewing OE systems only as a list of assets ignores these "kill chain" relationships.

In this view of systems, vulnerability and resilience are interdependent concepts. The purpose of vulnerability analysis techniques is to reveal what events and conditions (e.g., where in the OE kill chain) may prevent systems from being able to carry out critical functions. Resilience strategies, in turn, aim to develop mechanisms to adapt to failures when they occur or help to avoid them altogether. Thus, the goal of vulnerability analysis is to identify issues in OE systems that need to be managed with resilience strategies.

Unfortunately, it is not easy to identify the way in which the loss of one or more components in a system will lead to its failure. Similarly, it is difficult to recognize effective mitigations that achieve resilience outcomes to survive and adapt to change. This is in part because the connections between components can quickly become very complicated. Even when all dependencies are known, it can be challenging to find a single point of failure. A second reason is that in many cases, the behavior of these systems is governed by decision-makers (either human or automated) that adjust in the presence of a disruption. Thus, identifying failure modes requires consideration not only of how the system is currently operating, but how it could adjust its operation in response to disruption. A third reason identifying failure modes is hard is that typically not all system dependencies are identified, rather the system often contains a multitude of hidden dependencies that only reveal themselves at the most inopportune times – when the system fails.

An all-too-common experience when an OE system fails to provide a critical function is the discovery of vulnerabilities that could have been managed ahead of time. A transformer fails, a pump shuts down, a powerline disconnects, a backup generator does not turn on. In retrospect, these assets may not have been viewed as critical to the mission, even though the entire system function depended on them. These types of vulnerabilities are called "hidden in plain sight," that is, things that are obvious in retrospect but hard to see before the failure event. Thus, people often identify with perfect hindsight the resilience actions that could have been taken given knowledge of these vulnerabilities.

The overall goal of this chapter is to help officers learn how they can uncover potential problems and fix them before they risk the success of missions. Vulnerability and resilience analysis techniques provide a basis to identify issues "hidden in plain sight" and potential alternatives to manage them.

6.2 Vulnerability Analysis for OE Systems

OE systems are *vulnerable* if they are susceptible to events or conditions that can lead to loss of a critical function. All systems are vulnerable to something – the question is: what? As discussed in Chapter 4, OE systems must be concerned with both deliberate sources of harm (e. g., vandalism, sabotage, attack) and non-deliberate sources of harm (e. g., accidents, failures, natural disasters). But the list of potential threats to OE systems is long.

Several authors in the academic literature have tried to tackle this question to enable vulnerability analysis of infrastructure and OE systems. Vulnerability is defined across these works as:
- the manifestation of inherent states of a system that can be exploited;[297]
- the susceptibility and/or inability to cope and deal with a particular threat;[298]
- the conditional probability that damages occur given a specific threat or attack;[299]
- the uncertainty about and severity of the consequences of an activity given an initiating event;[300]
- the degree that a system can be affected by a particular risk;[301]
- the degree a system can withstand specified loads.[302]

Linking perspectives together, this examination of system vulnerability may consider one or both of the following: (1) analysis of the likelihood a system will experience an undesired event or condition (via system exploitation, susceptibility, probability of damage, etc.), and (2) analysis of the magnitude of damages experienced (via severity of consequences, the degree of consequences, degree to withstand loads, etc.). Given this view, vulnerability analysis is broad enough to encompass any technique that combines these analyses together.

For OE systems, vulnerability analysis relies on several methods to determine the susceptibility of systems to loss of function, namely reliability, risk, and adversarial analysis. Vulnerability analysis is the process of integrating knowledge from those methods into a comprehensive view of how systems may fail. Hence, vulnerability analysis informs management decisions that can improve the resilience of OE systems, where reliability, risk, and adversarial methods on their own are too narrow to produce such recommendations. The goal of vulnerability analysis is to compare and prioritize differ-

---

[297] Yacov Y. Haimes, "On the Definition of Vulnerabilities in Measuring Risks to Infrastructures," *Risk Analysis: An International Journal*, vol. 26, no. 2, 2006, pages 293–296.
[298] Barry Charles Ezell, "Infrastructure Vulnerability Assessment Model (I-VAM)," *Risk Analysis: An International Journal*, vol. 27, no. 3, 2007, pages 571–583.
[299] Henry H. Willis, "Guiding Resource Allocations Based on Terrorism Risk," *Risk Analysis: An International Journal*, vol. 27, no. 3, 2007, pages 597–606.
[300] Terje Aven, "On Some Recent Definitions and Analysis Frameworks for Risk, Vulnerability, and Resilience," *Risk Analysis: An International Journal*, vol. 31, no. 4, 2011, pages 515–522.
[301] Society for Risk Analysis, "Society for Risk Analysis Glossary" (https://sra.org/sites/default/files/pdf/SRA\%20Glossary\%20-\%20FINAL.pdf).
[302] Society for Risk Analysis, "Society for Risk Analysis Glossary" (https://sra.org/sites/default/files/pdf/SRA\%20Glossary\%20-\%20FINAL.pdf).

ent (and potentially conflicting) ways reliability, risk, and adversarial analysis indicate OE systems may fail.

Some may object to this framing as methods like risk analysis have significant development and application across OE systems. For example, one may argue that a comprehensive risk management program should be enough to support OE system resilience.

However, risk analysis is in fact a subset of vulnerability analysis because it creates a particular view of why OE systems fail to function. Specifically, reliability, risk, and adversarial analyses approach OE systems with different perspectives on what events or conditions can cause failure, which consequences matter, and how they should be measured. Accordingly, each analysis applied to the same OE system will produce different results. This chapter will discuss not only how methods like reliability, risk, and adversarial analyses differ in application, but also how they differ in outcomes – characteristically, they identify different system vulnerabilities.

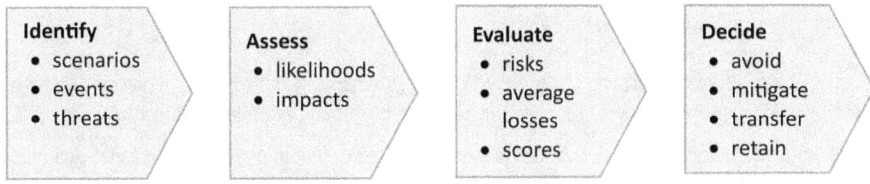

Traditional Risk Analysis

Step 1: Identify and list the scenarios, events, and/or threats of concern.

Step 2: For each entity identified in Step 1, estimate the likelihood the event will happen, as well as the potential impacts (e. g., consequences, damage, lives lost) if it does occur.

Step 3: Evaluate the risk (as some combined measure that combines likelihood and impact). A simple form of this is to evaluate the expected (or average) case and/or to assign a risk score.

Step 4: Decide whether to avoid the risk (don't proceed with the action), mitigate the risk (by altering the course of action), transfer the risk (for example, by buying insurance), or retain the risk (proceed as is).

6.3 Reliability, Risk, and Adversarial Analysis

6.3.1 The Basics

A key distinction between reliability, risk, and adversarial analysis is their treatment of uncertainty.[303] An important distinction between different sources of uncertainty is whether they are *non-deliberate* or *deliberate*.

Non-deliberate sources produce random events, sometimes referred to as "Mother Nature" uncertainty. The tools of probability and statistics appropriately study random events. The last decade has seen incredible growth in the use of advanced analytic tools (often based on statistics and probability) to identify patterns, predict potential failures, and even advise courses of action. These increasingly rely on techniques such as machine learning and artificial intelligence. It is important to recognize that these techniques rely on past data, and their ability to predict is often dependent on the quality of such data.

> **Statistics, Probability, and Possibility**
>
> *Statistics* is the study of methods for organizing and summarizing data and for drawing conclusions based on information contained in it – that is, characterizing things that *have happened*.
>
> *Probability* is the study of randomness and uncertainty. It includes mathematical methods for quantifying the likelihoods associated with the various outcomes of an experiment – that is, characterizing the things that *might happen*.
>
> *Possibility* is the study of what could happen, irrespective of whether it is likely or even realistic. Mathematical methods for studying possibility fall into discrete and combinatorial techniques that test multiple scenarios using specified settings (e.g., turning assets on or off) – that is, characterizing things that *could happen*.

In contrast, there is also uncertainty that comes from *deliberate* sources, such as adversaries. For example, in a game of chess a player does not know what the other player will do, but the player can assume that the adversary will behave in a manner that is deliberate and motivated by a desire to win (or to have the other player lose). The field of *game theory* is devoted to making the best possible decisions in the face of this type of uncertainty. Here, a slightly different look at uncertainty is applied, distinguishing between the *probable* and the *possible*. Things that are *probable* can be characterized using probability, typically based on experience or analysis designed to discover the

---

[303] Adversarial, reliability, and risk analyses are entire fields of study that cannot be adequately covered in a single book chapter. For interested readers, several related texts go into more detail on applying these techniques: Adversarial: Alan. R Washburn, *Two-Person Zero-Sum Games*, New York: Springer, 2014; Reliability: Kailash C. Kapur and Michael Pecht, *Reliability Engineering*, Hoboken, NJ: John Wiley & Sons, 2014; Risk: Terje Aven, *Risk Analysis*, Chichester: John Wiley & Sons, 2015.

frequency with which the event might occur. In contrast, things that are possible could happen but might seem strange, absurd, or unbelievable.

Importantly, officers should not treat adversarial behavior as random, in chess or in war. If there are significant concerns that adversaries intend to disrupt or harm a system, these potential disrupters should not be treated like random events (e. g., weather). Whereas random events might be appropriately represented by an average case, deliberate events are more likely to yield the worst case.

Accordingly, each analysis method considers uncertainty in a distinct way that, in turn, reveals different events and conditions that lead to system failure.

Reliability analysis considers uncertainty regarding the availability and functioning of assets within the system given estimates of the quality of these assets to perform their intended function (e. g., the failure rate of a transformer under normal operating conditions). Reliability methods are the most dependent on statistics and generally employ probability distributions to estimate asset quality and failure rate. Reliability methods also ignore the magnitude of the impacts caused when assets fail. This in turn focuses attention on system design that can meet minimum criteria for how well it will function under anticipated circumstances and prioritizes decisions for redundant, backup, or fail-safe systems. This is in contrast to other analysis techniques that aim to attenuate failure consequences when a failure eventually does occur.

Risk analysis considers uncertainty regarding the likelihood and magnitude of events that put assets in abnormal or extreme operating conditions (e. g., the return period on a storm that can flood the transformer's substation). Risk methods are the most reliant on probability to estimate threat likelihoods and consequences. Importantly, risk analysis often assigns probabilities to possible events that may lack sufficient statistical data, e. g., terrorist attacks, solar storms, extreme floods, etc. Hence, risk analysis prioritizes decisions that minimize the impacts of the most common (i. e., expected) events and consequences, and lowers the importance of decisions for events with rare or low impacts.

Adversarial Analysis considers uncertainty regarding the possibility that some assets may fail in detrimental combinations. The goal is to estimate the quantity of key assets that can be removed from service simultaneously and measure their impacts on system function (e. g., identifying the single, pair, or otherwise combination of worst transformers to lose). Adversarial analysis is most reliant on combinatorial methods to test possibilities by asking "what if" a particular combination of assets is not available, not when, why, or how this lack of availability may occur. The result is adversarial analysis will identify and recommend managing vulnerabilities that will cause the greatest disruption to system function and consequences irrespective of how likely the onset of such an event is.

6.3.2 The Details

This section provides more detail on each analysis method and an example of how each leads to different conclusions on vulnerability.

6.3.2.1 Reliability Analysis

Reliability deals with estimating the future performance of an OE system based on the quality of its assets. The key question reliability analysis is trying to answer is whether the OE system will be dependable in the future. It therefore focuses attention on the design and management of the system itself, including factors such as age, materials, environmental exposure, and maintenance history. Assessors use this information to estimate asset and system quality and to predict potential asset or system failure. An OE system is considered *reliable* if it is expected to perform its functional purpose to a defined quality within a particular future time horizon. Conversely, an OE system is *unreliable* if it will not perform its function within the established time frame and is expected to fail to meet required quality.

Failure in reliability is generally modeled as a binary state – either working (on) or not working (off). However, there are many different levels of failure that OE system operators may identify that define a spectrum of failure modes that are either desirable or undesirable. For example, having a fuse in a circuit overheat and turn off power may be a much more desirable failure state than burning out the wiring. Hence, failure for an OE system is a complex topic that requires a strong functional knowledge of the system's purpose, design, and existing mitigations.

Fault tolerance is the ability of an asset or system to function reliably despite stresses, and it is often measured as a probability of failure over a given amount of time into the future. This measure produces an estimate of asset or system *failure rate*, which is the fundamental measure dictating reliability-based decisions. Assets that have a low failure rate in the near or far future are assumed to be more reliable than assets with a higher failure rate. Reliability analysis is often reported as a *mean time to failure* (MTTF) or a related measure for this reason. MTTF and related measures are primarily used to inform preventive maintenance to keep systems operational. It is often prudent to be proactive and replace a component that is likely to fail before it actually does and causes an operational disruption.

There are also numerous techniques to transform asset-based measures like MTTF into system-wide measures to understand system reliability. For example, a *fault tree* is a tool that relates failure rates and related metrics of multiple assets together to determine when and how an asset failure may lead to system failure. Such analyses are often used to identify places where a system needs to be hardened or to have redundancy added.

6.3.2.2 Risk Analysis

Risk analysis deals with determining which threats to OE system assets and function are more or less important. The key question risk analysis is trying to answer is which threats should be expected to impact the OE system and how consequential these threats will be. Accordingly, risk analysis follows a well-established process that involves defining threats, measuring their likelihood and consequences, and then prioritizing threats based on these measures. An OE system is assumed to be low risk if there are no likely threats that can cause major disruption or damage. Conversely, an OE system is at higher risk if threats are identified that are likely to happen and cause significant impacts.

Threats to OE systems come in all shapes and sizes (see Chapter 4 for greater detail) but are generally categorized based on how they originate and challenge system performance. For example, the Homeland Security National Risk Categorization method developed by the Rand Corporation (see Table 6.1) defines twenty-eight different threats that can impact national critical infrastructure (including OE systems) and organizes them into seven different categories, including: terrorist threats, cyber threats, illegal activities, natural hazards, health hazards, infrastructure hazards, and other. A key step in risk analysis is defining which threats matter most to the OE system. For example, some natural hazards such as tsunamis that may be irrelevant to study for OE systems located inland, and vice versa.

Table 6.1: List of Threats Considered in the Homeland Security National Risk Categorization Framework by the Rand Corporation. Source: Henry H. Willis, Mary Tighe, Andrew Lauland, Lisa Ecola, Shoshana R. Shelton, Meagan L. Smith, John G. Rivers, Kristin J. Leuschner, Terry Marsh, and Daniel M. Gerstein, "Homeland Security National Risk Characterization: Risk Assessment Methodology," RAND Corporation, 2018.

Terrorist Threats	**Natural Hazards**
Attack on leadership	Drought
Attack targeting critical infrastructure	Earthquake
Biological weapon attack	Flooding
Chemical weapon attack	Hurricane
Nuclear attack	Space weather
Radiological attack	Tsunami
Small arms/explosive attack on populations	Volcano
Cyber Threats	Wildfire
Cyber attack on critical infrastructure networks	**Health Hazards**
Cyber attack that steals sensitive government data	Agricultural plant disease outbreak
Cyber attack on government networks	Foreign animal disease outbreak
Illegal Activities	Transnational communicable disease
Counterfeit goods	**Infrastructure Hazards**
Human trafficking	Technical failure or industrial accident of critical infrastructure cause by human error or age
Illegal migration	
Mass migration	
Transnational drug trafficking	

Once threats are determined, risk analysis requires measures of threat likelihood and consequences to identify system vulnerabilities. Threat likelihoods are generally estimates using statistical methods to relate the size and severity of a threat to its frequency or tendency to occur. For natural hazards, this is often based on historical records of past events, such as the *return period*[304] on a storm or the frequency of earthquakes of different magnitude. For terrorist threats, this may include intelligence estimates of an actor's capability and intent to act, which are then converted into numerical measures of likelihood.

Consequences are generally measured as the impact on the functioning of a system should assets be lost due to a threat. For example, the consequences of a flood on a pipeline system would be estimated given some flood event (either modeled or based on historical data), determining which assets are flooded, which of those assets will stop functioning, and in turn, how much loss of system function results.

The final step in traditional risk analysis is to combine these two measures and compare different threats. Generally, this includes the use of a table to compare threat likelihood and consequences and characterizing risks as high, medium, and low priority. Ideally, this process produces a nuanced view of the risk of each asset in the OE system and potential mitigations. This process means risk analysis will highlight threats that have a large, expected impact on system function, i.e., have high likelihood and consequence. In contrast, risk analysis will understate threats with high likelihood, but have little consequence on system function (e.g., normal rain), or events with enormous consequences, but are very rare (e.g., 1000-year flood). When risk analysis is conducted in this way, it is also referred to a *probabilistic risk analysis* (PRA). PRA is the most common form of risk analysis used across OE systems.

6.3.2.3 Adversarial Analysis

Adversarial analysis deals with finding the "worst-case" failures that challenge an OE system's function irrespective of why they occur. It focuses attention on identifying "bottlenecks" within the OE system, where the loss of few components can lead to a large loss in system function – i.e., locations in the system that would be "easy" for an adversary to interdict (stop, block, destroy, etc.) function with minimal effort.[305] A system is considered easy to interdict if few asset failures lead to a large reduction in system function. Conversely, a system is considered difficult to interdict if many failures are required to produce a reduction in system function.

---

[304] A return period, also known as a recurrence interval or repeat interval, is an average time or an estimated average time between events.

[305] David L. Alderson, Gerald G. Brown, W. Matthew Carlyle, and Louis Anthony Cox, "Sometimes There Is No 'Most-Vital' Arc: Assessing and Improving the Operational Resilience of Systems," *Military Operations Research*, vol. 18, no. 1, 2013, pages 21–37.

The reason this approach is called adversarial analysis is from its original mathematical development combining optimization and game theory techniques.[306] These techniques, referred to as two-player, zero-sum games, model how an intelligent adversary would inflict damage or disruption on a system – i.e., an adversary would choose to inflict the most damage with the least cost possible. However, this modeling approach is fundamental to finding the worst-case failures a system can experience irrespective of why they may occur (because of an intelligent adversary, or just by bad luck). More broadly, adversarial analysis uses a class of optimization techniques called "interdiction models" to study adversarial decisions and identify worst-case disruptions.

Adversarial analysis is dictated by a few key elements of an interdiction model. An interdiction model can be formulated as a mathematical optimization problem in which the notional "attacker" must choose between a limited set of actions that balance the preferences for disrupting the system with the constraints on the actions they can take.[307] A key metric to assess the actions available to an attacker is referred to as the attack "budget" which reflects the greatest disruption to an OE system that can be triggered by a given number of assets that fail. The most common forms of these models consider actions as binary decisions that turn assets on or off, and all decisions are assumed to occur simultaneously. For example, an adversarial analysis with a budget of three would find the combination of three assets that if turned off simultaneously would cause the greatest disruption to OE system function.

In practice, vulnerability analysis with adversarial modeling is conducted as follows: for different attack budgets (generally increasing from 1, 2, 3, …), identify which assets an adversary should attack with each budget to maximally disrupt the system, and measure how much impact that has on system function.[308] The results of such an analysis are not so simple – the assets that cause the worst-case disruption for a budget of two might be very different than the assets for a budget of three. The reason for this is straightforward: *the importance of a system asset depends on the other assets also available.* For example, consider a bridge that provides transport over a river. How important is this bridge? If there is a second bridge over the river, then the loss of either one in isolation might not cause a big problem. However, losing both bridges together (and interdicting any possible transport over the river) might be catastrophic for the mission.

---

306 Gerald Brown, Matthew Carlyle, Javier Salmerón, and Kevin Wood, "Defending Critical Infrastructure," *Interfaces*, vol. 36, no. 6, 2006, pages 530–544.
307 David L. Alderson, Gerald G. Brown, and W. Matthew Carlyle, "Assessing and Improving Operational Resilience of Critical Infrastructures and Other Systems," *Tutorials in Operations Research: Bridging Data and Decision*, October 27, 2014 (https://doi.org/10.1287/educ.2014.0131).
308 David L. Alderson, Gerald Brown, W. Matthew Carlyle, "Operational Models of Infrastructure Resilience," *Risk Analysis*, vol. 35, no. 4, 2015, pages 562–586.

The goal of this type of vulnerability analysis is to identify the components that, if lost together, would disrupt the system in the worst possible way and/or cause mission failure. Framing this problem from an adversarial perspective often reveals interdependencies and insights not easily obtained using other forms of system analysis.

Application of adversarial analysis across a diversity of critical infrastructure systems has consistently revealed two important implications. First, although it is common to design systems so that the loss of any single component does not compromise system function (this is known as "N-1 security"[309]), few systems are designed to withstand multiple, simultaneous failures (e.g., attacker budget greater than 2). Thus, it is important that designers and operators of OE systems "think beyond the first failure." Second, because the importance of a system component often depends on other components, in many cases it is not possible to rank components from most important to least important.[310] When prioritizing OE infrastructure, planners need to "think systems" and not get overly fixated on prioritized asset lists.

6.3.3 Example for How Reliability, Risk, and Adversarial Analyses Produce Different Results

Figure 6.2 demonstrates how these three analysis techniques differ in practice. In this OE example, a simple fuel network is located on the coast of a major body of water. Deliveries of fuel arrive at coastal pumping stations and are pumped uphill to a local terminal from which fuel is distributed to a community or military installation. The system also has a redundant pumping station and pipelines connecting the coast and the terminal. The pumping stations and terminal are relatively new (less than five years in operation), but the pipeline has been around for a long time (over thirty years).

As analytical assumptions for the reliability, risk, and adversarial methods, it is assumed that planners care about operations for the next year (for reliability analysis), have identified sea level rise, coast storms, and tsunamis as key threats (for risk analysis), and defined the attack budget as a single asset (for adversarial analysis).

These simple assumptions lead to widely different analysis results. Considering the system's history, construction, maintenance record, etc., reliability analysis may indicate the pipelines are the biggest vulnerability. They might be made of old materials and

---

[309] Electric power systems in the United States are required to be N-1 secure by regulation. However, there are no requirements for these systems to be N-2 secure.
[310] David L. Alderson, Gerald G. Brown, W. Matthew Carlyle, and Louis Anthony Cox, "Sometimes There Is No 'Most-Vital' Arc: Assessing and Improving the Operational Resilience of Systems," *Military Operations Research*, vol. 18, no. 1, 2013, pages 21–37.

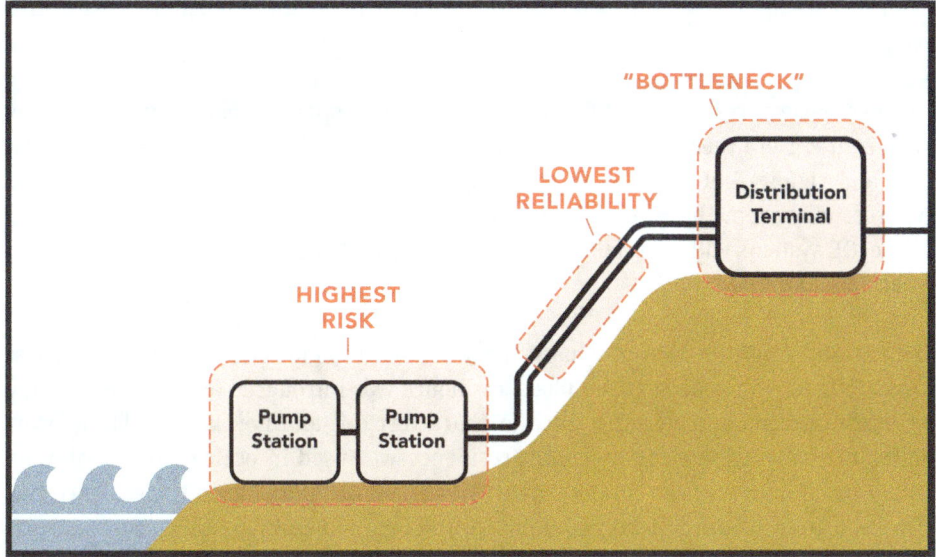

Figure 6.2: Reliability, risk, and adversarial analysis techniques can lead to different results in terms of what is a critical vulnerability.

likely to not function even with proper maintenance and management. In contrast, risk analysis may indicate the pumping stations are the most vulnerable due to their proximity to the coast and low-lying position. Sea level rise, coastal storms, and tsunami threats are most likely to impact pumping and the resulting consequences are sufficient to warrant concern. Finally, adversarial analysis may indicate the distribution terminal as the most vulnerable asset. The system possesses redundant pumping and pipelines, but only one terminal. Hence, the terminal serves as a bottleneck in that, if the terminal is lost for any reason, it will cause worst-case disruptions for fuel access.

6.4 Resilience Strategies for OE Systems

Whereas vulnerability analysis identifies key assets and systems to consider for protection and mitigation efforts, *resilience* involves ways in which to try to adapt and improve systems to avoid losses. A vulnerability analyst should expect reliability, risk, and adversarial analyses to point in different directions. Resilience theory and methods provide a suite of techniques to manage these inherent issues. Overall, it is up to decision-makers to decide how to use limited budgets and time to address vulnerabilities and improve resilience.

Resilience has become a popular term in the last decade for how to think about systems and the way that they deal with stress. The use (and overuse) of this term has resulted in considerable confusion about what it means for a system to be resilient and what we can do to make our systems resilient in the presence of potentially disruptive events.

To make sense of resilience, it helps to first consider its opposite, namely what it means to be *brittle*. Here there is considerable agreement. Something is *brittle* if it has hardness and rigidity but is prone to cracking and breaking when placed under stress. Whereas all systems have some inherent vulnerability, not all systems are inherently brittle. OE systems will experience stress, but soldiers do not want these systems to fail when this happens.

The use and interpretation of what it means to be resilient has evolved over the last few centuries. As far back as the 1800s, resilience was introduced as a mathematically technical concept in material science to characterize if and how a material deforms under stress. Much later, in the 1970s, resilience was used in ecology to describe the ability of an ecosystem to absorb changes and persist. More recently, resilience has also been used in the context of human psychology – alongside other concepts such as character, grit, and hardiness – in describing the factors that contribute to human well-being.

Over the last fifteen years, the concept of resilience has also become prominent in discussions of national security. One of the first mentions of resilience in this context was in the 2007 *National Strategy for Homeland Security* which recognized: "We will not be able to deter all terrorist threats, and it is impossible to deter or prevent natural catastrophes. We can, however, mitigate the Nation's vulnerability to acts of terrorism, other man-made threats, and natural disasters by ensuring the structural and operational resilience of our critical infrastructure and key resources."[311] It also offered important guidance: "We must now focus on the resilience of the system as a whole – an approach that centers on investments that make the system better able to absorb the impact of an event without losing the capacity to function."[312]

In military operations, the notion of resilience is often closely tied with *mission assurance*, as defined in DOD Directive 3020.40 as "A process to ensure that assigned tasks or duties can be performed in accordance with the intended purpose or plan. It is a summation of the activities and measures taken to ensure that required capabilities and all

---

[311] Homeland Security Council, *National Strategy for Homeland Security, 2007*, October 2007, page 27 (https://www.ojp.gov/ncjrs/virtual-library/abstracts/national-strategy-homeland-security-2007).
[312] Homeland Security Council, *National Strategy for Homeland Security, 2007*, October 2007, page 28 (https://www.ojp.gov/ncjrs/virtual-library/abstracts/national-strategy-homeland-security-2007).

supporting infrastructures are available [...] to mobilize, deploy, support, and sustain military operations throughout the continuum of operations."[313]

> **Origins of resilience – the verb *resile***
>
> Surprisingly, the approach to resilience stems all the way back to its original use and meaning in Latin, as a *verb* related to action.[314] Resilience was originally the verb *resilio* meaning to leap or bounce. Later, this entered early French as the verb *resilire*, meaning to desist, retract, or renege on one's position. The earliest use of resilience in the English language was in the 1500s as the verb *to resile*, with a similar definition to its partner in French. We highlight this form of the word because it is helpful for distinguishing resilience from other similar concepts, such as risk.
>
> Resilience and risk both have noun and verb forms, but they are grammatically and logically different. For example, it is grammatically correct to have one risk, but it makes no sense to have one resilience. Similarly, a system can risk something (e.g., hurricanes) because it is a linking verb, but a system cannot resile something – a system either resiles or does not. This is why risk must always involve the definition of external threats, where resilience is meant to adapt systems to anything.

6.5 Resilience Outcomes: What Should Systems Do (Rather than Fail)

A closer look across the many domains where the term resilience is commonly used reveals several distinct notions. There are four distinct notions of resilience originally identified by Woods[315] and expanded for vulnerability analysis of networked systems by Sharkey et al.:[316]

- **Resilience as robustness.**
  This involves managing a stressful event with limited-to-no impact on normal activities. It also involves the design and operation of systems that continue to function in the presence of stress. This notion of resilience as robustness is also known as *survivable design* or *fault tolerance*.
  An OE system does not exhibit resilience as robustness if it cannot maintain pre-defined operational thresholds during perturbations.
- **Resilience as rebound.**
  This involves returning system performance to normal (or an acceptable level)

---

[313] Department of Defense, "DOD Policy and Responsibilities for Critical Infrastructure, DOD Directive 3020.40," January 14, 2010 (https://policy.defense.gov/Portals/11/Documents/hdasa/newsletters/302040p.pdf).

[314] David E. Alexander, "Resilience and Disaster Risk Reduction: An Etymological Journey," *Natural Hazards and Earth System Sciences*, vol. 13, no. 11, 2013, pages 2707–2716.

[315] David D. Woods, "Four Concepts for Resilience and the Implications for the Future of Resilience Engineering," *Reliability Engineering & System Safety*, 141, 2015, pages 5–9.

[316] Thomas C. Sharkey, Sarah G. Nurre Pinkley, Daniel A. Eisenberg, and David L. Alderson, "In Search of Network Resilience: An Optimization-Based View," *Networks*, 2020, pages 1–30 (https://doi.org/10.1002/net.21996).

after a stressful event. Also called "bouncing back."

An OE system does not exhibit resilience as rebound if it cannot resume functioning after a stressful event.

- **Resilience as extensibility.**

This involves extending system performance or capabilities by reconfiguring and/or prolonging the use of constrained resources to accommodate new operations and survive stressful events. Extensibility is a dynamic capability that reflects how well a system can "stretch" to handle stress or unanticipated events.

Unlike robustness and rebound, which emphasize the continuation and restoration of existing network function, extensibility focuses on creating new system function to exceed predefined operational thresholds or change functional requirements.

An OE system does not exhibit resilience as extensibility if its function is so tightly constrained that minor perturbations in resource allocation or functional requirements lead to extreme and cascading losses. Moreover, a system that is unable to redistribute limited resources, adjust operational thresholds, or serve multiple purposes will likely experience brittle failure when unanticipated events require its operations to change.

- **Resilience as adaptability.**

This involves managing tradeoffs within continuously evolving contexts, often over long timescales, through *adaptive capacity*.

Adaptive capacity is a system's readiness or potential to adjust a system's operations – its processes, behaviors, relationships – to fit changing situations. Sometimes this is also called *sustained adaptability* because it tends to focus attention on how a system survives over the long term.

Unlike robustness, rebound, and extensibility, which are concerned with the impacts of stress on a network in a single event (or several events closely related in time), sustained adaptability is less concerned with the outcome of a single event, and more concerned with how a system survives many stressful events over its life cycle, considering tradeoffs between robustness, rebound, and extensibility.

A system might not exhibit resilience as adaptability in at least two ways: (1) not being able to manage short-term tradeoffs sufficiently to maintain, restore, or extend a system's structure or function, and (2) not being able to manage long-term tradeoffs to balance these adaptive capacities into the future.

Figure 6.3 summarizes each of these notions in terms of the way in which a system is prepared to respond to a stressful event. These four concepts are *resilience outcomes* as they orient resilience activities toward achieving a particular goal for system response. Robustness is really about the system holding onto its existing configuration. Rebound is typically about having the system return as quickly as possible to its previous configuration. A key difference with extensibility and adaptability is that they require the system to *reorganize* itself in order to extend and adapt.

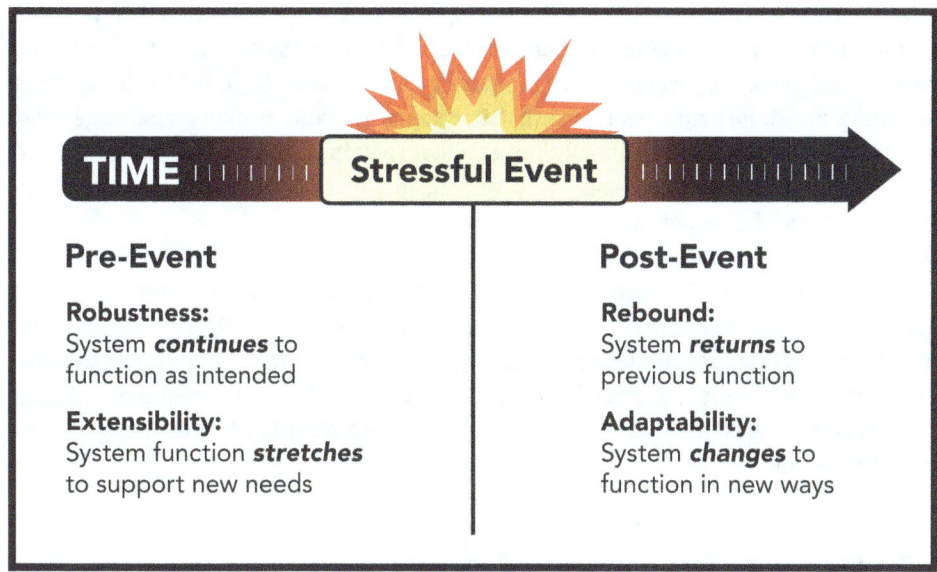

Figure 6.3: A conceptual view of four different notions of resilience.

Each concept of resilience is associated with particular strategies to achieve the intended outcome. For example, strategies to improve robustness of an OE system (e.g., via hardening or protecting existing infrastructure) can conflict with strategies for extensibility by making systems more difficult to reconfigure and extend operations. Similarly, strategies to rebound systems quickly may hinder capacities to adapt systems to have a new structure and function. As a result, there are tradeoffs between one resilience strategy and another. In the contingent case study, we explore vulnerability analysis techniques and tradeoffs between resilience strategies and outcomes through recent events involving energy systems in the US Virgin Islands.

6.6 A Final Thought: Efficiency vs Resilience

Over the last several decades, it has become increasingly fashionable to *optimize* systems – both for OE and in other contexts – in their design and operation. In common parlance, "optimized" is used synonymously with "efficient," suggesting that a system is inherently improved if it is faster, better, and/or cheaper. But a highly efficient system typically has little waste and/or slack, making it also brittle and fragile.

As a result, there is a grand challenge in the design and operation of OE systems to make them more efficient in using limited resources while still being able to respond and adapt to surprises (as illustrated by the Colonial Pipeline case in chapter 5). The goal in optimizing (a system or plan) should *not* be to eliminate all slack, but to have the right amounts of slack in the right places and at the right times. In practice, optimization should be about assessing tradeoffs between objectives, such as whether we want efficiency or resilience. It is important not to make lean, brittle OE systems. Assessing and improving resilience in OE systems remains a major challenge, both technologically and organizationally, but one that remains critical to the continued success of military operations. And there remain lots of opportunity for contributions from a variety of disciplines.

Tradeoffs exist for all OE systems. There is no one-size-fits-all solution for making OE systems more resilient. There are many ways that OE systems can fail, and there are many ways such failure can be mitigated. Perhaps more important than understanding any single strategy for resilience is understanding the tradeoffs between them. Vulnerability and resilience methods help us recognize these tradeoffs when adapting and improving systems.

6.7 Topics for Discussion and Research

- What are key vulnerability analysis techniques for OE systems? How do they consider uncertainty? How can they lead to different conclusions on how OE systems are vulnerable?
- Describe four different resilience strategies. How do they differ?
- Describe an OE system familiar to you. List all assets in ranked priority based on a chosen vulnerability analysis. Define real or fictitious situations that might lead to a change in vulnerabilities and associated priorities. How might we think of this system in a networked way and prioritize assets without using a list?
- For a given OE system, conduct a vulnerability analysis and define associated resilience strategies. Can you identify tradeoffs in how some resilience strategies either improve or exacerbate system vulnerabilities? Can you identify tradeoffs between resilience strategies and preferred outcomes?

6.8 Case Study: The US Virgin Islands – the Hurricanes of 2017

This case study illustrates concepts for vulnerability analysis and resilience strategies through examination of how US Virgin Islands (USVI) energy systems responded to the 2017 hurricane season.

The USVI Territory comprises three main islands – St. Croix, St. John, and St. Thomas – and several smaller surrounding islands. The islands are among the Leeward Islands of the Lesser Antilles approximately 40 miles east of Puerto Rico and more than 1100 miles from Miami, Florida. The United States acquired these islands in 1917, as part of a strategy to protect the approaches to the Panama Canal during World War I.[317]

In September 2017, Hurricane Irma and Hurricane Maria, both category-5 storms, struck the USVI within a two-week period. These storms devastated critical infrastructure systems, including energy, water, telecommunications, and transportation. Five years after the storms, the territory still had not recovered fully, despite receiving billions of dollars of US emergency federal funding. In the recovery plans, much of the emphasis focused on "bouncing back" to the way things were prior to the storms. However, it was logical that it was better to design systems that can adapt to a future filled with evolving challenges likely from weather and climate, and uncertain changes in technology, and economics.

Yet the story of infrastructure vulnerability and resilience in the USVI dates back long before the 2017 storms. The USVI's energy infrastructure, like many other USVI government services, had been plagued by problems for decades prior to the hurricanes.

The islands' rising energy demand during the twentieth century, highly affected the development of its energy infrastructure. In the mid-1950s, the USVI economy deliberately shifted from agriculture to tourism and manufacturing, and during this period the (permanent and temporary) population of the USVI increased dramatically. The number of tourists increased from approximately 16,000 in 1949 to more than 1.1 million in 1969, while the resident population grew from approximately 26,000 in 1950, to 62,000 in 1970 and 102,000 in 1990.[318]

USVI energy infrastructure includes fuel delivery systems and electric power systems. The islands of St. Thomas and St. John share a single power system, with generation coming from a single power plant in St. Thomas. St. Croix has its own independent power grid, powered by a single power plant. Both power plants burn fossil fuels, historically imported diesel fuel oil and more recently liquefied propane gas (LPG). The Virgin Islands Water and Power Authority (WAPA) owns, operates, and maintains the electric power infrastructure. WAPA is an autonomous government public utility that serves approximately 55,000 customers throughout the Territory.

Historically, power systems in the USVI relied on diesel fuel for power generation because they had a reliable source, a local petroleum refinery. The Hess Oil Virgin Islands Corporation opened a refinery in Limetree Bay, St. Croix in 1966, and it became one of the ten largest refineries in the world. Hovensa LLC, a joint venture between Hess Cor-

---

[317] Isaac Dookhan, *A History of the Virgin Islands of the United States*, Kingston, Jamaica: Canoe Press, 1994.
[318] Isaac Dookhan, *A History of the Virgin Islands of the United States*, Kingston, Jamaica: Canoe Press, 1994.

poration and Petroleos de Venezuela, took over operation of the refinery in 1998. In the late 2000s, the refinery began to lose money due to reduced demand caused by a global economic slowdown and increased refining capacity in emerging markets.[319]

By 2011, due to loss of revenue,[320] the Hovensa refinery stopped providing diesel fuel to WAPA and in 2012, closed down. The loss of this local source of diesel increased the length and cost of the fuel supply chain to the power system. Although WAPA has transitioned to using LPG as its primary fuel source for electric power generation to increase generator efficiency, save money, and reduce pollution and carbon emissions, the cost of fuel remains high.

Even during normal operations, a lack of generation reliability creates challenges for WAPA to provide stable power. However, during severe weather incidents, transmission and distribution infrastructure often fail. Hurricanes Irma and Maria caused significant damage to electric power infrastructure across the USVI. Nearly 100 percent of WAPA customers lost electricity. The storms damaged the electrical transmission and distribution networks in the territory: with 60 percent of such networks being affected on St. Croix, 80 percent on St. Thomas, and 90 percent on St. John. According to FEMA, WAPA did not restore electricity to 100 percent of eligible customers across the territory until January 2018.[321]

Recovery efforts included a variety of investments intended to increase system resilience. This case study demonstrates the four different notions of resilience in action.

6.8.1 Vulnerability Analysis of the USVI Energy System

- Reliability: the centralized system is highly unreliable based on national standards for power systems. This is compounded with very high electricity rates that many customers are unable to pay.
- Risk: the system is clearly at risk of major storms that bring wind and flood damage to the power system. Risk mitigation would entail hardening parts of the system exposed to hurricane-force winds, flying debris, and flooding.

---

[319] Associated Press (Business Staff), "Major Oil Refinery to Close in US Virgin Islands," January 18, 2012 (https://www.cleveland.com/business/2012/01/major_oil_refinery_to_close_in.html).
[320] Associated Press (Business Staff), "Major Oil Refinery to Close in US Virgin Islands," January 18, 2012 (https://www.cleveland.com/business/2012/01/major_oil_refinery_to_close_in.html).
[321] David L. Alderson, Brendan B. Bunn, Daniel A. Eisenberg, Alan R. Howard, Daniel A. Nussbaum, and Jack Templeton, "Interdependent Infrastructure Resilience in the US Virgin Islands: Preliminary Assessment," Naval Postgraduate School Technical Report, NPS-OR-18–005, December 2018 (https://faculty.nps.edu/dlalders/usvi/NPS-OR-18-005.pdf).

- Adversarial: there is little redundancy in the power system, where individual feeder power lines spread like branches and are subject to outage. This means each power line and all associated communities on that power line has at least one single point of failure. However, these branches are mostly independent, meaning that a failure in one branch often does not affect the others. Another issue is the size and management of generators. The oversizing of generators creates issues when trying to restart systems after a blackout (i.e., blackstart). Together, this means loss of generating assets and/or key substation equipment may be more impactful for the entire power system than bottlenecks that exist on each individual line.

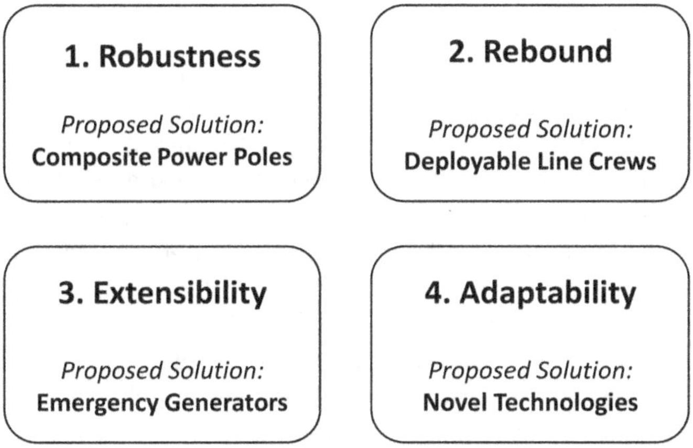

1. Robustness
Proposed Solution:
Composite Power Poles

2. Rebound
Proposed Solution:
Deployable Line Crews

3. Extensibility
Proposed Solution:
Emergency Generators

4. Adaptability
Proposed Solution:
Novel Technologies

Figure 6.4: Four strategies for creating a resilient energy system in the US Virgin Islands.

Four different resilience strategies for the USVI energy system:
1. Resilience as Robustness: composite power pole
   Power poles made from composite materials are considerably stronger than wooden poles and are capable of withstanding sustained winds up to 200 miles per hour. Installation of composite power poles provides robustness to help mitigate hurricane risk.
2. Resilience as Rebound: deployable line crews
   Being able to deploy trained personnel and equipment in the immediate aftermath of a storm helps manage unreliability with faster recovery times and emergency response.
3. Resilience as Extensibility: emergency generators
   Having the ability to put emergency generators into service on short notice helps mitigate against unreliability by providing additional backup assets to respond to

blackouts. Doing so also helps manage against adversarial attack by decentralizing generating resources.
4. Resilience as Adaptability: redesign of the electric grid to include renewable generation

    Reconfiguring the overall energy system helps mitigate against adversarial vulnerabilities by distributing generation resources and producing power from additional sources. It also helps mitigate hurricane risk by removing some of the most vulnerable infrastructure to hurricanes (e. g., the 240/120 V lines connecting a house to the distribution feeder).

Each of these strategies targets different aspects of resilience, and they can be used in combination as part of a broader resilience portfolio. However, there are tradeoffs and conflicts between these resilience strategies:
- Composite power poles actually *make it more difficult to recover* systems. The poles are so strong that they cannot be cut with a chainsaw or normal means available to onsite workers. In general, it is not possible to repair a broken power pole; it must be replaced, requiring significant cost and time to do so.
- Once in service, emergency backup generators are often used longer and/or more frequently than intended. This overuse can degrade their ability to provide service and can *render them unreliable* when needed for the next big emergency. Moreover, they add more assets to the system that will need regular management, potentially diverting limited resources and degrading the reliability of other assets in the system.
- Having readily deployable line crews is expensive and can create a burden on the local economy. Similar to backup generators, they are likely to be used in non-emergency situations and for non-energy-related purposes and/or may reduce staffing for other purposes due to limited budgets.
- Renewable energy sources in the USVI are only affordable to wealthy users and create incentive for *more* power use. They are more difficult to distribute across communities in need. Should solar panels become unavailable, residential power requirements may be larger than planned by the utility in an emergency, increasing response burden.

6.8.2 Case Conclusions

The lesson in this case is that resilience strategies need to be considered in combination, as part of a broader portfolio. It also illustrates that analysts should look at vulnerability and resilience of system as a whole.

Importantly, the case shows the tradeoffs between resilience strategies and how they can conflict with one another. For example, the USVI system has been vulnerable to major hurricanes for decades and experienced several storms prior to 2017 (and since). Hardening the power grid to withstand hurricane-force winds (i.e., making power poles more robust to storms) comes with the tradeoff that composite power poles are much more difficult and costly to replace (which reduces the ability of the system to rebound). Similarly, the USVI energy system was unreliable prior to the storms and remains unreliable today. Managing reliability would greatly improve the resilience of the system. Another key way to manage power outages is through greater use of backup generators and novel technologies like distributed generation and microgrids. These novel systems add complexity to the existing grid making it more difficult to maintain in lieu of benefits they may bring to respond to regular and extreme blackouts.

6.8.3 Topics for Discussion and Research

- Revisit a small OE system like that of the USVI, e.g., a military installation or other island location. Define vulnerabilities and resilience strategies. How do they differ to the USVI? How are they the same? Why might they differ or be the same?
- What OE challenges (and opportunities) exist for small island territories that don't exist for the mainland?
- The US DOD has expressed concern regarding climate change and how it potentially affects island territories disproportionately. How do concerns about a changing climate affect resilience strategy in the USVI? Of other island military installations?

7 Education and Training

This chapter discusses the main components of OE education and training and the vital role it should play in preparing future soldiers and military leaders. First it explains the importance of such military education. Secondly, it discusses the current gaps in OE education in the military. Then it outlines a course of professional military education in OE with three tiers at the undergraduate, graduate, and more specialized graduate levels. Finally, it describes how OE wargames and exercises can strengthen understanding of OE needs and raise broader awareness of OE demands.

As energy is an essential pillar in military power, the US military needs to develop a well-trained cadre of OE experts.

7.1 The Importance of OE Education to the Military Mission

Twenty-first-century battlespace realities demand sophisticated OE capacities, across potentially long supply chains, many of which are civilian owned and operated, highly vulnerable, and easily disrupted by a determined adversary. Future warfighting developments in mobility, lethality, and survivability will create increased demand for energy to complete military missions. However, most US military members lack OE competence, and this creates a knowledge and experience gap in a vital component of the US military as well as a potential challenge to US global power projection.

US military power projection in the twenty-first century relies on a technologically sophisticated operating environment, requiring high levels of cooperation across multiple domains and geographic regions. This modern operating environment, which emphasizes both kinetic and non-kinetic actions, allows peer adversaries to avoid potentially costly attacks on US or allied combat forces and instead target vulnerable logistical centers deep inside the battlespace. While the notion of a deep strike into the enemy's rear areas is not new, modern weapons and cyber tools give US adversaries considerable anti-access/area denial (A2/AD) capabilities. A well-planned attack on a key logistical node, such as an energy supply chain, could have a cascading effect with devastating impacts on forward-deployed assets. Under these conditions, the military needs to operate successfully despite OE sustainment challenges. This is a new situation for the military; since World War II, US forces have rarely lacked adequate energy supplies for extended periods, a condition that may not be a given when confronted by a peer adversary.

> The military will need to operate successfully with varying OE sustainment challenges. This is a new situation for the military; since World War II, US forces have rarely lacked adequate energy supplies for extended periods, a condition that may not be a given when confronted by a peer adversary.

To be successful, the twenty-first-century military must recognize OE as a critical mission enabler and possess more than a superficial knowledge of its application in the battlespace. Future leaders should also recognize how the challenges and opportunities related to OE can limit operational reach. Failing to educate soldiers and military leaders on OE could hamper operational performance, leading to elevated casualties and potential mission failure. Consequently, OE education and awareness is a necessary component of general military education and training.

7.2 Current Gap in OE Education

Until recently, US institutional military education has lacked a concentrated and institutionalized focus on OE. As a result, few service members have comprehensive OE knowledge. While some service members have deep experience and/or knowledge in certain specialty sectors related to energy, they may have shortcomings in others. For instance, a fuels expert may not have knowledge of battlefield power generation and distribution. While institutional training regimes have honed the Joint Force to an exceptional level of professionalism, that educational focus has been on mission execution, without the OE component. Despite its centrality on the modern battlefield, energy, more specifically, OE, often comes as an afterthought to military education curricula with fuel and battlespace power seen as an unlimited commodity – a luxury which a future adversary may not afford US forces.

> Logistics planners do not appreciate the tactical and operational impacts of energy, which could limit the ability to project kinetic effects beyond a single mission, particularly in a contested environment.

These challenges are exacerbated by the military services consistently (and necessarily so) acquiring new systems that enhance mobility, survivability, and lethality yet are also more energy intensive than predecessors. Such systems further tax OE resources and could potentially exhaust them altogether due to logistical or operational constraints. Moreover, planners that do not appreciate the tactical and operational impacts of energy could limit the ability to project force beyond a single mission, particularly in a contested environment.

To close these knowledge gaps, the military needs subject matter experts *and* a corresponding ethos within the officer and senior enlisted ranks, which can only be accomplished through a structured, accredited, and rigorous education and training effort.

7.3 Training Requirements and Structure

This section outlines an OE education and training program, establishing a foundation early in the military member's career and subsequently building and enhancing that knowledge over time in service.

> The services must create operational energy subject matter experts *and* a corresponding ethos within the officer and senior enlisted ranks, which can only be accomplished through a structured, accredited and rigorous education and training effort.

Key to success in this field is a cadre of experienced officers and senior enlisted personnel in the OE management field. Leaders must be exposed to OE concepts early in their careers and take regular refresher courses. Moreover, this instruction must be relevant to rank and position, and adequately framed within a real-world context.

The integrated force requires leaders, strategists, engineers, and operators who understand OE requirements within the Joint Force construct, ultimately functioning across domains, operational environments, and technologies. OE requirements include the importance of energy densities (liquid fuels); energy storage (batteries); energy distribution (refuel logistics); electrical generation, distribution, and demand (integrated power and energy, directed energy weapons); and energy command and control (balancing supply and demand).

> Standardized training and education in the operational energy field will institutionalize military professionalism and excellence, and allow the Joint Force to deter, fight, and win in the twenty-first century battlespace.

OE training should encompass four competencies: fuels, power generation and distribution (shipborne and land-based), energy storage, and energy management. Moreover, this instruction should concentrate on three skill levels commensurate with service member rank, occupational specialty, and time in service. These skill levels are: (1) Tactical or entry level (undergraduate), (2) Operational or professional level (graduate), and (3) Strategic or subject matter expert level (graduate). The goal being for service members to maintain OE currency throughout their careers.

7.3.1 A Multi-Tiered Solution

It is useful to envision OE instruction as organized into several tiers.

7.3.1.1 Tier 1: Foundational Instruction

Tier 1 should address foundational instruction needed by entry-level personnel, or those new to OE principles. This so-called General Military Training (GMT) focuses on OE fundamentals to provide personnel with an introductory level / basic knowledge of OE and how energy efficiency impacts warfighting capability. It could include a combination of web or classroom-based instruction, though it would not necessarily require field training.

OE Introduction, Level I

The OE Introduction Level I course should build upon the lessons learned in the GMT module, by enhancing this instruction with more challenging course content and real-world applications. A main component of OE Level I should be evaluating the basic tradeoffs between energy consumption and mission success, notably how OE impacts force mobility and lethality. Optimally, the OE Level I course should be designed for O-1 through O-3, and E-4 through E-6, and would have a field training component. The modules should be based on the four OE competencies with a culminating practical exercise that challenges the students and highlights the module lessons and real-world contingencies.

Table 7.1: Sample Modules for Operational Energy Level I.

Day/Module 1	Day/Module 2	Day/Module 3	Day/Module 4	Day/Module 5
Maritime fuel logistics/petroleum management	Power generation and distribution	Power storage	Management and measurement	Practical exercise (tactical)

7.3.1.2 Tier 2: Advanced OE Instruction

Tier 2 would build on lessons learned from Tier 1. It should focus on graduate-level instruction for mid-career officers and NCOs, notably for the O-4 through O-6 and E-7 through E-9 ranks. The level of instruction should provide students the opportunity to understand in greater detail the complex operational and strategic issues facing military leaders and how they impact operational capability. A certificate program should be designed to expose students to the technical, operational, and security aspects of DOD's energy needs.

OE Introduction, Level II

The OE Introduction II course would build on lessons learned from the OE Introduction Level I course. Therefore, the coursework demands are more rigorous than in OE Introduction and are designed for more advanced students, who anticipate greater operational responsibilities. While OE Level II would emphasize many of the same components of OE Level I, there must also be a focus on supply chain management, including refineries, port facilities, energy shipping and other transport, as well as analysis of how global markets can impact military operations. Ultimately, this requires broader knowledge of the risks, uncertainties, and tradeoffs related to the operational and strategic aspects of OE.

Table 7.2: Sample Modules Operational Energy Level II.

Day/Module 1	Day/Module 2	Day/Module 3	Day/Module 4	Day/Module 5
Maritime fuel logistics/petroleum management	Power generation and distribution	Power storage	Advanced management and measurement	Practical exercise (operational/strategic)

7.3.1.3 Tier 3: Future or Specialized Instruction

As energy-related technologies are constantly changing, the US military must also stay current in developing new, relevant coursework. Tier 3 is designed to meet future or specialized requirements. It builds on Tiers 1 and 2.

7.3.2 Potential Additional Curriculum Topics

There are several additional general fields which should be assessed for inclusion in curriculum.

7.3.2.1 Decision Support Tools

Decision support tools provide planners and operators with valuable insight to help leaders efficiently manage fuel/energy/ammunition consumption to maximize time on station and sustained fires on target. Additionally, indicator and warning (I&W) tools can give leaders advanced notice of pending kinetic or non-kinetic actions. Examples of logistic tools include, but are not limited to, Replenishment at Sea Planner (RASP), Optimized Transit Tool and Easy Reference (OTTER), Synthetic Theater Operations Research Model (STORM), Fuel Usage Study Extended Demonstration (FUSED), and Logistics Simulator (LOST).

7.3.2.2 Enhanced or Future OE Instruction

This is a broad category that recognize the OE field is dynamic, perpetually changing and evolving as new technologies or techniques are fielded. The following list provides sample topics for course offerings: Advanced Propulsion Systems, Hybridization Options, Advanced Power Generation and Distribution Technologies, Future Energy Storage Options, Unmanned Systems and OE Considerations, and Energy Weapons Implementation.

7.3.3 Critical Infrastructure Operators and Resilience Specialist Training

Critical infrastructure operators may not be adequately trained to operate microgrid or other systems under duress. This is particularly relevant for forward-deployed operational environments, where host nation conditions may not withstand intense kinetic or non-kinetic actions, as well as difficult weather conditions. It is vital these personnel are trained to operate these systems under a variety of challenging and hazardous conditions.

7.3.4 Climate and Weather Impact on OE

Certain weather and climate hazards impact specific regions of the world. Instruction could address how specific geographic regions of the world could be impacted more severely than others by the Joint Force's response. Finally, students could consider mitigating factors to those impacts in the short and long term, while, most importantly, maximizing operational reach and lethality.

7.4 An OE Education and Training Implementation Plan

Table 7.3: Operational Energy Education and Training Implementation Plan.

	Course/Module	
Tier 1 (Basic Instruction)	General Military Training (GMT)	Instruction on OE fundamentals
Tier 1	OE Introduction I	Instruction at the undergraduate level to junior or entry-level personnel
Tier 2 (Advanced Instruction)	OE Introduction II	Instruction at the graduate level to more experienced Joint Force leaders
Tier 3 (Future Instruction)	Decision Support Tools	Incorporating various tools into OE curricula
Tier 3	OE Enhanced Instruction	Rigorous technical and strategic instruction for specialists and/or senior leaders
Tier 3	Critical Infrastructure (CI) Operators	Specialist training dedicated to forward-deployed CI personnel
Tier 3	Climate and Weather Impacts on OE	Modules dedicated to impacts on the Joint Force and power projection capabilities

7.5 Education Tools: Wargames, Tabletop Exercises, Case Studies, Best Practices and Enhancing Cooperation with Allies and Partners

Another way to teach OE skills is the use of wargames and exercises. They allow the students to "act out" certain scenarios or responses, particularly those that might be counterintuitive or not normally recognized, in a compressed time schedule, allowing almost instantaneous feedback.

There are similarities between wargames and exercises, with each activity concentrating on different aspects of warfighting. Generally, exercises gauge the ability of forces to carry out a plan or procedure, while a wargame does not involve actual forces and is often more focused, usually on a unique situation or adversary.

7.5.1 Wargames

Wargames examine conditions in an operational setting, without actual military forces, with the flow of events affected by decisions made by students representing the opposing sides. OE wargames can focus on bulk petroleum deliveries and management, notably enemy A2/AD, maritime choke points, geopolitical conditions, and economic challenges. In wargames designed to teach about OE energy is often a constraint on the flow of the game, affecting operations.

The incorporation of OE as a function of the wargame has permitted more realism and enhanced communications between warfighters and logisticians. Furthermore, these changes have allowed a greater appreciation of the critical role that OE plays in the broader operational context, particularly to raise awareness of logistics constraints as operational rather than a purely logistics issue.

7.5.2 Exercises

A military exercise generally involves the operation of actual military forces, or other entities, in a simulated hostile environment. While exercises can be conducted in any variety of conditions, they are often characterized by real-time operation of personnel, ships, and aircraft, usually expending real or simulated weapons against an enemy.

An effective type of exercise is the tabletop exercise (TTX), which as the name indicates, is conducted in a small setting, usually in single or several rooms. A TTX is a facilitated discussion of a scenario in a formal or informal environment. Frequently, designed as an open, thought-provoking exchange of ideas on hypothetical, simulated incidents, it can enhance student awareness, validate current plans and procedures. An added value of an OE-centric TTX is it can employ a whole-of-government approach by bringing military, civilian, and private sector representatives to the table, thereby facilitating discussion between multiple players and perspectives. Moreover, tabletop exercises allow students to be immersed in all the OE competencies (fuels, power generation and distribution, storage, and command and control). For instance, a variety of simulated kinetic and non-kinetic actions on pipelines and power grids can be simulated, allowing for broader discussion on detection and mitigations.

7.5.3 Case Studies

Case studies of real-world or fictional events that illustrate various OE demands and challenges and analyze various planning and policy outcomes serve as great instruction tools for military officers and planners. Engagement in case study analysis can also raise awareness of OE needs and contribute to the identification of best practices. Case studies can reflect one or more of the OE competencies: fuels, power generation and distribution, and storage and management.

Instructors can assign writing case studies as part of the course work and then analysis of the cases in the classroom and in future classes, if the cases are worthy. Worthy case studies should be added to military data bases and libraries at DOD affiliated universities, colleges, and service academies.

7.5.4 Best Practices Analysis

Best practices codify standards or guidelines that establish reliable and superior courses of action in a set of scenarios or conditions. DOD continues to identify and codify best practices in the field of OE, based on real-world experience and research and analysis. OE best practices should continually be updated and integrated into US military publications and training programs and reflected in doctrine and strategy.

7.6 OE Education Cooperation with Allies and Partners

A vital component of joint operations is to develop higher levels of familiarity and cooperation with US allies and partners. Awareness of the importance of OE and related knowledge should be included in education programs with US military partners, both domestically and abroad. In the domestic arena, the Departments of Energy and Homeland Security are relevant partners for engagement in training and education related to OE. In parallel, education and training with US foreign allies and partners, including within the framework of NATO, should include OE.

7.7 Conclusions

As weapons and warfare become more sophisticated and require additional energy, OE expertise becomes vital for the Joint Force and US military leaders' need to recognize OE as a mission enabler, requiring more than a superficial knowledge of its application in the twenty-first-century battlespace. Failure to close this OE knowledge gap will result in poor coordination at the operational levels, missed opportunities on the battlefield, low deployment rates for equipment, or even tactical defeat or mission failure. While each of the services may approach this task differently, a tiered solution, coupled with a robust wargame and exercise regimen, as described in this chapter, allows for flexibility and oversight.

7.8 For Discussion in the Classroom and Study

- Discuss how training and education in OE will enhance Joint Force mobility and lethality.
- Discuss how training and education can address OE vulnerabilities.
- What specific OE skills need to be addressed in the officer and enlisted ranks?
- What OE training have you received during your career? Which OE skills and knowledge are missing in units you serve/have served? Discuss concrete examples. How should US military and training be designed to train for frequently changing OE needs and technologies?
- Develop an OE case study and share it with your classmates for feedback.

8 Operational Energy Challenges of the Armed Service Branches

The individual armed services that fall under the DOD share many common OE challenges. Due to the specialized role that each of the services perform within the larger Joint Force, each of these branches also faces unique quandaries. This chapter examines common predicaments that all the services face today, regardless of their role within the DOD or which operational domain that they tend to operate in. Next, the chapter analyzes service-specific problems. These are OE issues that are unique to the individual military branches, largely due to their operating concepts, or how they see their service contributing to the Joint Force.

8.1 OE Challenges for Today's Military

In a general sense the basic nature of the OE challenges faced by militaries today is the same as it has been throughout history: obtaining reliable access to required energy while at the same time limiting the impact these requirements have on operational freedom of maneuver, and denial of adequate energy supplies to one's adversary. This presents a particularly acute OE problem for the US military, which is charged with protecting and defending American interests across the globe.[322] Maintaining and employing such a military comes with enormous and specific OE challenges.

In fact, two of the OE problems faced by the US military are existential in nature. They are also inherently interrelated and exist within all the military services. The first challenge that each service must overcome is its enormous dependence on energy to fuel operations across all six operational domains.

Energy usage by the military services has increased steadily since the early 2000s as a reflection of the increased operational tempo after 9/11 but also because new equipment, down to the lowest levels, incorporates increasingly energy-consuming technology. The Biden administration's promotion of "electrification of the battlespace" also creates new OE challenges.[323]

The second problem, inherently related to the consumption issue, is a cultural issue that exists within each service: there is a lack of a fundamental understanding of the connection between energy and warfighting. The rank-and-file see OE as something

---

[322] The Joint Staff, "Description of the National Military Strategy 2018" (https://www.jcs.mil/Portals/36/Documents/Publications/UNCLASS_2018_National_Military_Strategy_Description.pdf).
[323] Alan Howard and Brenda Shaffer, "The Hidden Dangers of a Carbon-Neutral Military," *Foreign Policy*, August 12, 2021 (https://foreignpolicy.com/2021/08/12/the-hidden-dangers-of-a-carbon-neutral-military/).

that logisticians or other specialists should be concerned with as opposed to commanders. Despite some efforts to educate the force at large, OE is close to absent from service-level schools and their professional publications.

8.1.1 The Costs of Energy

To get an idea of the scope of the first OE challenge, dependency driven by high consumption rates and increasing demand, it's helpful to understand just how much energy the US military uses and at what cost. DOD is the largest institutional consumer of energy in the world. Of the funds DOD spends on energy, approximately 70 percent of that money goes to purchase the OE consumed by the military, the remaining 30 percent going to fund installation energy costs.[324] In FY 2020, the DOD purchased over 77 million barrels of fuel annually to power ships, aircraft, combat vehicles, and contingency bases at a cost of over $9 billion.[325] For the six years of actual costs depicted in Table 8.1, the DOD demand for fuel was 596.9 million barrels at a cost of over $74 billion. It should be noted, as evidenced in Table 8.1, that OE costs do vary from year to year depending on the scope of actual and anticipated military operations as well as the price of fuel.

Table 8.1: Operational Energy Demand (Million Barrels) and Costs.

	FY14	FY15	FY26	FY17	FY18	FY19	FY20	FY21e	FY22e
Army	10.1	7.3	7.1	7.6	9.2	9.0	8.1	9.3	9.3
Navy	28.2	28.5	28.5	28.4	26.0	28.1	27.9	25.3	25.3
Air Force	48.6	52.0	49.6	49.0	51.9	45.3	41.2	46.7	46.2
Marines	0.2	0.2	0.2	0.2	0.5	0.4	0.4	0.5	0.5
Other DOD	0.3	0.5	0.4	0.3	0.9	0.8	0.3	1.0	1.0
Total demand	87.4	88.6	85.7	85.5	88.5	83.6	77.6	82.8	82.3
Expenditure (billions)	$14.00	$14.10	$8.70	$8.20	$9.10	$11.00	$9.20	$8.24	$8.40

Source: Fiscal Year 2020 Operational Energy Annual Report (https://www.acq.osd.mil/eie/Downloads/OE/FY20%20OE%20Annual%20Report.pdf).

These OE costs largely consist of bulk purchases of jet fuel (JP-5 and JP-8) and diesel fuel. The Defense Logistics Agency (DLA), the DOD's executive agent for fuel procurement, purchase the bulk fuel that provides most of the OE from civilian sources. In addition to purchasing bulk fuel, the DLA also stores and maintains fuel stockpiles in the

---

[324] Office of the Assistant Secretary of Defense for Sustainment, "Installation Energy" (https://www.acq.osd.mil/eie/IE/FEP_index.html).
[325] Department of Defense, *2016 Operational Energy Strategy* (https://www.acq.osd.mil/eie/OE/OE_index.html).

United States and abroad. The DLA is also responsible for fuel delivery to the services, usually by contracting support, with truck transportation being the most common delivery method within the US. Maritime tanker vessels, combined with trucks for final stage transportation, deliver the lion's share of fuel to support overseas contingency operations.

Another factor to consider to fully appreciate the dangers associated with the US military's energy reliance is the Fully Burdened Cost of Fuel (FBCF). The FBCF affects all branches of service. It is defined as the total costs of fuel procurement, storage, and transportation. By the time a gallon of fuel gets to the warfighter in a contingency situation, the price of making that fuel available for use in an area of operations has grown exponentially. One report on DOD Energy Initiatives by the Congressional Research Service provided the following information regarding the FBCF in support of operations in Iraq and Afghanistan:

> In 2010, the Marine Corps estimated the fully burdened cost of fuel in Afghanistan at between $9 to $16 per gallon if delivered by land, and between $29 to $31 per gallon if delivered by air. An Army study estimated the fully burdened cost of fuel in Iraq at $9 to $45 per gallon, depending on the type of force protection used [...] and the delivery distance, while an Air Force study estimated the fully burdened cost of fuel delivered by land at $3 to $5 per gallon and $35 to $40 per gallon for aerial refueling. A report by the Army Environmental Policy Institute estimated that the fully burdened cost of fuel for a Stryker brigade in Iraq ranged from $14.13 to $17.44 per gallon ($3.73 to $4.61 per liter).[326]

Estimates of the FBCF also include casualties incurred in the delivery of that fuel, usually the result of attacks on ground supply convoys that are transporting fuel in theater. One Army study estimated that these casualty rates were as high as one casualty for every 39 fuel convoys in Iraq and one casualty for every 24 fuel convoys in Afghanistan.[327] In testimony to Congress in 2011, General James Mattis, then commander of US Central Command overseeing the wars in Iraq and Afghanistan, had the following to say about the impact of the US military's dependence on bulk liquid fuel on operations:

> On the fuel, it is a significant Achilles heel for us when you have to haul the amounts of fuel that we have to haul around the battlefield for the generators and for the vehicles [...]. I mean, it is an

---

[326] Moshe Schwartz, Katherine Blakeley, and Ronald O'Rourke, "Department of Defense Energy Initiatives: Background and Issues for Congress," Congressional Research Service, December 10, 2012 (https://sgp.fas.org/crs/natsec/R42558.pdf).

[327] Army Environmental Policy Institute, "Sustain the Mission Project: Casualty Factors for Fuel and Water Resupply Convoys," 2009 (https://apps.dtic.mil/dtic/tr/fulltext/u2/b356341.pdf).

amazingly complex effort to maintain the fuel lines. And it also gives the enemy an ability to choose the time and place of attacking us.[328]

An additional dimension to factor into understanding the scope of the US military's energy problem is that it continues to grow. The platforms that the services currently employ, or are procuring for future operational use, are steadily increasing OE demand. Despite a significant amount of rhetoric devoted to procuring ships, aircraft, and vehicles that are more energy efficient or that utilize some form of renewable energy, the fact of the matter is that most of the large defense platforms in the procurement cycle will continue to be heavily dependent on petroleum-based fuels for their energy for the foreseeable future.

The services are also fielding equipment that is creating more dependence on energy. Be it the result of fielding individual pieces of field equipment that consume more energy or energy-hungry platforms that facilitate command and control, the energy consumption levels (and associated costs) are rising at the tactical level, an echelon of command that was relatively free from energy dependency in the past. Military leaders like to talk about concepts like "net-centric warfare" or "Joint All-Domain Command and Control" when describing their vision for an internet-based system that links data from sensors and other operational information across all echelons of the services into one network. While the advantages of doing so are arguable, the costs associated with it are clear. Units that were once relatively unencumbered by the tether of fuel, are now firmly within its restraint.

8.2 What Changed?

If Vietnam was a helicopter war, then Iraq will be remembered as a vehicle war – one in which vehicle patrols became the norm over foot patrols or airborne operations. Prior to the wars in Iraq and Afghanistan, tactical units in the ground branches (Army and Marine Corps) had a similar OE footprint as did their counterparts in Vietnam. The primary energy-consuming platform in an infantry battalion was the High Mobility Multi-Wheeled Vehicle (HMMWV). Although the HMMWV was a gas guzzler (getting only about 12mpg on average) there were not enough of them in infantry units to have a massive impact on overall DOD energy consumption when compared to the amount of energy being consumed by aircraft and ships. In 2001, a typical Marine infantry battalion would have one or two HMMWVs per company; heavy weapons units were the exception requiring approximately sixteen vehicles to accommodate

---

[328] Mattis at the Committee on Armed Services, Hearing on National Defense Authorization Act for Fiscal Year 2012, March 3, 2011 (https://www.govinfo.gov/content/pkg/CHRG-112hhrg65114/html/CHRG112hhrg65114.htm).

transportation and use of crew-served weapons. When additional vehicles from headquarters and supporting units were added, the total number rose to sixty-four HMMWV-variant vehicles in the battalion. While this was not inconsequential from an energy consumption standpoint, it was not remarkable either. In the early day of the war in Iraq, the average number of gas-guzzling HMMWVs per company increased to somewhere between ten and twelve per company, each serving as both a mode of transportation and as an armored sanctuary from the increasing and ever-present threats of improvised explosive devices (IEDs) and sniper fire.

The evolution of armored vehicles that occurred during the conflict is well documented.[329] It began with individual units affixing scrap steel to their vehicles to provide occupants more protection, and reached its zenith with industrially modified vehicles that were specifically designed to withstand high explosive blasts. This extra protection came at a cost of adding thousands of pounds to an already underpowered vehicle, ultimately resulting in a significant decrease in its already poor fuel economy. When the newly "up armored" HMMWVs failed to provide adequate protection from the IED threat, the DOD procured and fielded thousands of Mine Resistant Ambush Protected Vehicles (MRAPs).[330] While it is debatable if these 40,000-pound, diesel-powered behemoths better shielded troops from IEDs than armored versions of existing vehicles combined with other IED mitigation techniques, they consumed nearly double the amount of fuel of HMMVWs.[331] By 2011, a typical Marine infantry battalion's motor pool had 173 MRAP-variant vehicles.[332] Ironically, the decrease in miles per gallon, as troops shifted from HMMWVs to MRAPs, resulted in a greater demand for fuel convoys which resulted in greater convoy casualties in both Iraq and Afghanistan.

8.2.1 Appearance of Digital Devices on the Battlefield

Changes in vehicles were not the only energy-related evolution to occur because of the wars in Iraq and Afghanistan. Prior to the late 1990s, the number of electrical devices in a typical infantry battalion had also not changed much since the Vietnam War. The

---

[329] Marne McEntee, "Troops Add Improvised Armor to Humvees," Stars and Stripes, February 3, 2004 (https://www.stripes.com/news/troops-add-improvised-armor-to-humvees-1.16236).

[330] The wisdom of this action is still debated to this day with some critics pointing out that the new up-armored HMMWVs offered nearly the same protection as the new MRAPs and that the fielding of the MRAPs, while well-intentioned, was more the result of a political requirement to demonstrate that something was being done to stem the highly publicized tide of dead and wounded troops returning from both wars.

[331] Alex Rogers, "The MRAP: Brilliant Buy, or Billions Wasted?," *Time Magazine*, October 2, 2012 (https://nation.time.com/2012/10/02/the-mrap-brilliant-buy-or-billions-wasted/).

[332] US Marine Corps, "USMC Expeditionary Energy Strategy and Implementation Plan," 2011 (https://www.hqmc.marines.mil/Portals/160/Docs/USMC%20Expeditionary%20Energy%20Strategy%20%20Implementation%20Planning%20Guidance.pdf).

primary sources of electricity consumption associated with infantry operations were non-rechargeable batteries used to power communication radios. The first significant change to this model occurred in the late 1990s, as digital devices began to appear on the scene. During this period, digital radios, along with associated devices such as GPS receivers and desktop computers, started showing up at the company level. Computer use is particularly emblematic of the exponential increase in electrical power consumption which took place during this timeframe as internet access and usage became widespread.

Accordingly, computers began to trickle into office spaces of tactical-level units just prior to the year 2000. At first, there were often one or two machines limited to the company commander and the company administrative clerk. Soon, however, they became as ubiquitous as M-16 service rifles. Still, even after computers became commonplace in garrison settings, they were largely considered administrative tools and were not taken to the field or used much at all in tactical operations. Most tactical units lacked organic power generation capability and the early generations of personal computers were not robust enough to survive outside of a garrison environment. All of that changed rapidly with subsequent technological advances which allowed computers to be miniaturized and ruggedized for field use. Concurrently, the proliferation of the internet, email accounts, and work productivity software such as Power Point became an impetus to expand computer usage to the field. Today, computers and computer-enabled devices are seen as indispensable tools in an increasingly connected, digital force, but their implementation uncovered new requirements for power generation capability within the services.

The benefit associated with the digitization of tactical-level units is the ability to communicate rapidly with anyone else who has a connected device and to share information. Electronic devices also enabled precision location of both friendly and enemy forces, which increased both safety and accuracy when linked with modern weapon systems. For obvious reasons these factors are considered beneficial to operations. The downside to all of this is that energy dependence at all levels increased exponentially.

The demand for copious amounts of reliable electricity created a fundamental change in the way that the military operates. For one, a soldier's individual load increased exponentially with electrically powered equipment and the batteries needed to power it. By the mid-point of the war in Iraq, circa 2007, the average soldier deployed in theater saw a dramatic increase in the amount of energy-consuming equipment that they were issued for personal use. Such devices included battery-operated night vision goggles, laser targeting devices for individual and crew-served weapons, battery-powered optics, digital cameras for recording evidence, and personal radios for communication between members of a rifle squad. In addition to vehicle-mounted radio sets, individual vehicles were equipped with GPS-enabled computers to aid in communication and in tracking a unit's location. Several vehicles in each squad also housed powerful IED jammers to disrupt electromagnetic signals from remote IED triggers. Some vehicles were even equipped with HMMWV-mounted multi-lens video cameras that would produce a 3-D rendering of the terrain that it recorded as vehicle patrols plodded through the area of operations.

Perhaps no addition to the soldier's basic load was as significant as the need to power much of this equipment with batteries. Examining the use of a single battery used in Iraq and Afghanistan, the BA-5590, illustrates the cascading effects of reliance on battery power. The BA-5590 is a disposable lithium battery used by the US military. It is responsible for powering over sixty systems used in combat. Arguably, the most important function the BA-5590 performs is powering the SINGARs family of digital radios used by most ground units of the US military. In the first two months of combat operations in Iraq, the US military used 620,000 BA-5590s at a cost of 100 dollars apiece. At one point during the initial operations in Iraq, the Marine Corps alone was consuming over 3028 BA-5590s a day. Overall, the US military would spend over 300 million dollars on BA-5590s in 2003. Such prolific battery usage had a direct impact on a soldier's load. At one point in the war in Iraq, it was estimated that each combat soldier carried approximately nine pounds of disposable batteries on a given mission to power the various electrical devices used in combat operations. As of 2024, a soldier on a three-day patrol required as much as 17 pounds of batteries.

> As of 2024, a soldier on a three-day patrol required as much as 17 pounds of batteries.

The impact of battery usage on the soldier's load is a tactical consideration but the impact of battery usage extends far beyond the tactical realm. In 2003, a shortage of BA-5590s had the potential to cause significantly degraded communication capabilities within the Marine Corps during a critical phase of the march to Baghdad. Even after defense logisticians managed to convince commercial producers to increase production by almost 300 percent, catastrophe was diverted only because that phase of the war ended as quickly as it did. Battery weight is also a concern at the operational level. The BA-5590 provides another useful lens to examine the costs of getting the large quantities of batteries required for operations from the manufacturer to the user in theater.

A pallet of BA-5590 batteries consists of 2000 batteries, weighs 4600 pounds, and takes up sixty-four cubic feet of cargo space.[333] In 2006, it cost $19,320 to ship a pallet of BA-5590s from Atlanta to Kuwait City. Steady state operations in Iraq, consumed ninety-

---

[333] Major C.B. Lynn, "Alternative Energy Harvesting: Turning Strategic Crisis Into Opportunity," Quantico, Virginia, Marine Corps University, School of Advanced Warfighting (SAW), 2011.

one pallets' worth of BA-5590s, on average, each month.³³⁴ This translates into a purchase cost of 18.2 million dollars and a transportation cost of over 1.75 million dollars a month. Those figures do not take into account the total transportation costs associated with BA-5590 use because once the batteries arrived in Kuwait, they still had to be either trucked or flown into Iraq and then distributed to combat units on the ground. Nor do those figures account for the lost opportunity costs associated with using precious cargo space for batteries versus any number of other sorely needed items. Finally, because BA-5590s are disposable lithium batteries, once they were depleted, they had to be transported back to the US at additional costs for proper disposal to avoid environmental damage. This final act did not take place in many cases and BA-5590s were either disposed of improperly by users leaving them on the ground or throwing them into burn pits. The latter course of action may have caused lingering illnesses to military personnel who were continuously exposed to the fumes emanating from these burn pits during deployment. In further illustration of the cascading costs of relying on batteries to power devices in combat, in October 2022 the US Congress allocated approximately 280 billion dollars to the Veteran's Administration to cover the costs of service-related disabilities for veteran's exposed to toxic fumes from burn pits in Iraq and Afghanistan.³³⁵

In the latter stages of the wars, a rechargeable version of the BA-5590 was fielded as a replacement for the disposable model but shared many of the weight and cost issues of the disposable battery as well as additional limitations. Specifically, these batteries lose power in extreme temperatures and require users to carry rechargers and have reliable access to electricity.

This last requirement, reliable access to electricity, once a luxury in combat, has now become a necessity as devices consuming electricity have been deemed essential to modern military operations. Electronic devices, particularly silicone-chip-based computers, don't tolerate heat well. Accordingly, a new requirement was added as a prerequisite to conduct operations at the tactical level; access to an adequate supply of electricity, both to power the equipment and to power the air conditioning units that are necessary to ensure that the equipment continues to operate as designed. With the US military conducting global operations over vastly different climates, OE needs are affected by the need to heat and cool electronic equipment and OE plans must take this into consideration.

---

334 Major C.B. Lynn, "Alternative Energy Harvesting: Turning Strategic Crisis Into Opportunity," Quantico, Virginia, Marine Corps University, School of Advanced Warfighting (SAW), 2011.
335 Sen. Kristen E. Gillibrand, "S.952 – Presumptive Benefits for War Fighters Exposed to Burn Pits and Other Toxins Act of 2021," March 24, 2021 (https://www.congress.gov/bill/117th-congress/senate-bill/952/text).

What this meant in practical terms was not clear until the US invasion of Iraq in 2003 and subsequent steady state operations focused on stabilizing the security situation in that country. Suddenly, platoon and company commanders who were used to living out of their backpacks with a tactical radio as their only means to communicate between echelons of command, had sophisticated and energy-hungry Forward Operating Bases (FOB) to manage. In many cases, these came complete with satellite-based internet and suites of computers, some dedicated to facilitating operations while others were part of the Moral Welfare and Recreation packages designed to provide the troops with a way to surf the net and communicate with family back home. Big screen television monitors replaced paper maps on the walls of their command post displaying real-time imagery and troop locations across the battlespace. Maps, acetate, and grease pencils, once the hallmark of an operations center, were replaced with laptops and projectors. Soon, company-level command posts were more sophisticated, and had a higher OE requirement, than battalion or regimental command posts in previous conflicts.

In addition to computers, company and battalion commanders were equipped with a plethora of other electronic gear to help them win the war. One common such item was the Ground Based Operational Surveillance System (G-BOSS), which was essentially a long view camera atop a tower mounted on a towable trailer. The camera could be monitored from a laptop and was principally used as part of the overall surveillance and IED detection effort. It consumed electrical power which was supplied by deep cycle, rechargeable batteries or it could be hard wired into a FOB's generator-based power grid. Electricity consuming cameras, along with other powered sensors, became common place at many FOBs.

These are some of many examples of technological advances and additions to tactical-level units in Iraq, all designed to help the military win a war, but at the costs of encumbering formerly light infantry units with enormous OE requirements. The requirements for electrical power were met with power produced by diesel-fueled generators at each Forward Operating Base. One Office of Naval Research Project found that the average Marine rifle company operating in an austere environment consumes 1000 kilowatt-hours of electricity per day.[336] One battalion, 2d Battalion, 8th Marines, which operated in Iraq for eight months in 2006 and 2007, used an average of 400 gallons of diesel fuel a day to power vehicles and generators at the battalion's five FOBs. Every drop of that fuel had to be trucked in from Kuwait. One way to put this increased demand for OE in perspective is the stark contrast between fuel usage per soldier in World War II, a four-year, global conflict, and the same metric during the wars in Iraq and Afghanistan. As pointed out in Chapter 2, the average use of fuel per soldier

---

[336] Office of Naval Research, "Request for Information, Experimental Forward Operating Base (EXFOB 4), RFI # 10-RFI-0007" (https://www.hqmc.marines.mil/Portals/160/Docs/RFI%20ExFOB%20Phase%204.pdf).

in World War II was one gallon per day. In Iraq and Afghanistan, it was somewhere between 15–20 gallons per soldier, per day.[337]

8.3 Military Approach to Energy Use

As stated earlier, decades of growing energy use have formed generational habits and assumptions about OE consumption and availability. In short, the prevalent notion seems to be that if there is a requirement, it will be met. To be sure there have been some energy-related operational events in the US wars of the early twenty-first century that foreshadowed what operations in an energy-scarce environment might be like. Before 2011, most bulk liquid fuel that supported Coalition operations in Afghanistan, some 1.8 million gallons a day, arrived by ship to the port of Karachi, Pakistan from DLA storage facilities in California. The fuel was then transported by truck through Pakistan and into Afghanistan. On November 26 of that year, a US strike on two Pakistani border checkpoints killed twenty-four Pakistani soldiers. The resulting ramifications for the Coalition's OE situation were significant. Pakistan closed their border for eight months, effectively shutting down all Coalition fuel transport routes through their country. Consequently, operations in Afghanistan slowed to a crawl for months until diplomatic agreements were reached with the Central Asian countries and Russia to open an alternative supply route. The costs of this incident, both in dollars and in lost opportunity costs were severe. The new supply routes ended up raising the costs of the war by hundreds of millions of dollars a month. Additionally, the near operational pause that Coalition forces had to take in the wake of the incident set back plans for Coalition forces to gradually begin withdrawing from the conflict.

Although the incident in Pakistan in 2011 did seem to get leaders within the DOD and Congress talking about OE, the effect was short-lived. In fact, serious education regarding OE, as of 2023, had only begun to surface at DOD educational institutions and within the operating forces, and in nascent forms. This emergence of OE considerations is largely the result of DOD war games that pit the US against a near-peer competitor in austere locations far from the continental US.[338] One of the outcomes of these simulations has been those forces fighting such a conflict would have difficulty sourcing the energy that the modern US military requires. How long this focus on OE will last before something else takes its place is anyone's guess. Efforts to moderate energy consumption in the operating forces have had episodic success, such as the Air Force's utilization of energy planning software JIGSAW to increase energy efficiency in Air Force sor-

---

[337] M.A. Vane and P.E. Roege, "The Army's Operational Energy Challenge," Association of the United States Army, Arlington, VA, 2011 (https://apps.dtic.mil/docs/citations/ADA543153).
[338] Brett Tingley, "Joint Chiefs Seek a New Warfighting Paradigm after Devastating Losses in Classified Wargames," *The Warzone*, July 27, 2021 (https://www.thedrive.com/the-war-zone/41712/joint-chiefs-seek-a-new-warfighting-paradigm-after-devastating-losses-in-classified-wargames).

ties in FY 2020 and save 180,000 gallons of jet fuel per week. Still, these successes are few and, when compared to total energy consumption by the services, often a drop in the bucket. More often than not, when it comes to OE, the services make marginal versus substantial changes to their *modus operandi*. In fact, as of FY 2021, the Assistant Secretary of Defense for Sustainment singled out two of the four major branches, the Air Force and the Marine Corps, for not doing enough to mitigate OE risk and invest in new systems that would improve their OE posture.[339]

At the time of publication, there is very little evidence that energy awareness, at a level that would change service culture, exists. Each service does emphasize the challenges that energy dependency presents for their respective service in their strategic documents and operating concepts. Still, outside of a few specialized communities across DOD, factoring energy considerations into training and education at the tactical and operational levels, a crucial step in fostering true organizational change lags behind. The focus instead has been on marquee initiatives such as Biden administration policies for achieving net-zero energy installations or electrifying vehicles at those installations.

8.4 Service-Specific OE Challenges

In addition to the common OE challenges described above that affect all the military services, each of the individual services has their own unique challenges. These challenges are largely the result of the way that the individual services think about warfighting, their own unique service cultures, and the core mission sets that they perform.

8.4.1 The US Air Force

With a total fleet of over 5200 aircraft, including more than 2100 high performance fighter jets, the Air Force is by far the biggest consumer of OE within the DOD (see Figure 8.1). Their most fuel-efficient fighter, the F-22 Raptor, burns through approximately 0.4 gallons per mile, depending on speed and flight conditions. Newer F35-A Joint Striker Fighters are said to be 40 to 60 percent less fuel efficient than that, although that is just an estimate due to lack of clear reporting regarding Air Force platform fuel efficiency. From a capability standpoint, the difference between the legacy platforms such as the F-22 and F-16, and the fifth-generation F-35 are remarkable. But that in-

---

[339] Office of the Assistant Secretary of Defense for Sustainment, "Fiscal Year 2022 Operational Energy Budget Certification Report" (https://www.acq.osd.mil/eie/Downloads/OE/FY22%20OE%20Budget%20Certification%20Report.pdf).

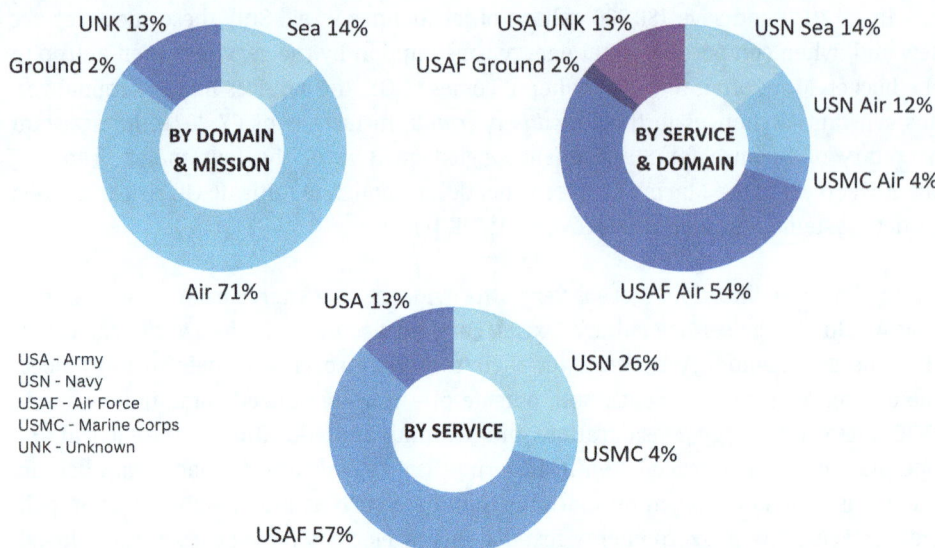

Figure 8.1: Military Fuel Use. Source: Department of Defense, *2016 Operational Energy Strategy*, December 3, 2015 (https://www.acq.osd.mil/eie/Downloads/OE/2016%20OE%20Strategy_WEBd.pdf).

creased capability comes with a significant tradeoff when it comes to OE expenditure. Aviation fuel consumption rates are the Air Force's primary OE challenge. As such, reducing consumption is the biggest objective in the Service Operational Energy Plan.

The Air Force's Approach to Reducing Energy Consumption
In addition to consuming billions of gallons of liquid fuel per year, the Air Force also consumes vast amounts of electricity each year in exercising command and control of aircraft and missiles. Airborne and ground-based sensors provide real-time positional data on hundreds of aircraft and send that data to air-conditioned command posts across the globe. The Air Force's idea of an expeditionary force carries an exponentially larger footprint than say the Marine Corps or even the Army. Even the ground support necessary to enable flight operations consumes a large amount of energy with $360 million per year spent on fuel for vehicles and ground equipment that allow the Air Force to conduct its mission.[340] It should be noted that the line between OE costs and installation energy costs begins to blur when the costs of support vehicles is added to the mix but the larger point remains that the Air Force consumes more energy than the other three services combined.

---

[340] Assistant Secretary of the Air Force for Installations/Logistics and Environment, "Air Force Energy Plan 2010" (https://apps.dtic.mil/sti/citations/ADA511964).

The Air Force also expends a lot of energy transporting people and things for its own operations, as well as in support of the other services. As the premier airlift provider in the DOD, the Air Force plays a critical role in extending the US military's operational reach. But that operational reach comes at a great cost. Airlift makes up 20 percent of all Air Force OE expenditure. That's the same amount of the Air Force's annual energy expenditure for its fighters. Unlike the Navy, the Air Force is inherently tied to land-based infrastructure for most of its operations and cannot remain untethered from land for extended periods of time. That means that energy generation and storage are relatively immobile, increasing the risk that access to that energy will be disrupted.

The Air Force also faces a serious threat to operations if its energy flow is disrupted. Physical and/or cyberattacks can accomplish just this sort of disruption. All the services are vulnerable to this threat, but the Air Force is especially vulnerable because of its enormous need for OE. If there is no fuel or electricity then jets, radars, missiles, and avionics equipment all become useless. Disruptions to energy supplies can and do also come in the form of severe weather, especially in typhoon-prone places such as the Philippines or Guam where the Air Force may operate from in a future conflict. The Air Force's Critical Infrastructure Protection (CIP) plans must factor in these kinds of manmade and natural events if the service is going to be able to continue to fulfill its mission to "Fly, Fight, and Win … Airpower Anytime, Anywhere."

The Air Force has initiated plans to reduce energy needs. In its 2010 Air Force Energy Plan, the service lists several goals it would like to reach prior to 2030.[341] Among these are:
- Reduced fuel consumption by using mission planning software and more efficient flying
- Increasing the use of non-fossil fuels, such as biofuels, where applicable
- Powering expeditionary bases with renewable power sources
- Prioritizing energy in all acquisitions
- Making energy a consideration in all actions.

The last point may be the toughest for a service that has had a heavy energy dependency since its inception. Air Force leaders acknowledge as much by stating, "Successful implementation of the Air Force Energy Plan is predicated on a culture change whereby Air Force members embrace saving energy as being part of their core competencies. Culture change is a long process that is best achieved through consistent delivery of awareness, training, and expectations."[342]

---

[341] Assistant Secretary of the Air Force for Installations/Logistics and Environment, "Air Force Energy Plan 2010," page 6 (https://apps.dtic.mil/sti/citations/ADA511964).
[342] Assistant Secretary of the Air Force for Installations/Logistics and Environment, "Air Force Energy Plan 2010," page 14 (https://apps.dtic.mil/sti/citations/ADA511964).

Figure 8.2: MQ-28 Ghost. Source: US Department of Defense.

While changing cultural attitudes regarding energy within the service may take time, there are several capabilities that the Air Force can explore today to help with reducing energy. The two most promising, in terms of the potential impact, are artificial intelligence and Unmanned Aerial Systems.

Advanced Unmanned Aerial Systems (UAS) show great potential in reducing energy consumption. As of 2023, the service is already experimenting with unmanned fighter aircraft such as Boeing's MQ-28 Ghost Bat. The MQ-28 is intended to operate as a "loyal wingman" in conjunction with manned fighter aircraft such as the F-35 and F-22 – what developers term Manned-Unmanned Teaming. The MQ-28 has several energy-related advantages over its manned counterparts. For one, it is far lighter because of not having to carry humans onboard. That avoids the need for systems to carry out manned flight and ensure pilot safety and comfort. A lighter aircraft means that it can be powered with less powerful engine which consume less fuel than conventional jets. Due to the lack of need for extensive safety testing, aircraft such as the MQ-28 also have a truncated timeline from drawing board to operational model. The MQ-28 went from conception to flight testing within two years, a process that can take decades with manned aircraft. In addition to unmanned fighters, the Air Force continues to experiment with other variants of UAS to include tankers and cargo craft.

Other initiatives underway in the Air Force are a combination of programs and technology. They include reducing energy consumption by replacing legacy engines, reducing drag on existing platforms through the use of new components and flight surface controls, gaining authorization from DOD aviation safety agencies to use commercially available biofuels, and investing in more efficient propulsion engines for future generations of aircraft.[343]

---

[343] Assistant Secretary of Defense for Sustainment, "Increased Resilience and Lethality through Opera-

8.4.2 The US Naval Services

The US Naval Services comprise the US Navy and the US Marine Corps. Although each of these services is a separate service within the DOD, it is useful to examine their approach to OE issues in tandem with one another as both services have somewhat complementary operating concepts. Both services reside within the common framework of guidance proffered by the Department of the Navy. In a theater-wide war against a near-peer competitor such as China or Russia, both services would presumably be operating as part of a naval campaign in roles that are mutually supportive. An example of this reciprocal relationship is the US Marine Corps' capture and defense of advanced naval bases to allow the US Navy to exercise sea control in its area of operations. The Marine forces that participate in this mission will likely be transported and supported by US Navy ships which in turn benefit from the security and access that the Marines provide once ashore. Contemporary concepts such as the Navy's Distributed Maritime Operations (DMO) and the Marine Corps' Expeditionary Advanced Base Operations (EABO) are merely adaptations of this basic mutually beneficial relationship that account for capabilities of specific strategic competitors.

There are, however, many other facets to Naval Services operations that impact each service's OE requirements in ways that somewhat separate the sister services. For instance, the Navy's blue water fleet, to include its submarines, must also conduct surface warfare against enemy fleets with little or no support from the Marine Corps. Likewise, the Marine Corps is often called upon to act in either a crisis response force role, or as a force provider to an extended ground campaign such as the ones in Iraq and Afghanistan, where there is little presence from the fleet. As a result of these divergent mission sets, both services have developed energy requirements that are often complimentary but can be service specific in certain circumstances.

Both services also have air wings that consume significant amounts of energy. The US Navy air wing consists of approximately 2600 aircraft ranging from jet fighters to propellor-driven support aircraft, as well as helicopters and unmanned aircraft systems (UAS). Likewise, the Marine air wing consists of approximately 1200 aircraft across similar categories. Although the purpose of the two services' air wings differ, they pose similar OE challenges. The consumption of jet fuel is the leading energy expenditure for the Marine Corps, and accounts for half of the OE usage of the Navy, the other half being fuel to power ships.

In total, the Navy accounts for approximately 26 percent of total US DOD fuel consumption. The Marine Corps accounts for just 4 percent. OE for the Naval Services over-

---

tional Energy Investment," January 2022 (https://www.acq.osd.mil/EIE/Downloads/OE/Increased%20Resiliency%20and%20Lethality.pdf).

whelmingly comes in the form of bulk liquid fuel, which is then consumed by ships, aircraft, ground vehicles, or generators. As discussed earlier in this chapter, getting this bulk fuel to naval forces that are conducting a mission in theater is a function of transporting it at sea and, in the case of ground forces, moving it ashore then transporting it overland. Unlike conflicts since WWII, where transportation and delivery were relatively uncontested, a conflict with a near-peer adversary would most certainly involve attacks at sea and ashore on these energy supply lines.

In addition to vessels that conduct Navy replenishment at sea, the Navy also has a small fleet of tanker ships that transport fuel from terminal to terminal. Some of these ships are capable of an instream offload of fuel to shore, negating the need for an established port facility on the receiving end but these are typically not ships that are hardened against enemy attack and would be extremely vulnerable in a combat environment.

Some of the ways that the Navy is attempting to mitigate this problem, as delineated in its 2022 Climate Action Plan, are to reduce overall consumption.[344] Conservation efforts and a desire to shift to non-fossil energy sources have been ongoing for the Navy. In 2009, the Secretary of the Navy Ray Mabus issued five goals pertaining to naval energy (fig. 8.3).

The Navy completely missed these goals, since they were unrealistic. Critics of Secretary Mabus' approach targeted the costs of some of the initiatives and asserted that some of the goals were based on political desires rather than operational benefits.

Reduction of consumption of fossil fuels may promote certain climate policy goals, but in most cases does little to mitigate OE challenges and actually increases them. Fossil fuels, especially oil and coal, are easy to store, are portable, and are energy dense. Renewable energy cannot be stored on a mass level, is not portable, and is not energy dense. Thus, they are not relevant for aircraft and ships which require energy-dense fuels.

The Great Green Fleet initiative is a good example of this. In 2012, the Navy successfully deployed a carrier strike group, built around the USS Nimitz, which used a 50:50 mix of petroleum and biofuel made from cooking oil and algae. The 2012 event was a demonstration of capability which saw the carrier group participate in the Rim of the Pacific exercise before returning to port. In 2016, the Navy repeated the experiment, this time sending a strike group built around the carrier John C. Stennis to conduct operations in the Indo-Pacific region. The Stennis Strike Group used an advanced 10:90 mixture of

---

[344] Department of the Navy, "Climate Action 2030" (https://www.navy.mil/Portals/1/Documents/Department%20of%20the%20Navy%20Climate%20Action%202030.pdf).

U.S. Secretary of the Navy 2009 Energy Goals

1. By 2020, at least 50% of total Department of the Navy energy will come from alternative energy resources.

2. By 2020, Department of the Navy will produce at least 50% of shore-based energy requirements from alternative resources and 50% of Department installations will be net-zero.

3. Department of the Navy will demonstrate a Green Strike Group in local operations by 2012 and sail the Great Green Fleet by 2016.

4. By 2015, Department of the Navy will reduce petroleum use in non-tactical vehicles by 50%.

5. Evaluation of energy factors will be used when awarding contracts for systems and buildings.

Figure 8.3: Secretary of the Navy 2009 Energy Goals. Source: Secretary of the Navy (2009), US Department of Defense.

beef tallow and marine diesel, respectively. It also incorporated various energy conservation measures and revised operational procedures designed around fuel conservation and efficiency.

While these two events might seem like successful milestones in transitioning the Navy away from petroleum-based fuel, strong criticism – within and outside the military – emerged to both of the Great Green Fleet experiments.[345] One of the most frequent critiques was that the costs and availability of the biofuel made adopting these practices across the fleet prohibitive. The Navy officially states that in support of the mission, the DLA purchased 77.66 million gallons of biofuel at a price of approximately $2.04 a gallon, a price that was reasonably competitive with the cost of marine diesel at the time. What they are not so forthcoming with is that the purchase price was heavily subsidized by money from the US Department of Agriculture to promote the biofuel industry. Without those subsidies, the true cost of the biofuel was closer to $26 a gallon when the FBCF is taken into account.[346] Some also claim that the Green Fleet experiment was based on a political desire of the Obama administration to create a demand for biofuel so that it could eventually become an industry of scale, thus ultimately lowering the

---

345 Mark F. Cancian, "Sink the Great Green Fleet," *Proceedings*, vol. 143, September 2007.
346 Mark F. Cancian, "Sink the Great Green Fleet," *Proceedings*, vol. 143, September 2007.

cost.[347] Proponents of this argument believe that the Navy was willing to sacrifice mission effectiveness in pursuit of larger economic goals of the administration and should have been more focused on warfighting. At the deckplate-level, the Green Fleet initiative also garnered a reputation for being hyper-focused on mundane issues such as turning off lights and closing hatches that formed air conditioning boundaries at the expense of more substantive energy conservation measures.

After the Green Fleet program, the Navy is still wrestling with conservation, efficiency, and transitioning to renewable sources of energy. In a 2020 article, James Caley, Director of Operational Energy, Office of the Secretary of Navy, highlighted some of the OE challenges facing the future fleet.[348] These included a naval fuel distribution system "characterized by critical assets and single points of failure along static lines of communication," advanced naval weapons systems and sensors which will more than double ships' energy demand, and challenges delivering fuel from the sea to the littorals in a contested environment.

The OE dilemmas that Caley highlighted should be especially concerning to the US Marine Corps whose Force Design 2030 effort is centered on creating a force to enable the Navy's sea control mission by using isolated outposts well within the adversaries' weapons engagement zone to deny them naval access. The Marine Corps concept of operating from these expeditionary bases, called Expeditionary Advanced Base Operations (EABO) is characterized by small, disaggregated forces which rely on stealth, advanced weapons and sensors, mobility, and maintaining a small footprint to avoid counterstrikes. These "stand-in forces" are heavily reliant on the Navy for their logistical supply. Given these requirements and the assumption that logistical support in such an environment will be contested by the adversary, it becomes evident rather quickly that access to reliable energy is an essential military requirement. One group of Marine Corps concept developers has described logistics as the pacing function of EABO, with energy being the pacing commodity, meaning that the concept is only valid as long as the Marine Corps and Navy figure out a way to meet the OE demand associated with it.[349]

To this end, the Marine Corps has identified numerous OE requirements as essential. Some of these requirements, the Corps identified coming out of the wars in Iraq and Afghanistan while others have become apparent through wargaming associated with Force Design and EABO.

---

[347] Mark F. Cancian, "Sink the Great Green Fleet," *Proceedings*, vol. 143, September 2007.
[348] J.C. Caley, "Meeting the Challenges of the Department of the Navy's Energy Goals" (https://nps.edu/web/eag/meeting-the-challenges-of-the-department-of-the-navy-operational-energy-goals).
[349] Capt. Walker D. Mills, Maj. Jacob Clayton, and Erik R. Limpaecher, "Powering EABO: Aluminum Fuel for the Future Fight," *Marine Corps Gazette*, August 2022.

One of the insights gained from the wars in Iraq and Afghanistan was to reduce the per Marine energy consumption metric by fielding more energy-efficient equipment and by introducing energy conserving practices to the operating forces. In 2009, then Commandant of the Marine Corps General James Amos established the Marine Corps Expeditionary Energy Office (E2O) and directed it to pursue initiatives that would accomplish these goals and meet the Corps OE requirements. Since then, the E2O has pursued efforts such as fielding more efficient batteries to lighten the Marine's load, solar power generation to meet small unit level command and control requirements, electrification of tactical vehicles, and standardization of bulk fuel distribution practices across the Marine Corps. Current and future operating concepts are forcing the Navy-Marine Corps team to address some difficult challenges associated with sourcing energy in a contested environment. For instance, what capability does the Navy have to refuel at sea in an area that is well within hypersonic, anti-ship missile range? Provided that the Navy can get energy sources such as bulk fuel or significant amounts of batteries to Marines on isolated outposts, how does that commodity then get transported from ship to shore and, subsequently from beach head to inland locations? Once Marines are supplied with an energy source such as bulk liquid fuel, how do they move with it quickly and stealthily when they have to displace to avoid detection by enemy intelligence, surveillance and reconnaissance units? Alternative energy sources also present a similar problem in that current technology does not account for the need to maintain a stealthy profile or to be able to displace quickly and frequently.

8.4.3 The US Army

The Army accounts for 13 percent of the total DOD OE consumption.[350] Much of that consumption fuels its fleet of over 225,000 tactical vehicles including tanks, armored personnel carriers, self-propelled howitzers, trucks, HMMWVs, and many other variants. In addition to its enormous vehicle fleet, the Army has an air wing consisting of over 4000 aircraft, the vast majority being helicopters. Accounting for differences in scope and scale, the Army's OE demands are similar to the Marine Corps in that, in addition to requiring fuel for vehicles and aircraft, it must also provide power to individual equipment, crew-served platforms, and robust command and control systems. The Army also shares the challenge of having reliable access to energy in expeditionary environments, although it must be noted that the term expeditionary is again relevant to the service. While the Army does still have light infantry units, such as their Airborne regiments, standard Army units tend to be much larger and heavier than their Marine Corps counterparts and are more dependent on logistically mature thea-

---

350 Office of the Assistant Secretary of Defense for Sustainment, "2016 Operational Energy Strategy" (https://www.acq.osd.mil/eie/Downloads/OE/2016%20OE%20Strategy_WEBd.pdf).

ters to operate effectively. Accordingly, these Army units also consume more energy than Marines.

Like the other services, the Army is using the passage away from Iraq and Afghanistan to reorient and reorganize itself toward a near-peer conflict with the assumption that rear area security is not assured. The Army details this shift in its 2019 Army Modernization Strategy.[351] To achieve this modernization, the Army is focused on six priorities; long-range precision fires, next-generation combat vehicles, vertical-lift aircraft, network technologies, air and missile defense capabilities, and soldier lethality.[352] A common thread among these priorities is an increase in systems that use energy. One program manager for ground soldier systems said that for soldiers to be able to use existing and forthcoming systems, they must have access to reliable power sources. "We've seen the demands on the soldier (are) just going to continue in the future," says Colonel Denny Dresch from the Army's Program Executive Office.[353]

In light of the Army's increasing attempts to "electrify" the battlefield, as commanded by the Biden administration, the Army is attempting to reduce or optimize its energy consumption as it evolves.[354] One method is by experimenting with both hybrid-electric and fully electric tactical vehicles. While the Army is moving full speed ahead to electrify its 170,000 non-tactical vehicles, it is taking a phased approach to electrify its tactical fleet due to the necessity to operate these vehicles in environments without reliable power grids. The Army's 2022 Climate Strategy directs that hybrid-electric tactical vehicles be introduced into the operating forces by 2035, with a transition to fully electric tactical vehicles to follow by 2050.[355] This creates certain new OE challenges,[356] including to supply reliable electricity.

---

351 US Army, "2019 Modernization Strategy" (https://www.army.mil/e2/downloads/rv7/2019_army_modernization_strategy_final.pdf).
352 Jen Judson, "Power Struggle: How the US Army Is Tackling the Logistics of Battlefield Electricity," *Defense News*, April 12, 2022 (https://www.defensenews.com/land/2022/04/12/power-struggle-how-the-us-army-is-tackling-the-logistics-of-battlefield-electricity/).
353 Jen Judson, "Power Struggle: How the US Army Is Tackling the Logistics of Battlefield Electricity," *Defense News*, April 12, 2022 (https://www.defensenews.com/land/2022/04/12/power-struggle-how-the-us-army-is-tackling-the-logistics-of-battlefield-electricity/).
354 Department of the Army, Office of the Assistant Secretary of the Army for Installations, Energy and Environment, "United States Army Climate Strategy," Washington, DC, February 2022 (https://www.army.mil/e2/downloads/rv7/about/2022_army_climate_strategy.pdf).
355 Department of the Army, Office of the Assistant Secretary of the Army for Installations, Energy and Environment, "United States Army Climate Strategy," Washington, DC, February 2022 (https://www.army.mil/e2/downloads/rv7/about/2022_army_climate_strategy.pdf).
356 Alan Howard and Brenda Shaffer, "The Hidden Dangers of Carbon Neutrality," *Foreign Policy*, April 12, 2021.

Another area of focus is battery standardization, as the abundance of batteries creates a significant logistics issue. "As you look at the battlefield of tomorrow and you look at what's going on [with] the soldier, there's going to be more computational power, there's going to be more devices that we plug into him or her, and all that's going to require more power," Dresch said.[357] In addition to improved battery capability, more fuel-efficient generators, combined with microgrids and the use of renewable energy, are ways that the Army is working to overcome its OE issues.

One additional challenge for the Army, perhaps owing to its vast size, is to accurately capture its energy logistics requirements in a way that provides clear direction for itself and for the defense industry that it relies on to provide technological solutions to enable its concepts. One defense industry leader, Chris Cavedo, President of Plasan North America, notes that the Army hasn't "conceived of taking all these different capabilities and putting them into one package because of the way that it writes requirements."

8.5 Conclusion

A key point raised in this chapter has been that the military branches all have similar OE challenges, irrespective of mission or organization. Primary among those are finding ways to reduce consumption, and to generate and use energy more efficiently. To be sure, each service's operating concepts influence how they are tackling those problems, often constrained by their own service culture and traditional means of operating.

It is imperative to foster a culture within the DOD that understands the criticality of energy to warfighting and actively seeks to incorporate energy considerations into mission planning and execution. The notion that energy is someone else's problem to figure out is misguided. Each of the services should move forward with ensuring that energy education and training is seeded throughout their institutions, especially their schoolhouses.

> A balance must be achieved between the potential benefits of increased situational awareness that these systems may provide with the energy requirements that they have.

Finally, there should be a recognition that despite the known challenges that exist with providing affordable, reliable energy to our military branches, none of the services are seriously considering pivoting away from systems that consume vast amounts of ener-

---

[357] Jen Judson, "Power Struggle: How the US Army Is Tackling the Logistics of Battlefield Electricity," *Defense News*, April 12, 2022 (https://www.defensenews.com/land/2022/04/12/power-struggle-how-the-us-army-is-tackling-the-logistics-of-battlefield-electricity/).

gy, rather the opposite: OE needs are increasing. There seems to be an acknowledgment within the DOD at large that the increasing reliance on systems that depend on energy to function is just a cost of fielding a modern, capable force. A balance must be achieved between the potential benefits of increased situational awareness that these systems may provide with the energy requirements that they have. More pointedly, with the exception of the Gulf War, one could make a case that the overwhelming technical advantage that US forces possess has not helped America to achieve strategic victories in war since World War II.

> With the exception of the Gulf War, one could make a case that the overwhelming technical advantage that US forces possess has not helped America to achieve strategic victories in war since World War II.

8.6 Case Study: Closure of the Red Hill Fuel Storage Facility at Pearl Harbor

Secretary of Defense Lloyd Austin's March 7, 2022 decision to shut down the Red Hill Underground Fuel Storage Facility at Pearl Harbor, Hawaii[358] reflects the challenges military officials face in squaring OE requirements with environmental challenges and domestic political concerns. In addition, the decision to close Red Hill sheds light on the greater challenge of the need for adequate fuel options in the Western Pacific theater.

Red Hill, which opened in 1943, is a military fuel storage facility operated by the US Navy, which supports all the service branches in the Pacific. Its location has become increasingly strategic for the growing US focus on deterring China and North Korea and the commensurate deployments of naval vessels and other fuel-thirsty military equipment to the Western Pacific.

The facility houses twenty steel-lined tanks, encased in concrete, and built into cavities that were mined inside of Red Hill. The facility's location within the Red Hill ridge was selected to allow fuel to flow from the storage tanks to Pearl Harbor by gravity. However – and here is the challenge military officials face in squaring OE requirements with environmental challenges and political concerns – the facility is also located directly above a freshwater aquifer that supplies Oahu with the bulk of the island's drinking water.

---

[358] US Department of Defense, "Statement by Secretary of Defense Lloyd J. Austin III on the Closure of the Red Hill Bulk Fuel Storage Facility" (https://www.defense.gov/News/Releases/Release/Article/2957825/statement-by-secretary-of-defense-lloyd-j-austin-iii-on-the-closure-of-the-red/).

Red Hill has stored more fuel than any other US facility – up to 250 million gallons. Each tank has a storage capacity of approximately 12.5 million gallons. The tanks are connected to three pipelines that run 2.5 miles through a tunnel to fueling piers at Pearl Harbor and nearby Hickam Air Field.

Red Hill was conceived on the cusp of World War II when military planners took note of the vulnerability of aboveground storage tanks at Pearl Harbor to enemy attack.[359] US military commanders have said that the United States was fortunate that the 1941 Japanese attack on Pearl Harbor did not strike the aboveground fuel storage tanks that were there. The fuel supplies at Pearl Harbor were viewed crucial for the US to bring the war to the Japanese. Admiral Chester W. Nimitz, who commanded the Pacific Fleet in the war, summed it up: "Had the Japanese destroyed POL stores and transport, it would have prolonged the war another two years."[360]

Red Hill's construction was already underway when the attack at Pearl Harbor occurred – nearly 3000 men worked around-the-clock for almost three years before completing the project in September 1942. Red Hill is a National Historic Civil Engineering Landmark, and it has been described as "one of the most remarkable engineering feats of World War II," with engineers boring vertical shafts into the mountain to take advantage of gravity.[361]

In peacetime, the Defense Logistics Agency provides fueling points throughout the region. However, in wartime, it is reasonable to expect that all these locations will be targeted, and Red Hill's solid fortifications could provide tactical, even strategic, advantages.[362]

On the other hand, the military had been moving toward more distributed refueling options. In his March 2022 announcement, Austin indicated that the Red Hill facility

---

359 Wyatt Olson, "Navy's Underground Fuel Tanks in Hawaii Are Impenetrable to Attack – and That's the Problem," *Stars and Stripes*, October 24, 2019 (https://www.stripes.com/theaters/asia_pacific/navy-s-underground-fuel-tanks-in-hawaii-ar e-impenetrable-to-attack-and-that-s-the-problem-1.604488).
360 RuthAnne Darling and Paul Mason Carpenter, "Energy: An Essential Element for Winning Future Wars – Operational Energy Part 1," *Surge*, Summer 2020, Naval Postgraduate School (https://nps.edu/web/eag/future-wars); Geoff Ziezulewicz, "How Shuttering Red Hill Could Make Fueling the Fleet More Complex," *Navy Times*, March 29, 2022 (https://www.navytimes.com/news/your-navy/2022/03/29/how-shuttering-red-hill-could-make-fueling-the-fleet-more-complex/); Gordon W. Prange, *At Dawn We Slept: The Untold Story of Pearl Harbor*, New York: McGraw-Hill, 1986, page 510.
361 Wyatt Olson, "Navy's Underground Fuel Tanks in Hawaii Are Impenetrable to Attack – and That's the Problem," *Stars and Stripes*, October 24, 2019 (https://www.stripes.com/theaters/asia_pacific/navy-s-underground-fuel-tanks-in-hawaii-ar e-impenetrable-to-attack-and-that-s-the-problem-1.604488).
362 Geoff Ziezulewicz, "How Shuttering Red Hill Could Make Fueling the Fleet More Complex," *Navy Times*, March 29, 2022 (https://www.navytimes.com/news/your-navy/2022/03/29/how-shuttering-red-hill-could-make-fueling-the-fleet-more-complex/).

would be replaced by a more decentralized approach: "The distributed and dynamic nature of our force posture in the Indo-Pacific, the sophisticated threats we face, and the technology available to us demand an equally advanced and resilient fueling capability," Austin said. "To a large degree, we already avail ourselves of dispersed fueling at sea and ashore, permanent and rotational. We will now expand and accelerate that strategic distribution."[363]

Soon after Austin's announcement, Navy Secretary Carlos Del Toro spoke at a conference in Washington, DC, saying there would not be a need to construct new facilities as there are several existing storage facilities in the Pacific that can be used to store the fuel. Del Toro said that a Navy assessment found it would give the US a strategic advantage to store fuel in a variety of land and sea facilities, instead of in one place.

"What might have made sense, perhaps during the days of World War II, given the threats that we face today, it doesn't make sense now," Del Toro said.[364]

However, other Pentagon analyses have claimed that current storage capacity in the region is insufficient: a Pentagon assessment, which appears in the long-term program planning document for the US Pacific Deterrence Initiative (PDI) submitted to Congress in April 2022 said that "Current theater logistics posture and capability to sustain the force are inadequate to support operations specifically in a contested environment."[365]

The Fiscal Year 2023 DOD authorization bill, in which Congress set policy for DOD from October 1, 2022 to September 30, 2023, required DOD to certify that the Indo-Pacific has been able to fully replace the 250-million-gallon fuel capacity that Red Hill previously provided. It requires DOD to report to the Congressional defense committees on how it will replicate the fuel storage capacity of the Red Hill Facility in the Indo-Pacific; generate a risk analysis of these new fuel storage options; and provide a timeline and cost analysis for establishing this storage capacity.[366]

As initial steps in fiscal year 2023, the Pentagon proposed expanding jet fuel storage capabilities at the US Marine air station at Iwakuni, Japan and sought military con-

---

[363] "Statement by Secretary of Defense Lloyd J. Austin III on the Closure of the Red Hill Bulk Fuel Storage Facility," US Department of Defense, March 7, 2022 (https://www.defense.gov/News/Releases/Release/Article/2957825/statement-by-secretary-of-defense-lloyd-j-austin-iii-on-the-closure-of-the-red/).
[364] "SECNAV Del Toro: Navy Will Not Need to Build Fuel Facilities to Replace Red Hill Fuel Depot," *USNI News*, March 11, 2022.
[365] Ryo Nakamura, "U.S. Lacks Asian Logistics Support for Armed Conflict: Pentagon," Nikkei Asia, May 4, 2022 (https://asia.nikkei.com/Politics/International-relations/Indo-Pacific/U.S.-lacks-Asian-logistics-support-for-armed-conflict-Pentagon).
[366] US Government Publishing Office, "National Defense Authorization Act for Fiscal Year 2023" (https://www.govinfo.gov/content/pkg/CRPT-117srpt130/html/CRPT-117srpt130.htm).

struction funds to add fuel storage at the US territory of Tinian in the Northern Marianas Islands.[367] Meanwhile, the Defense Logistics Agency planned to add a Defense Fuel Support Point in Darwin, Australia.[368] The latter sites will be aboveground, unhardened facilities.[369]

The decision to shut down Red Hill reflected the DOD's desire to address local environmental concerns, rather than a strategic calculation. Indeed, until Austin's announcement, DOD had resisted repeated pleas from local officials and residents to relocate the facility, citing Navy studies indicating that constructing a new jet fuel facility in Hawaii would cost between $4 billion and $10 billion and could take several decades to complete, according to a 2018 analysis commissioned by the Naval Facilities Engineering Systems Command.[370]

Between these conflicting needs, Secretary Austin made his decision to formally close Red Hill after Hawaii officials ordered the Navy to cease operations at the facility and defuel the storage tanks.[371] The Hawaii Department of Health was responding to repeated leaks of jet fuel from the facility into the local water supply which contaminated drinking water. The Navy had spent tens of millions of dollars over the past few decades in repairs on the facility.[372]

The most significant leak occurred in November 2021 when a release from Red Hill contaminated the Red Hill drinking water well. Hundreds of families living on Joint Base Pearl Harbor-Hickam (JBPHH) and the Army's Aliamanu Military Reservation and Red Hill Housing reported petroleum odors coming from residential tap water supplied by the US Navy water system. Residents also said they were sickened by the contaminated drinking water. The spill impacted about 92,000 US Navy water system users that were

---

367 Ryo Nakamura, "U.S. Lacks Asian Logistics Support for Armed Conflict: Pentagon," *Nikkei Asia*, May 4, 2022 (https://asia.nikkei.com/Politics/International-relations/Indo-Pacific/U.S.-lacks-Asian-logistics-support-for-armed-conflict-Pentagon); Abraham Mahshie, "Pacific Refueling," *Air and Space Forces Magazine*, August 29, 2022 (https://www.airandspaceforces.com/article/pacific-refueling/).
368 Seth Robson, "US Military's Footprint Is Expanding in Northern Australia to Meet a Rising China," *Stars and Stripes*, September 8, 2022 (https://www.stripes.com/theaters/asia_pacific/2022-09-08/australia-military-construction-projects-china-7251762.html).
369 Abraham Mahshie, "Pacific Refueling," *Air and Space Forces Magazine*, August 29, 2022 (https://www.airandspaceforces.com/article/pacific-refueling/).
370 Anita Hofschneider, "It Could Cost Billions for the Navy to Move Red Hill Fuel," *Civil Beat*, December 7, 2021 (https://www.civilbeat.org/2021/12/it-could-cost-billions-for-the-navy-to-move-red-hill-fuel/).
371 Department of Health, State of Hawaii, "Emergency Order: Docket No. 21-UST-EA-02," December 6, 2021 (https://health.hawaii.gov/about/files/2021/12/Emergency-Order-12.05.2021-signed.pdf).
372 Wyatt Olson, "Navy's Underground Fuel Tanks in Hawaii Are Impenetrable to Attack – and That's the Problem," *Stars and Stripes*, October 24, 2019 (https://www.stripes.com/theaters/asia_pacific/navy-s-underground-fuel-tanks-in-hawaii-are-impenetrable-to-attack-and-that-s-the-problem-1.604488).

unable to use or drink it for months.[373] Many residents were forced to relocate to temporary housing during the drinking water crisis.[374]

A Navy investigation found a cascading series of mistakes, complacency, and a lack of professionalism over the course of six months led to the November 2021 fuel spill.[375]

More than 1600 current and former residents have sued the US government for their exposure to the contaminated drinking water, with at least another thousand expected to file before the November 2023 submission deadline.[376] A federal grand jury conducted a criminal investigation into the spills, Hawaiian media reported.[377]

The US Environmental Protection Agency (EPA) coordinated with the Navy, Army, and the Hawaii Department of Health in an Interagency Drinking Water System Team (IDWST) to restore safe drinking water to the affected residents and workers. The team launched in December 2021 and completed work to restore the drinking water system in March 2022.[378]

After several rounds of legal motions and interventions by the Hawaiian government and the Navy, the EPA on June 2, 2023, finalized and signed the 2023 Administrative Consent Order with the US Department of the Navy and the Defense Logistics Agency that requires steps to ensure the safe defueling and closure of the Red Hill Facility.

---

[373] Anita Hofschneider, "It Could Cost Billions for the Navy to Move Red Hill Fuel," *Civil Beat*, December 7, 2021 (https://www.civilbeat.org/2021/12/it-could-cost-billions-for-the-navy-to-move-red-hill-fuel/).
[374] United States Environmental Protection Agency, "About Red Hill Fuel Releases" (https://www.epa.gov/red-hill/about-red-hill-fuel-releases).
[375] Diana Stancy Correll, "Pentagon Accelerates Timeline to Defuel Red Hill Facilities," *Navy Times*, May 17, 2023 (https://www.navytimes.com/news/your-navy/2023/05/17/pentagon-accelerates-timeline-to-defuel-red-hill-facilities/); see Department of the Navy, "Command Investigation into the 6 May 2021 and 20 November 2021 Incidents at Red Hill Bulk Storage Facility," June 13, 2022 (https://www.epa.gov/system/files/documents/2022-07/FOIA-Release-Red%20Hill-CI-%28June%202022%29.pdf for details of the Navy investigation).
[376] Patricia Kime, "1,000 More Pearl Harbor Area Residents Join Lawsuit over Red Hill Fuel Spill," Military.com, June 20, 2023 (https://www.military.com/daily-news/2023/06/20/1000-more-pearl-harbor-area-residents-join-lawsuit-over-red-hill-fuel-spill.html).
[377] Rick Daysog, "Federal Grand Jury Conducting Criminal Probe into Red Hill Fuel Spills," *Hawaii News Now*, April 12, 2023 (https://www.hawaiinewsnow.com/2023/04/13/federal-grand-jury-is-conducting-criminal-probe-into-red-hill-fuel-spills/).
[378] United States Environmental Protection Agency, "About Red Hill Fuel Releases" (https://www.epa.gov/red-hill/about-red-hill-fuel-releases); United States Environmental Protection Agency, "Drinking Water Incident Response at Joint Base Pearl Harbor-Hickam, Honolulu, Hawai'i, November 2021-March 2022" (https://www.epa.gov/red-hill/drinking-water-incident-response-joint-base-pearl-harbor-hickam-honolulu-hawaii-november).

Under the Consent Order, the Navy has committed to properly operate and maintain the JBPHH drinking water system to protect the health and safety of its consumers.[379]

Meredith Berger, the Biden administration Assistant Secretary of Navy for Energy, Installations and Environment, said the Navy's plan "continues to prioritize the Navy's commitment to the safety of the Oahu community and environmental health, and reinforces our assurance of transparency."[380]

The Navy began repairs to the facility to prepare it for defueling soon after the Consent Order was signed with the repairs to be validated by the Hawaii Department of Health. Defueling commenced on October 16, 2023.[381]

8.6.1 Questions for Discussion

- How might the DOD most effectively replace the Red Hill facility's capacity and capabilities, particularly its benefits for forward-deployed forces in the Western Pacific?
- Which of the following options are the most appropriate? Putting more fuel afloat via tankers; building more aboveground tanks; building another Red Hill-type facility in Hawaii; building another Red Hill-type facility elsewhere?
- What are the costs and benefits both financially and in value to the military of these alternative courses of action? What are some appropriate metrics to assess these costs and benefits?
- How should the military evaluate strategic needs versus public concerns about placement of energy infrastructure in their areas of residence?
- Discuss the state of US OE capacity for engagement in Asia versus Europe.
- Do the storage fuel depots that serve the Asian theater adequately provide for the OE needs of the US military?

---

[379] United States Environmental Protection Agency, "Red Hill: 2023 Consent Order" (https://www.epa.gov/red-hill/red-hill-2023-consent-order#docs).
[380] Doug G. Ware, "Navy Says It Will Dismantle Fuel Pipelines at Red Hill Facility in Hawaii to Prevent Future Use of Storage Tanks," *Stars and Stripes*, June 1, 2023 (https://www.stripes.com/branches/navy/2023-06-01/red-hill-hawaii-fuel-pipelines-10306728.html).
[381] Heather Mongilio, "Red Hill Repairs Finished, Awaiting DoH Validation and Approval before Defueling," *USNI News*, June 29, 2023 (https://news.usni.org/2023/06/29/red-hill-repairs-finished-awaiting-doh-validation-and-approval-before-defueling).

9 Looking Ahead: Operational Energy Adoption of Technology

In the early 2020s, the world experienced the worst energy crisis since World War II. This energy crisis triggered a wider global economic crisis and food crisis, and exposed national security weaknesses in Europe and the United States. This civilian energy crisis illustrated that lack of adequate energy supplies projects onto every major sphere: food supply, economy, national security, social stability, and more. The same is true in the military: getting energy right is essential for the military to fulfill its missions, win wars, and safeguard national security.

Energy policy formation in the civilian, commercial, and military spheres demands decisions under conditions of significant uncertainty. Decisions on energy infrastructure, systems, investments, and more need to take into consideration long-term trends of: the economy, energy supply and demand, society, geopolitics, and technological developments, each of which is quite difficult to predict.

Energy decision-making for the military is even more complicated than in the civilian and commercial sectors. First, the price of miscalculation is higher: loss of life, loss of territory, national security threat, and potential loss of sovereignty. Second, weapons and military platforms like ships and aircraft are built with an intended shelf-life of twenty to thirty years. Decisions on weapons and platform design lock the military into requirements for certain types of fuel and quantities for several decades. For instance, a fighter plane design based on access to energy-dense petroleum derived liquid fuels can likely not be adapted to electricity as a fuel source. This demands correctly assessing significant energy-related developments over a longer horizon than the civilian and commercial sectors require. Third, the military requires a higher degree of energy security than the civilian sector: the civilian sector can tolerate periodic blackouts and fuel disruptions; the military needs its energy needs met at all times. The civilian sector can tolerate insufficient energy supplies during "peak demand" periods while during "peak demand" is precisely when the military needs its energy supplies.

In addition to requiring decisions under high uncertainty, energy policy must provide for secure and affordable energy supplies for today, while planning for very different energy supply and demand trends in the future. This sounds basic, but lack of regard for current energy needs was the major factor in the 2020s energy crisis: the West and many international institutions believed they no longer needed to provide for today's energy needs, since an energy transition to renewable energy was presumed to be underway. This is despite the fact that there had not emerged a major shift in the global fuel mix toward renewable energy and no technological spark appeared that ushered in a new energy transition.

As part of this policy of attempting to force the transition to renewable energy, government stifled investments in production of energy supplies needed today. For this end, Western governments created impediments to commercial investments in fossil fuels and halted all public finance for fossil fuel projects. This is despite the fact that in the 2020s fossil fuels supply over 80 percent of the global fuel demand, and at the time of publication, this trend did not seem to be declining.

As part of this policy of attempting to increase demand for renewables, through blocking fossil fuel supplies, Europe did not import sufficient natural gas. Lack of gas supplies triggered high prices, which led to an economic crisis and the closure of many fertilizer factories in Europe (natural gas is the feedstock in fertilizer production) triggering a global food crisis.

The 2020s global energy crisis illustrates the need for both the civilian and military sectors' to identify a model that allows for adoption of new technologies as they emerge, while at the same time providing energy supplies based on current technologies, and energy supply and demand trends. Both sectors need to make room for technological developments, but at the same time not to develop infrastructure or assumed new energy supplies based on non-existent technologies. Counting on non-existing technologies that may or may not emerge to provide energy is dangerous in both the civilian and the military spheres. However, not being able to take advantage of new technologies and energy products as they emerge can leave a state or a military behind its competitors as well. The challenge is to find the balance.

> Counting on non-existing technologies that may or may not emerge to provide energy is dangerous in both the civilian and the military spheres.

Some technological developments will radically change how the military uses energy and which energy is available to the military.[382] In its forming of OE policy, the military and DOD should map out likely technological developments that will fundamentally change energy supply and demand.

In pursuing development of energy technologies, the military should employ the principle of technology neutrality. Western governments like to pick specific technologies and subsidize and promote them. It is not likely that politicians do a better job at predicting technologies than the private sector or scientists. Examples of political promotions of types of energy are biofuels, hydrogen, and the electrification of transportation. The military should develop the technologies that provide for the most energy

---

382 A potential example is energy beaming. Energy beaming is an emerging technology where power is transferred across great distances wirelessly. "Power Beaming Comes of Age," *MIT Technology Review Insights*, October 6, 2022 (https://www.technologyreview.com/2022/10/06/1060650/power-beaming-comes-of-age/).

advantage gains at the lowest cost. But, not be beholden to a certain technology or type of technology.

OE needs are increasing and anticipated to grow. The needs are not just in quantities, but in the range of specifications. The purposes of energy are changing as well. It is clear that the US DOD and the US Congress recognize these growing OE needs, as illustrated by the OE strategy requirements and the establishment of dedicated institutions to formulate and implement that strategy. The next stage of OE policy development requires increased OE education and training, deployment of dedicated OE officers, a flexible workforce that can provide the technical needs of changing energy supplies and needs, and the formulation of an OE doctrine to complement the OE strategy.

Appendix

A.1 OE Ontologies

Ontologies are a form of modeling that can be used to organize and understand a discipline. Ontologies instruct how individual aspects of a discipline integrate with one another and compose the whole. An ontology helps individuals understand a defined concept, individual components, and how they relate.[383]

A crucial first step in ontology development is to define the discipline and the specific areas that make up the greater system. It is important that when all the specific areas are combined, they complete the whole. If the combined specific areas fail to make a whole or exceed the whole, the ontology requires adjustment. Ontology visualization is an important second step. It must visually depict the whole, all the individual aspects, and how they relate.[384]

The Office of the Secretary of Defense Operational Energy-Innovation has developed an energy ontology model to aid analysis of OE tasks. It is comprehensive, begins with energy sources, and works through to energy users. The OE ontology includes energy sub-systems, enablers, systems, and operations.

A.2 Operational Energy Ontology

The following sections describe the OE ontology[385] in more detail. It is important to note that the left-hand side of the ontology represents a linear relationship. However, decisions on the left-hand side have exponential impacts on the right-hand side of the ontology. For instance, an improvement in an "energy sub-system" such as "energy storage," can have multiple and cascading impacts on "systems" and "operations."

---

[383] Natalya F. Noy and Deborah L. McGuinness, "Ontology Development 101: A Guide to Creating Your First Ontology" (https://protege.stanford.edu/publications/ontology_development/ontology101-noy-mcguinness.html).

[384] Natalya F. Noy and Deborah L. McGuinness, "Ontology Development 101: A Guide to Creating Your First Ontology" (https://protege.stanford.edu/publications/ontology_development/ontology101-noy-mcguinness.html).

[385] RuthAnne Darling, Mace Carpenter, and Clint Novotny designed as a working operational energy ontology for Office of the Secretary of Defense, Operational Energy-Innovation.

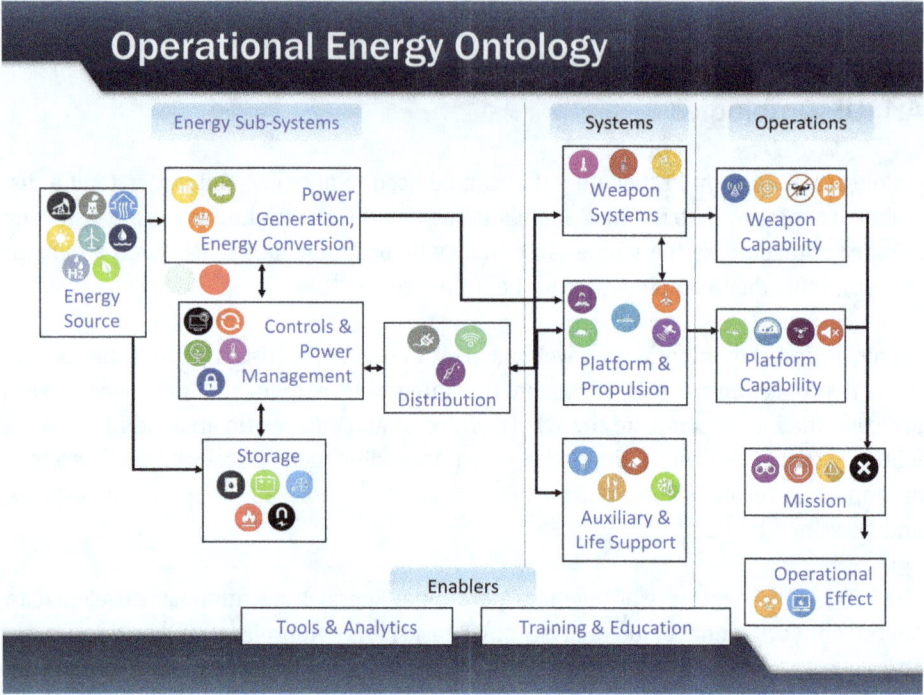

Figure A.1: Operational Energy Framework. Source: Operational Energy Ontology, RuthAnne Darling, Mace Carpenter, and Clint Novotny, designed as a working OE ontology for Office of the Secretary of Defense, Operational Energy-Innovation.

A.2.1 Energy Sub-Systems

Sources

Energy sources are the beginning of the energy chain. Energy sources include fossil fuels (oil, coal, natural gas, shale, tar sands, etc.), renewable (solar, wind, hydroelectric, hydrogen, geothermal, biofuels, etc.), and nuclear. The transportation sector typically has relied on fossil fuels to power internal combustion platforms.[386] Fixed facilities primarily use electrical power generated from coal, natural gas, and nuclear power. However, renewable sources increasingly are being used for electricity generation.[387] Oil, coal, etc., are often moved over long distances and refined before they can be exploited.

---

[386] Beata Caranci, Francis Fong, and Mekdes Gebreselassie, "Decarbonization: A Simple Framework for a Complex Problem," October 27, 2021 (https://economics.td.com/esg-understanding-energy-transition).

[387] US Energy Information Administration, "Electricity Explained: Electricity Generation, Capacity, and Sales in the United States" (https://www.eia.gov/energyexplained/electricity/electricity-in-the-us-generation-capacity-and-sales.php).

Natural gas is often cooled to a liquid state before it is transported. Nuclear materials must be mined, moved through a series of steps to produce nuclear fuel, and the fuel must be distributed to nuclear power plants.

Currently, fossil fuels are the most important energy source for military applications. Today, military systems rely on fossil fuels for forward base microgrids and platforms (air, land, sea, and space mobile systems). Fossil fuels enjoy a high energy density and can be stored for long periods.

Controls and Power Management
Effective energy command and control (EC2) is essential to (1) ensuring forces have the power they need to conduct required military operations and (2) assuring maximum efficiency to conserve resources and protect the environment. EC2 is important at the strategic, operational, and tactical levels of conflict. At the strategic level, senior leaders, planners, and logisticians must understand how much energy to allocate and these decisions, in turn, require very large logistics movements. At the operational and theater levels of conflict, leaders and their staffs must understand tactical requirements and link the strategic energy movements to the tactical units. All types of energy sources, generation, conversion, storage, and distribution are involved. It is highly desirable to establish an Energy Common Operating Picture (ECOP). An ECOP can provide users and leaders near real-time energy information to identify energy shortfalls and quickly adjust distribution.

At the micro level (computers, sensors, system controllers, moderators, etc.), EC2 involves the information necessary to operate energy systems. These systems are required for effective and efficient energy production, storage, and distribution and are vulnerable to cyber interference or attack. Professionals who develop energy systems must also design and maintain system cyber protections.

Microgrids benefit from standardization and commonality, which allows different systems to integrate with one another, whether from different services or countries.

Power Generation / Conversion
Power generation and conversion involves converting energy sources into usable power. For most transportation platforms today, power generation is generated from fossil fuels. Of the remainder, some mobile vehicles are hybrid (fossil fuel engine with battery power) and others are fully electric (battery only); other platforms use natural gas. Most electrical generation occurs at power plants that then distribute the electricity to fixed users via electrical lines. Over 80 percent of power plant electrical generation in the US is generated from coal, natural gas, or nuclear power. Solar and wind power generation remains a small part of the US and global power production and the energy mix. US hydroelectrical generation capacity is static or at times,

decreasing because of its impact on the physical environment and the lack of unexploited productive hydropower sources. Forward base microgrids are primarily powered by fossil fuels, although more effort is being accomplished to efficiently use renewable energy.[388] US nuclear power capacity is declining, mainly due to costs. The US military is examining developing mobile nuclear power plants.

Distribution
Most electrical power is distributed to fixed locations via metal, electrical power lines. Some distributed electricity is lost in the process (about 5 percent in the continental United States), but this number is significantly less over short distances. In general, longer distribution distances lose more electricity. While most permanent electrical grids are interconnected, microgrids normally stand alone. Researchers are working on ways to transmit electricity by wireless power beaming or by electro-optical cable, but in late 2023, these technologies were not yet commercial or operational.

DOD defines a microgrid as a forward and/or isolated energy distribution system and/or backup energy distribution system. Generally, it operates independently from other power grids but may be connected to larger grids. Microgrids are especially useful for forward basing of military forces. They can be powered by a combination of different sources such as fossil fuel generators, or renewables like solar or wind. In the future, small nuclear reactors, hydrogen, and wave energy may power microgrids. A microgrid can connect to the grid at a point of common coupling. They maintain voltage at the same level as the main grid unless there exists some sort of problem on the grid or other reason to disconnect. A switch can separate the microgrid from the main grid automatically or manually, allowing it to then function as an "energy island."

Microgrids not only provide backups for the grid in case of emergencies but can also be used to cut costs or connect to a local resource that is too small or unreliable for traditional grid use. A microgrid enables forward bases to be energy independent and can help reduce carbon emissions. Microgrids may be adjusted to specific unit requirements such as taking advantage of different energy sources, power generation, and storage systems that best suit a particular environment and operational needs.[389]

---

[388] Beata Caranci, Francis Fong, and Mekdes Gebreselassie, "Decarbonization: A Simple Framework for a Complex Problem," October 27, 2021 (https://economics.td.com/esg-understanding-energy-transition).
[389] Beata Caranci, Francis Fong, and Mekdes Gebreselassie, "Decarbonization: A Simple Framework for a Complex Problem," October 27, 2021 (https://economics.td.com/esg-understanding-energy-transition).

Storage
Storing large amounts of electricity for extended periods is costly and technologically challenged. In contrast, fossil fuels – especially oil and coal – can easily be stored. However, fossil fuel storage requires significant volume to support significant numbers of military platforms. During conflict, this storage can be vulnerable to attack.

As of publication, electricity storage on a scale to support major weapons platforms is not available. Not only is electricity storage technology limited, but it is also very expensive. In addition, electricity storage adds significant costs to power provision.

On a small scale, electrical energy can be stored in batteries that provide from minutes to months of power (depending on demand). Modern military forces depend on batteries. A combat equipped soldier may carry up to 17 pounds of batteries when entering a combat area. A modern naval destroyer uses as many as 30,000 batteries when it is operational. Many different types of batteries exist – voltaic, fuel, galvanic, electrolytic, flow cells, etc. They involve differing chemical processes to store or produce electricity. Primary batteries are charged but cannot be reused. Secondary batteries are rechargeable.

Energy may also be stored through other methods. Some of these are thermal (e.g., molten salts), mechanical (e.g., flywheels), and pumped hydro power. Some developing technologies include compressed air, hydrogen storage, and magnets.[390]

A.2.2 Enablers

Tools and Analytics
Tools and analytics play a critical role in OE. All elements within the ontology should be monitored with objectives of improved energy output and efficiency. Tools can measure energy output for systems of any size, scale, or level. Further analysis can produce system and operation understandings that can lead to improvements in reliability and/or operations.

Training and Education
Training and education are critical for optimal energy exploitation. This includes the training and education not only of those developing energy systems, but of those who maintain and employ these energy systems. Inefficient maintenance and employment can result in failure to optimize energy use and may reduce the mean time between system failures and add expense.

---

390 US Environmental Protection Agency, "Electricity Storage" (https://www.epa.gov/energy/electricity-storage).

A.2.3 Systems

Weapons Systems

Energy is a critical element of modern weapons systems.[391] Weapons systems are complete structures that are developed to support military requirements. They may or may not involve the employment of weapons. Weapons systems normally refer to a platform and its weapons. For some systems, a separate launcher may be mounted on the platform. One example is a naval gun. It involves a platform (ship), the gun, and a projectile. Other weapons systems do not require a platform. A fighter carrying a bomb is one example – the fighter provides the velocity and trajectory required to employ the weapon.

Platforms and Propulsion

Platforms generally require mobility. Energy directed through engines or rockets results in propulsion at varying speeds that meet platform and mission requirements. Most propulsion today is accomplished through fossil fuels such as reciprocating or turbine engines. Some major naval combatants make use of nuclear power.

Auxiliary Systems

Auxiliary systems support other weapons systems and microgrids. Types of auxiliary systems include generators, auxiliary power units, batteries, solar/wind/wave systems, and nuclear power. Most auxiliary power systems in use rely on fossil fuels.

A.2.4 Operations

Weapon Capability

In terms of energy, weapons fall into three general types – explosive, kinetic energy, and directed energy.[392] Explosive weapon detonation is the result of the instantaneous release of stored energy – bombs, grenades, torpedo warheads, etc. Kinetic energy weapons involve the rapid movement of non-explosive matter (e.g., bombs or rods

---

[391] The DOD defines a weapon system as, "A combination of one or more weapons with all related equipment, materials, services, personnel, and means of delivery and deployment (if applicable) required for self-sufficiency." Reference: Joint Chiefs of Staff, *DOD Dictionary of Military and Associated Terms*, March 2017, page 253 (https://apps.dtic.mil/sti/pdfs/AD1029823.pdf).

[392] Explosive material is any substance or device that can be made to produce a volume of rapidly expanding gas in an extremely brief period to neutralize, or destroy a target. Types of explosives include mechanical, nuclear, and chemical. A kinetic attack is the use of any solid matter that inflicts physical damage into targeted object to neutralize, or destroy a target. It may or may not contain explosive material. A non-kinetic attack is the use of information/cyber to intrude, jam, meacon, interfere so as to neutralize, or destroy a target.

with no explosive material). Directed energy weapons concentrate energy on selected targets to disable or destroy enemy targets. Some weapons involve a combination of more than one of these types.

Some weapons may have self-contained propulsion – missiles, powered bombs, rockets, etc. The energy required for weapon propulsion should be optimized for density, reliability, maintainability, and overall effectiveness.

Many weapons require energy for sensors and guidance. Weapons such as the GBU-24 do not have propulsion but require stored energy (batteries) for sensors and guidance systems. An AGM-65 has a rocket motor for propulsion, but also requires batteries for sensors and guidance. Battery life limits the range over which these weapons can be deployed.

Platform Capability
All modern military platforms (aircraft, ground vehicles, ships, satellites, etc.) require energy to operate. Platforms will be more effective (speed, range, endurance, payload, etc.) if the energy is effective and efficient. Improvements in energy result in platform improvements. Some weapons require high speed platforms. Others may be launched from stationary platforms.

Mission
A military mission is, "The task, together with the purpose, that clearly indicates the action to be taken and the reason therefore."[393] Energy is an underpinning element – a foundation – of modern military missions and subsequent effectiveness. All military energy development should support given missions. The *National Security Strategy* provides the overarching guidance, followed by the *National Defense Strategy*, which provides more detail. After considering these documents, DOD and combatant command plans should be studied further to determine the most important energy development. In many instances, specific energy guidance may not be given. However, those developing plans should tailor efforts to consider how energy might support these strategies.

Operational Effect
An operational effect is the result of applying a specific capability against a given objective. Desired operational effects are designed to support accepted strategies, plans, and combat execution. A simple example is a petroleum storage facility that is located near an area where a mechanized assault is to be conducted. The operational effect is

---

393 Joint Chiefs of Staff, *DOD Dictionary of Military and Associated Terms*, March 2017, page 157 (https://apps.dtic.mil/sti/pdfs/AD1029823.pdf).

the armored vehicles have the fuels required to conduct the attack on enemy positions. All military energy development and resourcing should be executed with desired operational effects.[394]

---

[394] Paul Carpenter and William Andrews, "Effects Based Operations: Combat Proven," *Joint Force Quarterly*, issue 52, 1st quarter, January 2009, pages 78–81.

Index

Note: Page numbers in *italics* indicate figures, and page numbers in **bold** indicate tables in the text

accidents, 80–81
adaptive capacity, 144
adversarial analysis, 135, 138–140
– goal of, 140
– interdiction model, 139
– optimization and game theory techniques, 139
– uncertainty and, 135
adversaries of the United States, 50
– China, 94–97
– Iran, 97–99
– Russia, 97
aerial bombings, 93
aging or poorly constructed infrastructure, 81
Air Force Energy Plan 2010, 173
Afghanistan, 42
Alterman, Eric, 82
Amos, James, 179
Amenas Natural Gas Plant (Algeria), 85
Armenia-Azerbaijan War 2020, 53–64
– attacks on international pipelines during the war, 59–60
– background, 54–55
– energy – as catalyst for war, 56–59
– energy export, 55–56
– Metsamor nuclear power plant, 61–62
– Mingachevir hydropower station, 60–63
– Russia in, 54–56
– tunnels, 57, 62
armored vehicles, 165
Army Modernization Strategy 2019, 180
Ashley, Robert, 91
AUKUS, 52
Austin, Lloyd, 182, 183–184, 185
Axis powers, 22
Azerbaijan, 17, 22, *see also* Armenia-Azerbaijan War 2020

Baku oil fields, 22–26, 93, *see also* Operation Edelweiss
baseload, 34
battery-powered equipment, 167–168
battery standardization, 181
battlefields, modern, 4–7
Battle of the Bulge, 21
Berger, Meredith, 187

best practices analysis, 159
Biden administration
– efforts to moderate operational energy consumption, 170–171
– electrifying the battlefield, 180
– energy policies, 43–44
biofuel industry, 177–178
blockade, 92
Blount, Joseph, 122

Caley, James C., 7, 73, 178
Carpenter, Paul Mason, 15
Carter, Ashton, 42
Case studies, as education tools, 159
Cavedo, Chris, 181
Center of Gravity (COG) analysis, 74–76
Chernobyl, 65, 67, 68, 70
Chia-ya Lee, 84–85
China
– cyberattacks on American critical infrastructure, 90, 95–96
– plans to target adversaries' energy systems, 96–97
– potential conflict with Taiwan, 95
– as threat to US energy security, 38, 39–40, 41, 47, 48, 51, 86
– vulnerability due to Malacca Straits, 95
view of US vulnerabilities, 94–97
– chokepoints, 39, 47
Churchill, Winston, 14
civilian energy security, 7–8
civilian energy supply lines, 46–47
clean energy, 33
– climate, 157
Climate Strategy 2022, 180
coal, 30–31
– as energy source, 14
– transportation, 31
Colonial Pipeline cyberattack, 118–128
Congress, 7, 111
conversion, power, 193–194
costs
– of battery-powered equipment, 167–168
– of biofuel for navy, 177
– Fully Burdened Cost of Fuel, 163

– of operational energy, 162–163
critical capability, 75
critical requirement, 75
critical vulnerability, 75
cross-agency cooperation, 51–52
Curzon, George, 15
cyberattacks, 45, 88–91, 97, 124–125

Darling, RuthAnne, 15, 100
DarkSide, 122, 124–125
Defense Logistics Agency (DLA), 117, 162–163, 183
Defense Science Board, 111–112
deliberate threats to OE, 78
– aerial bombings / indirect military fires, 93
– blockade, 92
– cyberattack, 88–91
– looting, 87
– sabotage, 87–88
– terrorism, 82–87
Del Toro, Carlos, 184
Deptula, David, 93
digital devices on battlefield, 165–170
distribution of electricity, 194
DLA, *see* Defense Logistics Agency (DLA)
DOD, *see* US Department of Defense (DOD)
Dresch, Denny, 180, 181

E2O, *see* Marine Corps Expeditionary Energy Office (E2O)
EABO, *see* Expeditionary Advanced Base Operations (EABO)
economic tools of geopolitics of energy, 40
ECOP, *see* Energy Common Operating Picture (ECOP)
education tools, 158–159
efficiency
– *vs.* resilience, 145–146
electricity, 32–34
– distribution, 194
electronic equipment in military, 165–170
Energy Common Operating Picture (ECOP), 193
energy crisis 2020, 188–189
energy density, 29, 30
energy ontology model, 10
energy security, definition, 36
energy security policies, 40–41
energy sources in wars
– coal, 14
– crude oil and refined products, 14–15
– nuclear technologies, 15–16

– steam power, 14
– wood and animal products, 14
energy sub-systems, 192–195
– controls and power management, 193
– distribution, 194
– power generation / conversion, 193–194
– sources, 192–193
– storage, 195
energy supply
– capacities, role of, 2
– civilian supply lines, 46–47
– disruption of, 40, 46
energy technologies, 189–190
energy transitions, 12–21
– anticipating and developing, 20–21
– catalysts for, 12
– meaning of, 12
– and militaries, 12–13
– and war, 13–16
exercises, 158–159
Expeditionary Advanced Base Operations (EABO), 178

fault tolerance, 136
fault tree, 136
FBCF, *see* Fully Burdened Cost of Fuel (FBCF)
FOB, *see* Forward Operating Base (FOB)
Forward Operating Base (FOB), 169
France, 16
– oil imports during World War I, *17*
fuel convoys, 19, 163
fuel mix, global, 27–28
Fully Burdened Cost of Fuel (FBCF), 163

game theory, 134
Gaza Strip, 104
General Military Training (GMT), 155
geography, 78–80
geopolitics, definition, 36
geopolitics of energy, 34–40
Germany, 22–26, 79, 92
Gilday, Michael, 92
GMT, *see* General Military Training (GMT)
Granholm, Jennifer, 126
Great Green Fleet initiative, 176–178
green energy, 33
Grossi, Rafael, 67–70
Ground Based Operational Surveillance System (G-BOSS), 169

Hamas, 51, 91, 101, 103–105
Hayward, Joel, 23, 25
Hezbollah, 85–86, 98
High Mobility Multi-Wheeled Vehicle (HMMWV), 164–165
Hitler, Adolf, 22–26
HMMWV, see High Mobility Multi-Wheeled Vehicle (HMMWV)
Homeland Security National Risk Categorization method, 137
Houthis, 86, 92, 99
Hurricane Irma, 147
Hurricane Maria, 147
hybrid warfare, 2, 45–46

IAEA, see International Atomic Energy Agency (IAEA)
– implementation plan, 157
indirect military fires, 93
installation energy, 3
institutions
– international and regional, 52
– operational energy, 115–116
intelligence, 51–52
– International Atomic Energy Agency (IAEA), 52, 64–70
international conventions, 47
International Energy Agency (IEA), 52, 64–71
International Maritime Organization, 52
Iran
– attacks on energy tankers, 98–99
– cyberattacks by, 98
– naval guerilla warfare, 98–99
– proxy forces, 98, 99
– terrorism by, 86
– view of American vulnerabilities, 97–99
Iraq, 42
– history of looting, 87
– war in, 164–165, 166, 167
Israel, 51, 91, 101, 103–105
– Israel-Hamas war tunnels, 103–104

Japan, 17, 56, 183
Joint Intelligence Preparation of the Operational Environment (JIPOE), 73
– planning and targeting, 76–77

Kemp, Brian, 126
kill-chain analysis, 130

looting, 87
Ludendorff, Erich, 15
Lynn, William, 19

Mabus, Ray, 176
Malacca Straits, 95
Marine Corps Expeditionary Energy Office (E2O), 179
Marine infantry battalion, 164–165
maritime delimitation conflicts, 38
Mattis, James, 46, 112, 163–164
mean time to failure (MTTF), 136
metals, 38
Metcalf electricity substation, attack on, 105–110
– assessment of, 108–109
– role of transformers in energy grid, 106–107
microgrid, 194
military decisions, effect of energy, 16–21
military mission, 197
military platforms, 196, 197
Military Sealift Command, 117
Miller, Erin, 83
minerals, geopolitics of, 38
Mine Resistant Ambush Protected Vehicles (MRAPs), 165
MRAPs, see Mine Resistant Ambush Protected Vehicles (MRAPs)
MTTF, see mean time to failure (MTTF)

National Defense Authorization Act (NDAA), 111, 115
National Defense Authorization Legislation, 113
National Strategy for Homeland Security, 142
NATO, 37, 37, 37, 48, 48, 48, 52, 52, 88, 93, 93, 93
natural gas, 31, 189, 193
– challenges in storage of, 37–38
– geopolitics of, 37–38
– supply of, 31
naval guerilla warfare
– Iran, 98–99
NDAA, see National Defense Authorization Act (NDAA)
Netanyahu, Benjamin, 103
Nimitz, Chester W., 183
non-deliberate threats to OE, 78, 80–81
– accidents/safety, 80–81
– aging or poorly constructed infrastructure, 81
– geography, 78–80
– poor decision-making and policies, 81
– theft, 81–82
– North Korea, 91

nuclear energy, 15–16, 32–33
nuclear power plants, 61–62, 64–71
– Metsamor nuclear power plant, 61–62
– Zaporizhzhya Nuclear Power Plant (ZNPP), *see* Ukraine

Obama administration, 177–178
OE Education Cooperation with Allies and Partners, 159
OE Introduction, Level I course, 155
OE Introduction, Level II course, 155–156
Office of the Secretary of Defense Operational Energy-Innovation, 191
oil, 29–30
– benchmarks for prices, 30
– geopolitics of, 36–37
– liberalization of trade, 36
– trading, 29–30
– transportation, 29–30
ontologies, operational energy (OE), 191–198, *192*
– enablers, 195
– energy sub-systems, 192–195
– operations, 196–198
– systems, 196
On War (von Clausewitz), 74
OPEC, 36–37
Operational energy, definition, 2, 3
Operational Energy Strategy, 7, 43–44, 113, 114–115
Operational Energy superiority, 4
Operation Allied Force, 93
Operation Desert Storm, 93
Operation Edelweiss 1942, 21–26, 93
operations
– mission, 197
– operational effect, 197–198
– platform capability, 197
– weapon capability, 196–197

Pearl Harbor, 182–187
Petraeus, David, 3
People's Liberation Army's (PLA), 95
petroleum
– for air warfare, 15
planning
– geopolitical factors for OE, 50–51
platforms, military, 196, 197
policy for operational energy (OE), 111–117
poor decision-making, 81
possibility, 134
power generation, 193–194

probabilistic risk analysis (PRA), 138
probability, 134
protection of energy infrastructure, 48–50

railroads, 14
rare earth, 38
Red Hill (Pearl Harbor, Hawaii) fuel storage closure, 182–187
refineries, 30
reliability analysis, 135–136
renewable energy, 13, 31–32
– electricity generation, 32
– geopolitics of, 38
– price of, 32
– transition to, 189
resilience, 142–143
– as adaptability, 144
– different notions of, 145, *145*
– as extensibility, 144
– outcomes, 143–145
– as rebound, 143–144
– as robustness, 143
– *vs.* efficiency, 145–146
resilience specialist training, 157
resilience strategies for OE systems, 131, 141–146
Rickover, Hyman, 15
Rommel, Erwin, 17
Russia, 46
– cyberattacks by, 89, 97, 124–125
– invasion of Ukraine, 81, 89–90, 101–103
– "non-linear warfare," 97
– OPEC and, 37
– as threat to US energy security, 86
– view of American vulnerabilities, 97

sabotage, 87–88
safety, 80–81
sea chokepoints, OE and, 47
Secretary of the Navy 2009 Energy Goals, *177*
Serbia, 93
shale revolution, 13
Soleimani, Qassem, 86
Southern Gas Corridor, 17, 56–58, 62
Southeast Asia Treaty Organization (SEATO), 52
Stalingrad, 23–25
statistics, 134
steam power, 14
storage, 195
sustained adaptability, 144

tabletop exercise (TTX), 158–159
tactical-level units, 166–170
telegraph communications in the US Civil War, 18–19
terrorism, 82–87
theft, 81–82
threats to OE, 72–73
– Center of Gravity analysis, 74–76
– control and weaponization of energy, 77
– deliberate *vs.* non-deliberate threats, 78
– JIPOE, planning and targeting, 76–77
– meaning of, 72–73
training, in operational energy (OE), 154–157
TTX, *see* tabletop exercise (TTX)
Turner, Eric, 5

UAS, *see* Unmanned Aerial Systems (UAS)
Ukraine
– destroying Russia's energy supplies, 101–105
– nuclear power plants in war, 64–71
– *see also* Russia
uncertainty, 134–135
United States
– adversaries, 39–40, 39–40, 51, 51, 94–99
– allies and partners, 48–50
– government and public limitations on OE, 43–45
– greenhouse gas emissions, 41
– oil storage in, 37
– "Pivot to Asia," 47–49
– primary energy consumption in 2020, *28*
– procurement of energy products, 42
– protection of energy infrastructure, 48–50
– terrorism in, 82–87
Unmanned Aerial Systems (UAS), 174
Unmanned Underwater Vehicle (UUV), 86–87
US Air force, 171–174
– consumption of energy, 2
– efforts to reduce energy consumption, 170–171, 172–174
– operational energy challenges, 171–174
– operational energy demand, **162**, 171–173
– operational energy office, 116
– threats to operations, 173
US Army, 179–181
– Army Modernization Strategy 2019, 180
– Climate Strategy 2022, 180
– energy consumption, 179–180
– operational energy challenges, 179–181
– operational energy demand, **162**
– operational energy office, 116

US Civil War, 18–19
US Cyber Command, 91
US Department of Defense (DOD), 1
– institutions, 117
– interest in policy for operational energy, 111–112
– largest consumer of energy within US government, 43
– *National Defense Strategy*, 113, 114, 117
– *Operational Energy Strategy*, 7, 43–44, 113, 114–115
US Marines
– efforts to reduce energy consumption, 179
– energy consumption, 175–176
– Force Design 2030, 178
– mutually beneficial relationship with US Navy, 175
– operational energy demand, **162**
US National Security Strategy (NSS), 113–114
US Naval Services, 175–179
– energy consumption, 175–176
US Navy
– efforts to reduce energy consumption, 176–179
– energy consumption, 175–176
– Military Sealift Command, 117
– mutually beneficial relationship with US Marines, 175
– operational energy challenges, 175–179
– operational energy demand, **162**
– operational energy office, 116
– Secretary of the Navy 2009 Energy Goals, *177*
USS Cole, 84
USS Nautilus, 15–16
USSR, *see* Operation Edelweiss
US Transportation Command, 117
US Virgin Islands – the hurricanes of 2017, 146–151
– vulnerability analysis of the USVI energy system, 148–150
UUV, *see* Unmanned Underwater Vehicle (UUV)

Van Ovost, Jacqueline, 117
von Clausewitz, Carl, 74
von Holtzendorff, Henning, 92
von Manstein, Erick, 23–24
vulnerability, 8–9, 46, 50
vulnerability analysis
– adversarial analysis, 135, 138–140
– goal of, 132–133
– for operational energy (OE) systems, 131–133
– reliability analysis, 135, 136

– risk analysis, a subset of, 133, 135, 137–138
– techniques, 131

wagons used in wars, 18, *19*, *20*
warfighter's look, *76*
wargames, 158
waterways for energy transport, 39
weapon capability, 196–197

weaponization of energy, 50, 54, 60, 63, 77
weapons, 196–197
weather, 157
Wellinghoff, Jon, 83, 108–109

Yergin, Daniel, 84, 87

Zaporizhzhya Nuclear Power Plant (ZNPP), 64–71

www.ingramcontent.com/pod-product-compliance
Lightning Source LLC
Chambersburg PA
CBHW080805300426
44114CB00020B/2830